AMERICAN POLITICAL, ECONOMIC, AND SECURITY ISSUES

CONSTITUTION: OVERVIEW, ISSUES AND INTERPRETATIONS

American Political, Economic, and Security Issues

Additional books and e-books in this series can be found on Nova's website under the Series tab.

AMERICAN POLITICAL, ECONOMIC, AND SECURITY ISSUES

CONSTITUTION: OVERVIEW, ISSUES AND INTERPRETATIONS

JACKELYN HAGGERTY

New York

Library of Congress Cataloging-in-Publication Data

ISBN: 978-1-53614-198-6

Published by Nova Science Publishers, Inc. † New York

CONTENTS

PREFACE

While exercising its power to review the constitutionality of governmental action, the Supreme Court has relied on certain "methods" or "modes" of interpretation – that is, ways of figuring out a particular meaning of provision within the Constitution. The first chapter or report broadly describes the most common modes of constitutional interpretation. The next chapters herein examine the Speech or Debate Clause of the US Constitution; provides an overview of Congress's power under the Constitution and Congress's role in interpreting the nation's founding document; and discusses contemporary issues for Congress with regards to Article V of the US Constitution, and the two methods by which the nation's founding charter may be amended.

In: Constitution
Editor: Jackelyn Haggerty
ISBN: 978-1-53614-198-6

Chapter 1

MODES OF CONSTITUTIONAL INTERPRETATION*

Brandon J. Murrill

SUMMARY

When exercising its power to review the constitutionality of governmental action, the Supreme Court has relied on certain "methods" or "modes" of interpretation—that is, ways of figuring out a particular meaning of a provision within the Constitution. This chapter broadly describes the most common modes of constitutional interpretation; discusses examples of Supreme Court decisions that demonstrate the application of these methods; and provides a general overview of the various arguments in support of, and in opposition to, the use of such methods of constitutional interpretation.

Textualism. Textualism is a mode of interpretation that focuses on the plain meaning of the text of a legal document. Textualism usually emphasizes how the terms in the Constitution would be understood by people at the time they were ratified, as well as the context in which those terms appear. Textualists usually believe there is an objective meaning of

---

* This is an edited, reformatted and augmented version of Congressional Research Service report 7-5700, R45129, www.crs.gov, dated March 15, 2018.

the text, and they do not typically inquire into questions regarding the intent of the drafters, adopters, or ratifiers of the Constitution and its amendments when deriving meaning from the text.

Original Meaning. Whereas textualist approaches to constitutional interpretation focus solely on the text of the document, originalist approaches consider the meaning of the Constitution as understood by at least some segment of the populace at the time of the Founding. Originalists generally agree that the Constitution's text had an "objectively identifiable" or public meaning at the time of the Founding that has not changed over time, and the task of judges and Justices (and other responsible interpreters) is to construct this original meaning.

Judicial Precedent. The most commonly cited source of constitutional meaning is the Supreme Court's prior decisions on questions of constitutional law. For most, if not all Justices, judicial precedent provides possible principles, rules, or standards to govern judicial decisions in future cases with arguably similar facts.

Pragmatism. Pragmatist approaches often involve the Court weighing or balancing the probable practical consequences of one interpretation of the Constitution against other interpretations. One flavor of pragmatism weighs the future costs and benefits of an interpretation to society or the political branches, selecting the interpretation that may lead to the perceived best outcome. Under another type of pragmatist approach, a court might consider the extent to which the judiciary could play a constructive role in deciding a question of constitutional law.

Moral Reasoning. This approach argues that certain moral concepts or ideals underlie some terms in the text of the Constitution (e.g., "equal protection" or "due process of law"), and that these concepts should inform judges' interpretations of the Constitution.

National Identity (or "Ethos"). Judicial reasoning occasionally relies on the concept of a "national ethos," which draws upon the distinct character and values of the American national identity and the nation's institutions in order to elaborate on the Constitution's meaning.

Structuralism. Another mode of constitutional interpretation draws inferences from the design of the Constitution: the relationships among the three branches of the federal government (commonly called separation of powers); the relationship between the federal and state governments (known as federalism); and the relationship between the government and the people.

Historical Practices. Prior decisions of the political branches, particularly their long-established, historical practices, are an important source of constitutional meaning. Courts have viewed historical practices as a source of the Constitution's meaning in cases involving questions about the separation of powers, federalism, and individual rights, particularly when the text provides no clear answer.

INTRODUCTION

Early in the history of the United States, the Supreme Court began to exercise the power that it is most closely and famously associated with—its authority of judicial review. In its 1803 decision in *Marbury v. Madison*,[1] the Supreme Court famously asserted and explained the foundations of its power to review the constitutionality of federal governmental action.[2] During the two decades following its holding in *Marbury*, the Court decided additional cases that helped to establish its power to review the constitutionality of state governmental action.[3] If a challenged governmental action is unconstitutional, the Court may strike it down, rendering it invalid.[4] When performing the function of judicial review,[5] the Court must necessarily ascertain the meaning of a given provision within the Constitution, often for the first time, before applying its interpretation of the Constitution to the particular governmental action under review.

The need to determine the meaning of the Constitution through the use of methods of constitutional interpretation and, perhaps, construction,[6] is

---

[1] 5 U.S. (1 Cranch) 137 (1803).

[2] *Id.* at 180.

[3] *See, e.g.*, Cohens v. Virginia, 19 U.S. (6 Wheat.) 264, 430 (1821); Martin v. Hunter's Lessee, 14 U.S. (1 Wheat.) 304, 362 (1816); Fletcher v. Peck, 10 U.S. (6 Cranch) 87, 139 (1810).

[4] *Id.* The Court first struck down an action of the executive branch of the federal government as unconstitutional in Little v. Barreme, 6 U.S. (2 Cranch) 170, 177–79 (1804). The Court first struck down a state law as unconstitutional in *Fletcher v. Peck*. *See* 10 U.S. at 139.

[5] The term "judicial review" refers to "a court's power to review the actions of other branches or levels of government[, and especially] the courts' power to invalidate legislative and executive actions as being unconstitutional." *Black's Law Dictionary* 976 (10th ed. 2014).

[6] Professor Keith Whittington has distinguished between the concepts of "constitutional interpretation" and "constitutional construction." In an influential book on the subject, he wrote that both interpretation and construction of the Constitution "seek to elaborate a meaning somehow already present in the text." However, constitutional interpretation relies on traditional legal tools that look to internal aspects of the Constitution (e.g., text and structure) to ascertain meaning, whereas constitutional construction supplements the meaning derived from such traditional interpretive methods with materials outside of the text (e.g., moral principles or pragmatic considerations) "where the text is so broad or so undetermined as to be incapable of faithful but exhaustive reduction to legal rules." Keith Whittington, *Constitutional Construction: Divided Powers and Constitutional Meaning* 1, 5–7 (1999).

apparent from the text of the document itself.[7] While several parts of the Constitution do not lend themselves to much debate about their preferred interpretation,[8] much of the Constitution is broadly worded, leaving ample room for the Court to interpret its provisions before it applies them to particular legal and factual circumstances.[9] For example, the Second Amendment reads, "A well regulated Militia, being necessary to the security of a free State, the right of the people to keep and bear Arms, shall not be infringed."[10] The text of the Amendment alone does not squarely resolve whether the "right of the people to keep and bear arms" extends to all citizens or merely is related to, or perhaps conditioned on, service in a militia. This ambiguity prompted a closely divided 2008 decision of the Supreme Court that ruled in favor of the former interpretation.[11]

The text of the Constitution is also silent on many fundamental questions of constitutional law, including questions that its drafters and those ratifying the document could not have foreseen or chose not to address.[12] For example, the Fourth Amendment, ratified in 1791, does not on its face resolve whether the government may perform a search of the digital contents of a cell phone seized incident to arrest without obtaining a warrant.[13] Thus, interpretation is necessary to determine the meaning of ambiguous provisions of the Constitution or to answer fundamental questions left unaddressed by the drafters. Some commentators have also noted the practical need for constitutional interpretation to provide principles, rules, or standards to govern future conduct of regulated parties, as well as political institutions, branches of government, and regulators.[14]

---

[7] Erwin Chemerinsky, Constitutional Law 11 (4th ed. 2013).

[8] For example, the Constitution provides a clear, bright-line rule that individuals who have not yet "attained to the Age of thirty five Years" are ineligible to be President. *See* U.S. CONST. art. II, § 1, cl. 5.

[9] Chemerinsky, *supra* note 7, at 11; Cass R. Sunstein, *The Partial Constitution* 93–94 (1993).

[10] U.S. CONST. amend. II.

[11] *See* District of Columbia v. Heller, 554 U.S. 570, 573–619, 635–36 (2008) (examining historical sources to determine the original meaning of the Second Amendment).

[12] Laurence H. Tribe, *The Invisible Constitution* 1–4 (Geoffrey R. Stone ed., 2008).

[13] The Court resolved this question in *Riley v. California*, holding that a warrant is needed to search the contents of a cell phone incident to an individual's arrest. *See* 573 U.S. ___, No. 13-132, slip op. at 28 (2014).

[14] Harry H. *Wellington, Interpreting The Constitution: The Supreme Court And The Process Of Adjudication* 3 (1990).

When deriving meaning from the text of the Constitution, the Supreme Court has relied on certain "methods" or "modes" of interpretation—that is, ways of figuring out a particular meaning of a provision within the Constitution.[15] There is significant debate over which sources and methods of construction the Court should consult when interpreting the Constitution—a controversy closely related to more general disputes about whether and how the Court should exercise the power of judicial review.

Judicial review at the Supreme Court, by its very nature, can involve unelected judges[16] overturning the will of a democratically elected branch of the federal government or popularly elected state officials. Some scholars have argued that in striking down laws or actions, the Court has decided cases according to the Justices' own political preferences.[17] In response to these concerns, constitutional scholars have constructed theories designed to ensure that the Justices following them would be able to reach principled judgments in constitutional adjudication. In 1987, Professor Richard Fallon of Harvard Law School divided "interpretivists," or those purporting to prioritize the specific text and plain language of the Constitution above all else, into two basic camps: "On one side stand 'originalists,'" whom he characterized as taking "the rigid view that only the original understanding of the language and the framers' specific intent ought to count. On the other side, 'moderate interpretivists' allow contemporary understandings and the framers' general or abstract intent to enter the constitutional calculus."[18]

---

[15] Professor Philip Bobbitt defines a modality for interpreting the Constitution as "the way in which we characterize a form of expression as true." Philip Bobbitt, *Constitutional Interpretation* 11 (1991). *See also* Richard H. Fallon, Jr., *Stare Decisis and the Constitution: An Essay on Constitutional Methodology*, 76 N.Y.U. L. REV. 570, 592 (2001) ("The power to say what the Constitution means or requires—recognized since *Marbury v. Madison*—implies a power to determine the sources of authority on which constitutional rulings properly rest.").

[16] The President appoints the Justices of the Supreme Court, who serve for life terms unless impeached and removed from office. U.S. CONST. art. II, § 2, cl. 2; *id.* art. III, § 1.

[17] *See, e.g.*, Hon. Antonin Scalia, *A Matter of Interpretation: Federal Courts and the Law* 37–41, 44–47 (Amy Gutmann ed., 1997) [hereinafter Scalia, *A Matter of Interpretation*] ("The ascendant school of constitutional interpretation affirms the existence of what is called the Living Constitution, a body of law that...grows and changes from age to age, in order to meet the needs of a changing society. And it is the judges who determine those needs and 'find' that changing law.")

[18] Richard H. Fallon, Jr., A Constructivist Coherence Theory of Constitutional Interpretation, 100 *Harv. L. Rev.* 1189, 1211 (1987).

Whether or not Professor Fallon's precise description at the time was accurate, those regarding themselves as originalists have clarified that the Court should rely on the fixed meaning of the Constitution as understood by at least the public at the time of the Founding.[19] This has become known as the original public meaning of the Constitution.

On the other hand, still other commentators have questioned the legitimacy of fixating on what the Framers, ratifiers, or members of their generation might have considered the core meaning of a particular provision of the Constitution, and have instead suggested interpretive methods that ensure the Court's decisions allow government to function properly, protect minority rights, and safeguard the basic structure of government from majoritarian interference.[20] Although the debate over the proper sources of the Constitution's meaning remains unresolved, several key methods of constitutional interpretation have guided the Justices in their decision making and, more broadly, have influenced constitutional dialogue.[21]

It is possible to categorize the various methods that have been employed when interpreting the Constitution.[22] This chapter broadly

---

[19] Scalia, *A Matter of Interpretation, supra* note 17, at 44–47.

[20] *E.g.*, Paul Brest et al., *Processes of Constitutional Decisionmaking: Cases and Materials* 54–55 (2006) (discussing the argument that the Constitution should "be interpreted to facilitate the performance of government functions"); Hon. William J. Brennan, Jr., *The Constitution of the United States: Contemporary Ratification*, 27 S. Tex. L. Rev. 433, 436 (1986) ("A position that upholds constitutional claims only if they were within the specific contemplation of the Framers in effect establishes a presumption of resolving textual ambiguities against the claim of constitutional right....Those who would restrict claims of right to the values of 1789 specifically articulated in the Constitution turn a blind eye to social progress and eschew adaption of overarching principles to changes of social circumstance."); Hon. Stephen Breyer, *Active Liberty* 25 (2008) ("[O]ur constitutional history has been a quest for...workable democratic government protective of individual personal liberty... And...this constitutional understanding helps interpret the Constitution—in a way that helps to resolve problems related to *modern* government.").

[21] *See* Laurence H. Tribe, *American Constitutional Law: Volume One* 32 (3d ed. 2000) ("[T]he subject and substance of constitutional law in the end remains the language of the United States Constitution itself and the decisions and opinions of the United States Supreme Court. Modes of interpretation are means—however intricate—of explicating this subject and substance."). As discussed below, whether any particular source of meaning may serve as a proper basis for interpreting the Constitution is subject to debate.

[22] Philip Bobbitt, *Constitutional Fate: Theory of the Constitution* 6–7 (1982). This report does not examine the potential role of politics in judicial decision making. *See, e.g.*, Lee Epstein

describes the most common modes of constitutional interpretation; discusses examples of Supreme Court decisions that demonstrate the application of these methods; and provides a general overview of the various arguments in support of, and in opposition to, the use of such methods by the Court. The modes discussed in detail in this chapter are (1) textualism; (2) original meaning; (3) judicial precedent; (4) pragmatism; (5) moral reasoning; (6) national identity (or "ethos"); (7) structuralism; and (8) historical practices.

In explaining these modes, this chapter is merely describing the most common methods on which the Justices (and other interpreters) have relied to argue about the meaning of the Constitution.[23] Depending on the mode of interpretation, the Court may rely upon a variety of materials that include, among other things, the text of the Constitution; constitutional and ratification convention debates; prior Court decisions; pragmatic or moral considerations; and long-standing congressional or legislative practices.[24] It is important to note that the Court may use more than one source in deciding a particular case, and the Justices must exercise some discretion in choosing or coordinating the sources and materials they will consult in making sense of those sources.[25]

Understanding these methods of interpretation may assist Members of Congress in observing the oath they take to uphold the Constitution when performing their legislative functions and fulfilling Congress's role as a coequal branch of government.[26] For example, Members of Congress may

---

& Thomas G. Walker, *Constitutional Law for a Changing America: Rights, Liberties, And Justice* 22 (8th ed. 2013).

[23] This report does not provide an exhaustive list of the modes of interpretation. There is unlikely to be agreement on which methods such a list would include. *See* Bobbitt, *supra* note 22, at 8.

[24] *See also* Fallon, *supra* note 15, at 592; Sunstein, *supra* note 9, at 95 ("It is impossible to interpret any written text without resort to principles external to that text.").

[25] For example, in *New York v. United States*, the Court held that Congress could not directly compel states to participate in a federal regulatory program. 505 U.S. 144, 188 (1992). In so holding, the majority opinion relied upon the text of the Tenth Amendment; historical sources; the structural relationship that the Constitution establishes between the federal government and states; and judicial precedent, among other sources. *Id.* at 174–83.

[26] *See* U.S. Const. art. VI ("The Senators and Representatives before mentioned, and the Members of the several State legislatures, and all executive and judicial Officers, both of the United States and of the several states, shall be bound by Oath or Affirmation, to support this Constitution; but no religious Test shall ever be required as a Qualification to

interpret the Constitution when considering whether to vote for proposed legislation[27] or when a dispute arises regarding the boundaries between Congress's own constitutional authority and that of the executive branch (e.g., a dispute over the reach of Congress's oversight power or the scope of Executive privilege).[28] And knowledge of the most common methods for elaborating on the Constitution's meaning may aid Senators and the Senate Judiciary Committee in examining the judicial philosophy of individuals the President nominates to serve on the federal courts.[29] It may also assist Members and congressional committees in evaluating executive branch officials' interpretations of the Constitution.[30]

---

any Office or public Trust under the United States."). Fulfilling this oath requires Members of Congress to read and understand the nation's founding document. *See also* Nixon v. United States, 506 U.S. 224, 228–29 (1993) (holding that the Constitution gave the Senate alone the power to determine whether it had properly "tried" an impeachment); Edwin Meese III, *The Law of the Constitution*, 61 Tul. L. Rev. 979, 985–86 (1987) ("The Supreme Court, then, is not the only interpreter of the Constitution. Each of the three coordinate branches of government created and empowered by the Constitution—the executive and legislative no less than the judicial—has a duty to interpret the Constitution in the performance of its official functions.").

[27] *See, e.g.,* Russ Feingold, *The Obligation of Members of Congress to Consider Constitutionality While Deliberating and Voting: The Deficiencies of House Rule XII and A Proposed Rule for the Senate,* 67 Vand. L. Rev. 837, 846–49, 856 (2014) ("While members should vote upon legislation based on their own constitutional interpretations, which may be at odds with the Court's, they should not vote for legislation without any thought whatsoever regarding its constitutionality.").

[28] *See, e.g.,* Youngstown Sheet & Tube Co. v. Sawyer, 343 U.S. 579, 637 (1952) (Jackson, J., concurring) ("When the President acts in absence of either a congressional grant or denial of authority, he can only rely upon his own independent powers, but there is a zone of twilight in which he and Congress may have concurrent authority, or in which its distribution is uncertain. Therefore, congressional inertia, indifference or quiescence may sometimes, at least, as a practical matter, enable, if not invite, measures on independent presidential responsibility.").

[29] *See, e.g., The Nomination of Elena Kagan to Be an Associate Justice of the Supreme Court of the United States: Hearing Before the S. Comm. on the Judiciary Part 1*, 111th Cong. 62 (2010) (statement of Elena Kagan in response to a question from Senator Patrick Leahy) ("And I think that [the Framers] laid down—sometimes they laid down very specific rules. Sometimes they laid down broad principles. Either way we apply what they say, what they meant to do. So in that sense, we are all originalists.").

[30] See, e.g., Letter from Jefferson B. Sessions III, Attorney General, U.S. Dep't of Justice, to Elaine C. Duke, Acting Sec'y, Dep't of Homeland Sec. (Sept. 4, 2017), https://www.dhs.gov/sites/default/files/publications/17_0904_DOJ_AG-letter-DACA.pdf (advising the Department of Homeland Security that, in the opinion of the Attorney General, the Deferred Action for Childhood Arrivals (DACA) immigration policy is unconstitutional, stating, "As Attorney General of the United States, I have a duty to defend the Constitution and to faithfully execute the laws passed by Congress.").

TEXTUALISM

Textualism is a mode of legal interpretation that focuses on the plain meaning of the text of a legal document. Textualism usually emphasizes how the terms in the Constitution would be understood by people at the time they were ratified, as well as the context in which those terms appear.[31] Textualists usually believe there is an objective meaning of the text, and they do not typically inquire into questions regarding the intent of the drafters, adopters, or ratifiers of the Constitution and its amendments when deriving meaning from the text.[32] They are concerned primarily with the plain, or popular, meaning of the text of the Constitution. Textualists generally are not concerned with the practical consequences of a decision; rather, they are wary of the Court acting to refine or revise constitutional texts.[33]

The Justices frequently rely on the text in conjunction with other methods of constitutional interpretation.[34] The Court will often look to the text *first* before consulting other potential sources of meaning to resolve ambiguities in the text or to answer fundamental questions of constitutional law not addressed in the text.[35] For example, in *Trop v. Dulles*, a plurality of the Court held that the Eighth Amendment prohibited the government from revoking the citizenship of a U.S. citizen as a punishment.[36] When determining that a punishment that did not involve physical mistreatment violated the Constitution, the Court first looked briefly to the text of the Amendment, noting that the "exact scope" of the phrase "cruel and unusual punishment" in the Eighth Amendment had not been "detailed by [the]

---

[31] *See* Scalia, *A Matter of Interpretation*, *supra* note 17, at 23–38.

[32] *See id.*

[33] *See id.* at 23.

[34] Epstein & Walker, *supra* note 22, at 26. For additional examples of the Court's use of a textualist approach, see "Original Meaning" below.

[35] Chemerinsky, *supra* note 7, at 16; TRIBE, *supra* note 12, at 2–4; Sotirios A. Barber, *On What the Constitution Means* 9 (1984).

[36] 356 U.S. 86, 100–04 (1958) (plurality opinion). Justice William Brennan, providing the fifth and deciding vote in *Trop*, did not base his decision on the Eighth Amendment, instead concluding that denationalization exceeded Congress's war powers. *Id.* at 105–14 (Brennan, J., concurring).

Court."[37] The plurality then turned to other modes of interpretation, such as moral reasoning and historical practices, in deciding the case.[38]

The *Trop* plurality's use of textualism in combination with other interpretive methods is distinguishable from a stricter textualist approach espoused most famously by Justice Hugo Black.[39] Consistent with his view that those interpreting the Constitution should look no further than the literal meaning of its words, Justice Black contended that the text of the First Amendment, which states, "Congress shall make no law…abridging the freedom of speech, or of the press" absolutely forbids Congress from enacting any law that would curtail these rights.[40]

An example of Justice Black's use of textualism in a First Amendment case is his dissent in *Dennis v. United States*.[41] In that case, the Court held that Congress could, consistent with the First Amendment's guarantee of freedom of speech, criminalize the conspiracy to advocate the forcible overthrow of the United States government.[42] The Court determined that the severity of potential harm to the government from the speech in question justified Congress's restrictions on First Amendment rights.[43] In accordance with his views that the text of the Constitution should serve as the sole source of its meaning, Justice Black dissented on the grounds that the Court should not have applied a balancing test to uphold the law against First Amendment challenge.[44] He wrote, "I cannot agree that the

---

[37] *Id.* at 99–101 (plurality opinion).

[38] *Id.* at 100–03 (stating that the Eighth Amendment "must draw its meaning from the evolving standards of decency that mark the progress of a maturing society").

[39] Epstein & Walker, *supra* note 22, at 25–26.

[40] Justice Black once wrote that the First Amendment's statement that "Congress shall make no law...abridging the freedom of speech, or of the press" amounted to an "absolute command...that no law shall be passed by Congress abridging freedom of speech or the press." Hon. Hugo L. Black, *A Constitutional Faith* 45–46 (1968). This form of textualism is sometimes referred to as *pure textualism* or *literalism*. Epstein & Walker, *supra* note 22, at 26. Justice Antonin Scalia, who was both a textualist and an originalist, criticized this sort of "strict constructionist" approach to textualism. He wrote that a "text should not be construed strictly, and it should not be construed leniently; it should be construed reasonably, to contain all that it fairly means." Scalia, *A Matter of Interpretation*, *supra* note 17, at 23.

[41] 341 U.S. 494 (1951).

[42] *Id.* at 509, 513–17.

[43] *Id.*

[44] *Id.* at 580 (Black, J., dissenting) ("At least as to speech in the realm of public matters, I believe that the 'clear and present danger' test does not 'mark the furthermost constitutional

First Amendment permits us to sustain laws suppressing freedom of speech and press on the basis of Congress' or our own notions of mere 'reasonableness.' Such a doctrine waters down the First Amendment so that it amounts to little more than an admonition to Congress."[45]

Another classic example of a self-consciously textualist opinion is Justice Black's dissent in *Griswold v. Connecticut*.[46] In *Griswold*, the majority struck down as unconstitutional a Connecticut law that criminalized the furnishing of birth control to married couples based on a view that the Due Process Clause of the Fourteenth Amendment provides a general right to privacy.[47] Justice Black criticized the majority for straying too far from the text of the Bill of Rights and relying on "nebulous" natural law principles to find a "right to privacy in marital relations" in the Constitution that—at least in his view—did not exist.[48] Adhering to his preference for interpreting the Constitution in line with its text, Justice Black wrote, "I like my privacy as well as the next one, but I am nevertheless compelled to admit that government has a right to invade it unless prohibited by some specific constitutional provision."[49]

Proponents of textualism point to the simplicity and transparency of an approach that focuses solely on the objectively understood meaning of language independent of ideology and politics.[50] They argue that textualism prevents judges from deciding cases in accordance with their personal policy views, leading to more predictability in judgments.[51] Proponents also argue that textualism promotes democratic values because

---

boundaries of protected expression,' but does 'no more than recognize a minimum compulsion of the Bill of Rights.'") (citation omitted).

[45] *Id.*

[46] 381 U.S. 479 (1965).

[47] *Id.* at 485–86.

[48] *Id.* at 507–27 (Black, J., dissenting).

[49] *Id.* at 510.

[50] Epstein & Walker, *supra* note 22, at 26. However, some textualist approaches may allow for consideration of contemporary values. For example, approaches based on present textual meaning may allow for consideration of these values to the extent that they have become incorporated in modern understandings of phrases in the Constitution (e.g., "cruel and unusual punishment"). *Trop,* 356 U.S. at 100–03; BOBBITT, *supra* note 22, at 36.

[51] Epstein & Walker, supra note 22, at 26; Scalia, *A Matter of Interpretation*, supra note 17, at 37–41, 44–47.

it adheres to the words of the Constitution adopted by the "people" as opposed to what individual Justices think or believe.[52]

Opponents of a strict reliance solely on the text in interpreting the Constitution suggest that judges and other interpreters may ascribe different meanings to the Constitution's text depending on their background[53]—a problem compounded by textual provisions that are broadly worded[54] or fail to answer fundamental constitutional questions.[55] In addition, opponents argue that judges should consider values not specifically set forth in the text, such as those based on moral reasoning, practical consequences, structural relationships, or other considerations.[56] In other words, establishing textual meaning may not be straightforward, and a more flexible approach that does not bind the Court and policymakers to words written 300 years ago may, in the view of those who argue against textualism, be necessary to ensure preservation of fundamental constitutional rights or guarantees.[57]

ORIGINAL MEANING

Whereas textualist approaches to constitutional interpretation focus solely on the text of the document, originalist approaches consider the meaning of the Constitution as understood by at least some segment of the populace at the time of the Founding. Though this method has generally

---

[52] *See* Hon. William H. Rehnquist, *The Notion of a Living Constitution*, 54 TEX. L. REV. 693, 695–97 (1976) ("The ultimate source of authority in this Nation, Marshall said, is not Congress, not the states, not for that matter the Supreme Court of the United States. The people are the ultimate source of authority; they have parceled out the authority that originally resided entirely with them by adopting the original Constitution and by later amending it.").

[53] Bobbitt, *supra* note 22, at 37.

[54] McCulloch v. Maryland, 17 U.S. (4 Wheat.) 316, 407 (1819) ("A constitution, to contain an accurate detail of all the subdivisions of which its great powers will admit, and of all the means by which they may be carried into execution, would partake of the prolixity of a legal code, and could scarcely be embraced by the human mind"); Epstein & Walker, *supra* note 22, at 26.

[55] Bobbitt, *supra* note 22, at 38; Tribe, *supra* note 12, at 1–4.

[56] *Cf.* Bobbitt, *supra* note 22, at 26.

[57] *Id.* at 24, 37–38.

been called "originalism," constitutional scholars have not reached a consensus on what it means for a judge to adopt this methodology for construing the Constitution's text.[58] Disagreements primarily concern which sources scholars should consult when determining the fixed meaning of the Constitution.[59] Originalists, however, generally agree that the Constitution's text had an "objectively identifiable" or public meaning at the time of the Founding that has not changed over time, and the task of judges and Justices (and other responsible interpreters) is to construct this original meaning.[60]

For many years, some prominent scholars (such as Robert Bork) argued that in interpreting the Constitution, one should look to the *original intent* of the people who drafted, proposed, adopted, or ratified the Constitution to determine what those people wanted to convey through the text.[61] According to this view, original intent may be found in sources outside of the text, such as debates in the Constitutional Convention or the Federalist Papers.[62] For example, in *Myers v. United States*,[63] Chief Justice William Howard Taft, writing for the majority, held that the President did not need legislative approval to remove an executive branch official who was performing a purely executive function.[64] The Court sought the original meaning of the President's removal power by looking at English common law, the records of the Constitutional Convention, and the actions of the first Congress, among other sources[65] Relying on these various sources, in his opinion for the Court, Chief Justice Taft wrote that "the debates in the Constitutional Convention indicated an intention to create a strong Executive."[66] Notably, in *Myers* the Court did not look at sources that

---

[58] Gregory E. Maggs & Peter J. Smith, *Constitutional Law: A Contemporary Approach* 39 (3rd ed. 2015).

[59] *Id.*

[60] *Id.*

[61] *Id.* at 17; Robert H. Bork, *Tradition and Morality in Constitutional Law: The Francis Boyer Lectures on Public Policy* 10 (1984) ("[T]he framers' intentions with respect to freedoms are the sole legitimate premise from which constitutional analysis may proceed.").

[62] Myers v. United States, 272 U.S. 52, 136 (1926); Hon. Antonin Scalia, *Originalism: The Lesser Evil*, 57 U. Cin. L. Rev. 849, 852 (1989) [hereinafter Scalia, *Originalism*].

[63] 272 U.S. 52 (1926).

[64] *Id.* at 176.

[65] *Id.* at 109–21.

[66] *Id.* at 116.

would likely indicate what ordinary citizens living at the time of the Founding thought about the President's removal power.

Over the course of Justice Antonin Scalia's near thirty-year tenure on the Supreme Court, he and several prominent scholars explained that, as originalists, they were committed to seeking to understand *original public meaning* of the Constitution.[67] This method considers the plain meaning of the Constitution's text as it would have been understood by the general public, or a reasonable person, who lived at the time the Constitution was ratified.[68] This approach has much in common with textualism, but is not identical. The original public meaning approach to understanding the Constitution is not based solely on the text, but, rather, draws upon the original public meaning of the text as a broader guide to interpretation. Justice Scalia's majority opinion in *District of Columbia v. Heller*[69] illustrates the use of original public meaning in constitutional interpretation. In that case, the Court held that the Second Amendment, as originally understood by ordinary citizens, protected an individual's right to possess firearms for private use unconnected with service in a militia.[70] Justice Scalia's opinion examined various historical sources to determine original public meaning, including dictionaries in existence at the time of the Founding and comparable provisions in state constitutions.[71]

Those in favor of the use of original meaning as an interpretive approach point to its long historical pedigree[72] and its adherence to the democratic will of the people who originally framed and ratified the Constitution.[73] They point as well to the basic logic that a law, in order to

---

[67] Scalia, *A Matter of Interpretation*, *supra* note 17, at 17, 44–45.
[68] *Id.*
[69] 554 U.S. 570 (2008).
[70] *Id.* at 635–36.
[71] *Id.* at 573–619.
[72] Maggs & Smith, *supra* note 58, at 18.
[73] Paul Brest, *The Misconceived Quest for the Original Understanding*, 60 B.U. L. REV. 204, 204 (1980) (discussing arguments made by supporters of originalism). Proponents of original meaning generally oppose the use of foreign law to establish the original meaning of the Constitution unless it is English common law that predates the founding era. *See* Knight v. Florida, 528 U.S. 990, 990 (1999) (Thomas, J., concurring in denial of cert.); Thompson v. Oklahoma, 487 U.S. 815, 868 n.4 (1988) (Scalia, J., dissenting) ("But where there is not first a settled consensus among our own people, the views of other nations, however enlightened the Justices of this Court may think them to be, cannot be imposed

function as law, has to have a fixed or settled meaning until it is formally amended or discarded.[74]

Proponents of originalism also argue that the approach limits judicial discretion, preventing judges from deciding cases in accordance with their own political views.[75] Some originalists argue that changes to the Constitution's meaning should be left to further action by Congress and the states to amend the Constitution in accordance with Article V.[76] Proponents also credit the approach with ensuring more certainty and predictability in judgments.[77]

Those who are skeptical of this mode of interpretation underscore the difficulty in establishing original meaning. Scholars cannot always agree on original meaning, and, perhaps, people living at the time of the Constitution's adoption may not have agreed on a particular meaning either.[78] As such, critics argue, originalists will have merely constructed a meaning that had never actually been approved by the people who drafted or ratified the actual text being construed.[79] Such a view may stem from

upon Americans through the Constitution."*);* Myers v. United States, 272 U.S. 52, 118 (1926) (discussing when English common law could be relevant to original meaning). Treaties to which the United States is party (or customary international law that is incorporated into domestic law) might be cited by a proponent of original meaning when interpreting the Constitution. *See* Ganesh Sitaraman, *The Use and Abuse of Foreign Law in Constitutional Interpretation*, 32 Harv. J. L. & Pub. Pol'y 653, 689 (2009) ("In cases where the fundamental rights that a court seeks to protect are described in a treaty or convention or are a matter of customary international law, the question is merely whether those rights are incorporated by domestic law.").

[74] Maggs & Smith, *supra* note 58, at 17.

[75] Epstein & Walker, *supra* note 22, at 27; Scalia, *Originalism*, *supra* note 62, at 852, 862–64. A textualist approach based on the original meaning may allow for consideration of contemporary values to the extent that a court finds the original meaning counsels for an application of contemporary values to modern factual circumstances. Maggs & Smith, *supra* note 58, at 36.

[76] Scalia, *Originalism*, *supra* note 62, at 852, 862–64.

[77] Maggs & Smith, *supra* note 58, at 39.

[78] Epstein & Walker, *supra* note 22, at 28; Maggs & Smith, *supra* note 58, at 40. Furthermore, opponents argue that original meaning is of little use when the provision of the Constitution to be interpreted and applied is broadly worded and open to several meanings, or when the Constitution is silent on an issue. *Id.* at 20. Arguably, the "original meaning" of some provisions of the Constitution (e.g., the Ninth Amendment) contemplates constitutional rights that exist independent of the text, and thus the drafters contemplated that interpreters of the Constitution would consider sources of meaning outside of the text and historical sources from the time of the Founding. *See* John Hart Ely, *Democracy and Distrust: A Theory of Judicial Review* 14, 33–40 (1980).

[79] *See* Maggs & Smith, *supra* note 58, at 40–41.

the potentially wide variety of sources of such meaning; conflicting statements by these sources; conflicting understandings of statements in these sources; and gaps in historical sources.[80] Thus, because of this lack of consensus on the original meaning of the Constitution, judges may simply choose the original view that supports their political beliefs.[81] Opponents also argue that originalism requires judges to act as historians—a role for which they may not be well suited—as opposed to as decisionmakers.[82]

While Justice Elena Kagan, for example, has conceded that "we [the Justices] are all originalists,"[83] many critics question the extent to which originalism is a workable theory of constitutional interpretation. They argue that originalism is an inflexible, flawed method of constitutional interpretation,[84] contending that the Constitution's contemporaries could not have conceived of some of the situations that would arise in modern times.[85] They argue further that interpreting the Constitution based on original meaning may thus fail to protect minority rights because women and minorities did not have the same rights at the time of the Founding (or ratification of the Civil War Amendments) as they do today.[86] In addition, some skeptics of originalism challenge the view that Article V should be the exclusive vehicle for constitutional change,[87] as that article requires a

---

[80] Bobbitt, *supra* note 22, at 7, 10–12. Justice Scalia acknowledged the limits of historical sources. Scalia, *Originalism*, *supra* note 62, at 856–57.

[81] Maggs & Smith, *supra* note 58, at 40–41.

[82] Darrell A.H. Miller, *Text, History, and Tradition: What the Seventh Amendment Can Teach Us About the Second*, 122 Yale L.J. 852, 935 (2013) ("Judges are not historians, and so, in addition to the risk that they will not understand the materials they are charged to consult, there is the additional risk that they will not conduct a dispassionate examination of the historical evidence and will simply marshal historical anecdotes to achieve what they have already decided is the preferred outcome.").

[83] *The Nomination of Elena Kagan to Be an Associate Justice of the Supreme Court of the United States: Hearing Before the S. Comm. on the Judiciary Part 1*, 111th Cong. 62 (2010) (statement of Elena Kagan in response to a question from Senator Patrick Leahy) ("And I think that [the Framers] laid down—sometimes they laid down very specific rules. Sometimes they laid down broad principles. Either way we apply what they say, what they meant to do. So in that sense, we are all originalists.").

[84] Maggs & Smith, *supra* note 58, at 21.

[85] Sunstein, *supra* note 9, at 103.

[86] Brennan, *supra* note 20, at 436–37; Sotirios A. Barber, *The Constitution of Judicial Power* 7 (1993). For example, it seems possible that many of the ratifiers of the Fourteenth Amendment would have favored segregation by race and gender. SUNSTEIN, *supra* note 9, at 121.

[87] C. Herman Pritchett, Constitutional Law of the Federal System 37 (1984).

two-thirds majority vote of the House of Representatives and Senate to propose an amendment,[88] and ratification by three-fourths of the states for the amendment to become part of the Constitution.[89] The high threshold the Constitution creates for formal amendment has prompted arguments that the Constitution's meaning should not be fixed in time, but, rather, should accommodate modern needs.[90]

JUDICIAL PRECEDENT

The most commonly cited source of constitutional meaning is the Supreme Court's prior decisions on questions of constitutional law.[91] For most, if not all Justices, judicial precedent provides possible principles, rules, or standards to govern judicial decisions in future cases with arguably similar facts.[92] Although the Court routinely purports to rely upon precedent,[93] it is difficult to say with much precision how often precedent has actually constrained the Court's decisions[94] because the Justices plainly

---

88 Under Article V, two-thirds of the states' legislatures may also call a constitutional convention to propose amendments. *See* U.S. CONST. art. V.

89 *Id.*

90 Pritchett, *supra* note 87, at 37.

91 Michael J. Gerhardt, *The Power of Precedent* 147–48 (2008) ("[I]t is practically impossible to find any modern Court decision that fails to cite at least some precedents in support."). This report's concept of "judicial precedent" is limited to prior decisions of the Supreme Court. However, the concept of "precedent" is arguably much broader, encompassing "norms," "historical practices," and "traditions." *Id.* at 3. For a discussion of the use of historical practices in interpreting the Constitution, see "Historical Practices" below.

92 Bobbitt, *supra* note 22, at 7. Black's Law Dictionary 1366 (10th ed. 2014) (defining "precedent" as "a decided case that furnishes a basis for determining later cases involving similar facts or issues"). The Court may also rely on commentary on these cases by academics and judges. *Id.* This report does not examine in any detail reliance on such commentary or the precedents of state courts or foreign tribunals in constitutional interpretation. *See* Brest et al., *supra* note 20, at 56.

93 Epstein & Walker, *supra* note 22, at 29.

94 *See* Michael J. Gerhardt, *The Role of Precedent in Constitutional Decisionmaking and Theory*, 60 Geo. Wash. L. Rev. 68, 76 (1991) ("Precedents commonly are regarded as a traditional source of constitutional decisionmaking, despite the absence of any clear evidence that they ever have forced the Court into making a decision contrary to what it would rather have decided.").

have latitude in how broadly or narrowly they choose to construe their prior decisions.[95]

In some cases, however, a single precedent may play a particularly prominent role in the Court's decisionmaking. For example, a plurality of Justices relied on *Roe v. Wade* as controlling precedent in their opinion in *Planned Parenthood v. Casey*.[96] In that case, the plurality reaffirmed *Roe*'s holding that a woman has a protected liberty interest in terminating her pregnancy prior to fetal viability, stating that the essential holding of *Roe* "should be retained."[97] Another example of the heightened role that precedent can play in constitutional interpretation is the Court's decision in *Dickerson v. United States*, which addressed the constitutionality of a federal statute governing the admissibility of statements made during police interrogation, a law that functionally would have overruled the 1966 case of *Miranda v. Arizona*.[98] In striking down the statute, the majority declined to overrule *Miranda*, noting that the 1966 case had "become embedded in routine police practice to the point where the warnings have become part of our national culture."[99]

More often, the Court reasons from the logic of several precedents in rendering its decisions. An example is *Arizona State Legislature v. Arizona Independent Redistricting Commission*, which held that the voters of Arizona could remove from the state legislature the authority to redraw the boundaries for legislative districts and vest that authority in an independent

[95] Gerhardt, *supra* note 91, at 34–35.

[96] 505 U.S. 833 (1992) (plurality opinion).

[97] *Id.* at 845–46 ("After considering the fundamental constitutional questions resolved by *Roe*, principles of institutional integrity, and the rule of stare decisis, we are led to conclude this: the essential holding of *Roe v. Wade* should be retained and once again reaffirmed."). Although the plurality in *Casey* declined to overrule the core aspects of *Roe*, it discarded *Roe*'s "trimester approach" to evaluating the constitutionality of a state's restrictions on abortion in favor of a balancing test that considers whether such restrictions impose an "undue burden" on a woman's privacy interests protected by the Fourteenth Amendment. *Id.* at 872–77.

[98] 530 U.S. 428, 431–32 (2000).

[99] *Id.* at 443; *see also id.* at 432 ("We hold that *Miranda*, being a constitutional decision of this Court, may not be in effect overruled by an Act of Congress, and we decline to overrule *Miranda* ourselves. We therefore hold that *Miranda* and its progeny in this Court govern the admissibility of statements made during custodial interrogation in both state and federal courts.").

commission.[100] In so holding, the Court examined the Elections Clause, which states that the "Times, Places, and Manner of holding Elections for Senators and Representatives, shall be prescribed in each State by the Legislature thereof."[101] The Court determined that the term "Legislature" encompassed the voters of a state making law through a referendum.[102] In reaching this determination, the Court relied on three cases from the early twentieth century to support a more expansive view of the term "Legislature,"[103] including one case from 1916, *Ohio ex rel. Davis v. Hildebrant*, which the Court described as holding that a state referendum was "part of the legislative power" and could be "exercised by the people to disapprove the legislation creating congressional districts."[104]

Proponents of the primacy of precedent as a source of constitutional meaning point to the legitimacy of decisions that adhere to principles set forth in prior, well-reasoned written opinions.[105] They contend that following the principle of stare decisis[106] and rendering decisions grounded in earlier cases supports the Court's role as a neutral, impartial, and consistent decisionmaker.[107] Reliance on precedent in constitutional interpretation is said to provide more predictability, consistency, and stability in the law for judges, legislators, lawyers, and political branches and institutions that rely on the Court's rulings;[108] prevent the Court from overruling all but the most misguided decisions;[109] and allow constitutional norms to evolve slowly over time.[110]

---

[100] 576 U.S. ___, No. 13-1314, slip op. at 3 (2015).

[101] U.S. CONST. art. I, § 4, cl. 1.

[102] *Ariz. State Leg.*, slip op. at 35.

[103] *Id.* at 15 ("Three decisions compose the relevant case law: *Ohio ex rel. Davis v. Hildebrant*, 241 U.S. 565 (1916); *Hawke v. Smith (No. 1)*, 253 U.S. 221 (1920); and *Smiley v. Holm*, 285 U.S. 355 (1932).").

[104] *Id.* at 16.

[105] Bobbitt, *supra* note 22, at 42.

[106] "Stare decisis" refers to the "doctrine of precedent, under which a court must follow earlier judicial decisions when the same points arise again in litigation." *Black's Law Dictionary* 1626 (10th ed. 2014).

[107] *See* Gerhardt, *supra* note 94, at 70–71 (discussing arguments in support of the use of precedent).

[108] Epstein & Walker, *supra* note 22, at 29; Gerhardt, *supra* note 94, at 85–87.

[109] Henry P. Monaghan, *Stare Decisis and Constitutional Adjudication*, 88 COLUM. L. REV. 723, 749–50 (1988); Fallon, *supra* note 15, at 585.

[110] Maggs & Smith, *supra* note 58, at 19.

Some argue that judicial overreliance on precedent can be problematic. For one thing, certain precedents might have been wrongly decided, in which case relying on them merely perpetuates their erroneous construction of the Constitution.[111] Indeed, critics argue that, if the Court strictly adheres to precedent, once a precedent has been established on a question of constitutional law, the only way to alter that ruling is to amend the Constitution.[112] This inflexibility is particularly problematic when those outside the Court begin to disagree about general background principles underlying a precedent; as such, disagreements arguably cause that precedent to lose its authority.[113] For example, when precedent offends basic moral principles (e.g., *Plessy v. Ferguson*),[114] the power of the Court's precedent may necessarily be weakened.[115] Other commentators argue that "consistency," "predictability," "stability," and "neutrality" are not actually benefits of reliance on precedent, as judges may choose among precedents and, to some extent, interpret precedents in accordance with their own views in order to overrule them implicitly; to expand them; or to narrow them.[116] In addition, some proponents of original meaning as a method of constitutional interpretation object to the use of judicial precedent that conflicts with original meaning, because it favors the views of the Court

---

[111] Raoul Berger, *Original Intent and Boris Bittkey*, 66 IND. L.J. 723, 747 (1991) (citation omitted).

[112] *See, e.g.*, Burnet v. Coronado Oil & Gas Co., 285 U.S. 393, 406–10 (1932) (Brandeis, J., dissenting) ("[I]n cases involving the Federal Constitution, where correction through legislative action is practically impossible, this Court has often overruled its earlier decisions."); Smith v. Allwright, 321 U.S. 649, 665 (1944) ("[W]hen convinced of former error, this Court has never felt constrained to follow precedent. In constitutional questions, where correction depends upon amendment and not upon legislative action this Court throughout its history has freely exercised its power to reexamine the basis of its constitutional decisions.").

[113] Bobbitt, *supra* note 22, at 52.

[114] 163 U.S. 537 (1896). In *Plessy*, the Court upheld the constitutionality of a Louisiana law mandating racial segregation in railway cars, determining that "separate but equal" public accommodations did not violate Thirteenth or Fourteenth Amendment guarantees. *Id.* at 542, 550–51.

[115] Gerhardt, *supra* note 91, at 35–36.

[116] *Id.* at 34–35 ("Applying precedents requires interpreting them, interpreting them frequently entails modifying them, and modifying them often entails extending or contracting them."); Epstein & Walker, *supra* note 22, at 30.

over the views of those who ratified the Constitution, thereby allowing mistaken interpretations of the Constitution to persist.[117]

PRAGMATISM

In contrast to textualist and some originalist approaches to constitutional interpretation, which generally focus on the words of the Constitution as understood by a certain group of people, pragmatist approaches consider the likely practical consequences of particular interpretations of the Constitution.[118] That is, pragmatist approaches often involve the Court weighing or balancing the probable practical consequences of one interpretation of the Constitution against other interpretations.[119] One flavor of pragmatism weighs the future costs and benefits of an interpretation to society or the political branches,[120] selecting

[117] *See* Monaghan, *supra* note 109, at 769–70 ("In the interpretation of this written Constitution, we may assume that the founding generation was much attached to the original, publicly shared understanding of the document. Thus, one can make a good case that, as historically understood, the written Constitution was intended to trump not only statutes but case law. This argument is reinforced if one recalls that to the founding generation it was not clear that judicial opinions would need to play such a dominant role in establishing the meaning of the Constitution.").

[118] Hon. Richard A. Posner, *The Problems of Jurisprudence* 31 (1990).

[119] *See* Hon. Richard A. Posner, *Cardozo: A Study In Reputation* 28 (1990) (discussing Justice Benjamin Cardozo's views on pragmatism, as reflected in his jurisprudence, as contemplating a method "in which social interests behind competing legal principles are identified and (roughly speaking) weighed against each other to determine how a case lying at the intersection of those principles should be decided"); Hon. Richard A. Posner, *What Has Pragmatism to Offer Law?*, 63 S. Cal. L. Rev. 1653, 1670 (1990) ("All that a pragmatic jurisprudence really connotes...is a rejection of a concept of law as grounded in permanent principles and realized in logical manipulations of those principles, and a determination to use law as an instrument for social ends.").

[120] Justice Byron White often argued that the Court should adopt a functionalist approach in separation-of-powers cases by considering the extent to which a particular reading of the Constitution would promote a workable government. *See, e.g.*, INS v. Chadha, 462 U.S. 919, 984 (White, J., dissenting) ("It is long settled that Congress may 'exercise its best judgment in the selection of measures, to carry into execution the constitutional powers of the government,' and 'avail itself of experience, to exercise its reason, and to accommodate its legislation to circumstances.'") (quoting McCulloch v. Maryland, 17 U.S. (4 Wheat.) 316, 415–16, 420 (1819)) (internal quotation marks omitted); William J. Wagner, *Balancing as Art: Justice White and the Separation of Powers,* 52 Cath. U. L. Rev. 957, 962 (2003) ("Where he encountered silence in the constitutional text, Justice White consistently deferred to congressional judgments on the best structure and functioning of government. The

the interpretation that may lead to the perceived best outcome.[121] For example, in *United States v. Leon,* the majority held that the Fourth Amendment does not necessarily require a court to exclude evidence obtained as a result of the law enforcement's good faith reliance on an improperly issued search warrant.[122] Justice Byron White's majority opinion in *Leon* took a pragmatic approach, determining that "the [exclusionary] rule's purposes will only rarely be served" by applying it in the context of a good faith violation of the Fourth Amendment.[123] Notably, the Court determined that adoption of a broader exclusionary rule would result in significant societal costs by undermining the ability of the criminal justice system to obtain convictions of guilty defendants.[124] Such costs, the Court held, outweighed the "marginal or nonexistent benefits."[125]

Another case in which the Supreme Court accorded weight to the likely practical consequences of a particular interpretation of the Constitution is *United States v. Comstock.*[126] In *Comstock*, the Court considered whether Congress had the power under Article I, Section 8 of the Constitution to enact a civil commitment law authorizing the Department of Justice to cause to be detained indefinitely convicted sex offenders who had already served their criminal sentences but were deemed "mentally ill" and "sexually dangerous."[127] Such a power is not among those specifically enumerated in Article I, Section 8 of the Constitution, but the Court held that Congress could enact the law under a combination of (1) its implied constitutional powers to, among other things, legislate criminal offenses, provide for the imprisonment of offenders, and regulate prisons and prisoners; and (2) Article I, Section 8, Clause 18 of the Constitution, which provides Congress the power to "make all Laws which shall be necessary and proper for carrying into

---

judiciary's role in these cases was simply to unmask any congressional attempts to deprive another branch of its constitutional power, not to apply formulaic rules.").

[121] Brest et al., *supra* note 20, at 54–55.

[122] 468 U.S. 897, 926 (1984).

[123] *Id.*

[124] *Id.* at 907–08, 922.

[125] *Id.*

[126] 560 U.S. 126 (2010).

[127] *Id.* at 129–32.

Execution...all other Powers vested by this Constitution in the Government of the United States."[128] Justice Stephen Breyer, writing for the Court, listed several factors that weighed in favor of the Court's determination that Congress possessed the authority to enact the civil commitment law.[129] One of these factors rested primarily on pragmatic concerns about the potential detriment to society of releasing dangerous offenders into the community.[130] The Court held that the civil commitment law represented a rational means of implementing Congress's implied criminal justice powers "in light of the Government's custodial interest in safeguarding the public from dangers posed by those in federal custody."[131]

Using another type of pragmatist approach, a court might consider the extent to which the judiciary could play a constructive role in deciding a question of constitutional law.[132] According to this approach, a judge might observe the "passive virtues" by declining to rule on the constitutional issues in a case by adhering to certain doctrines, including those under which a judge will avoid ruling on political or constitutional questions.[133] This may allow the Court to avoid becoming frequently embroiled in public controversies, preserving the Court's institutional capital for key cases and giving more space for the democratic branches to address the issue and reach accommodations on questions about the meaning of the Constitution.[134] The Supreme Court's decision in *Baker v. Carr*[135] illustrates the application of this second type of pragmatism. In that case, Justice William Brennan, writing for the majority, debated a dissenting Justice Felix Frankfurter about whether the Court was the proper actor to review

---

[128] *Id.* at 135–37.

[129] *Id.* at 149–50. The factors included "(1) the breadth of the Necessary and Proper Clause, (2) the long history of federal involvement in this arena, (3) the sound reasons for the statute's enactment in light of the Government's custodial interest in safeguarding the public from dangers posed by those in federal custody, (4) the statute's accommodation of state interests, and (5) the statute's narrow scope." *Id.*

[130] *Id.* at 142–43, 149–50.

[131] *Id.*

[132] Bobbitt, *supra* note 22, at 7. Brest et al., *supra* note 20, at 55.

[133] Alexander M. Bickel, *The Least Dangerous Branch: The Supreme Court at the Bar of Politics* 199–201 (1962). Alternatively, the court could rule on the merits on narrow grounds. Cass R. Sunstein, *One Case at a Time: Judicial Minimalism on the Supreme Court* ix–xiv (2001).

[134] Brest et al., *supra* note 20, at 55.

[135] 369 U.S. 186 (1962).

the constitutionality of a state's apportionment of voters among legislative districts, or whether the plaintiffs should have sought remedies from the state legislature.[136] Justice Brennan's majority opinion in *Baker* ultimately concluded that a state's apportionment decisions are properly justiciable matters, as an alternative holding would require those harmed by malapportionment to seek redress from a political process that was skewed against such plaintiffs.[137]

Those who support pragmatism in constitutional interpretation argue that such an approach takes into account the "political and economic circumstances" surrounding the legal issue before the Court and seeks to produce the optimal outcome.[138] Such an approach may allow the Court to issue decisions reflecting contemporary values to the extent that the Court considers these values relevant to the costs and benefits of a particular interpretation.[139] On this view, pragmatism posits a view of the Constitution that is adaptable to changing societal circumstances, or that at least reflects the proper role of the judiciary.[140]

Critics of pragmatism argue that consideration of costs and benefits unnecessarily injects politics into judicial decisionmaking.[141] They argue that judges are not politicians. Rather, a judge's role is to say what the law is and not what it should be.[142] In addition, some opponents of the pragmatic approach have argued that when the Court observes the "passive virtues" by dismissing a case on jurisdictional grounds, it fails to provide guidance to parties for the future and to fulfill the Court's duty to decide important questions about constitutional rights.[143]

---

[136] *Id.* at 231–37, 266–68. The majority opinion announced a standard to determine when a case presents a political question not suitable for resolution by the courts. *See id.* at 217.

[137] *See id.* at 208–09.

[138] Bobbitt, *supra* note 22, at 61; Brest et al., *supra* note 20, at 54–55.

[139] Breyer, *supra* note 20, at 11–12.

[140] *Id.*

[141] *See* Scalia, *A Matter of Interpretation*, *supra* note 17, at 45–47.

[142] *See id.*

[143] Gerald Gunther, *The Subtle Vices of the "Passive Virtues": A Comment on Principle and Expediency in Judicial Review*, 64 Colum. L. Rev. 1, 15–16, 21–23 (1964).

MORAL REASONING

Another approach to constitutional interpretation is based on moral or ethical reasoning—often broadly called the "ethos of the law."[144] Under this approach, some constitutional text employs or makes reference to terms that are infused with (and informed by) certain moral concepts or ideals, such as "equal protection" or "due process of law."[145] The moral or ethical arguments based on the text often pertain to the limits of government authority over the individual (i.e., individual rights).[146] The Court has derived general moral principles from the broad language of the Fourteenth Amendment in cases involving state laws or actions affecting individual rights.[147] For example, in *Lawrence v. Texas*, the Court struck down a Texas law that banned private, consensual same-sex sexual activity as violating the Due Process Clause of the Fourteenth Amendment.[148] That clause provides, in relevant part, that states shall not "deprive any person of...liberty...without due process of law."[149] The Court held that the concept of liberty "presumes an autonomy of self that includes freedom of thought, belief, expression, and certain intimate conduct."[150] Notably, the text of the Fourteenth Amendment does not define "liberty," and the Court's holding in *Lawrence* is more broadly grounded in general views about the proper role of government in not punishing behavior that provides no discernible harm to the public at large.[151]

A particularly famous example of an argument based on the "ethos of the law" is contained in the Court's decision in *Bolling v. Sharpe*.[152] The Court decided *Bolling* on the same day it decided *Brown v. Board of Education*, which held that a state, in segregating its public school systems

---

144 Some scholars refer to the general moral or ethical principles underlying the text of the Constitution as the "ethos of the law." Bobbitt, *supra* note 22, at 142.
145 *Id.* at 126.
146 *Id.* at 162.
147 *Id.* at 142.
148 539 U.S. 558, 578 (2003).
149 U.S. Const. amend. XIV, § 1.
150 *Lawrence*, 539 U.S. at 562.
151 *See id.* at 578.
152 347 U.S. 497 (1954).

by race, violated the Fourteenth Amendment.[153] Specifically, the Court held that the practice of "separate but equal" as applied to schools violated the Equal Protection Clause, a provision that prohibits state governments from depriving their citizens of the equal protection of the law.[154]

Bolling, however, involved the District of Columbia school system, which was not subject to the Fourteenth Amendment because the District of Columbia is not a state, but rather a federal enclave.[155] Furthermore, the Fifth Amendment, which applies to the actions of the federal government, provides that no person shall "be deprived of life, liberty, or property, without due process of law" but does not explicitly contain an Equal Protection Clause.[156] Nevertheless, the Court struck down racial segregation in DC public schools as a violation of the Fifth Amendment's Due Process Clause, determining that due process guarantees implicitly include a guarantee of equal protection.[157] The Court's reasoning was based on the Due Process Clause being derived "from our American ideal of fairness," ultimately holding that the Fifth Amendment prohibited the federal government from allowing segregation in public schools.[158]

Proponents of using moral or ethical reasoning as an approach for making sense of broad constitutional text, such as the Due Process Clause of the Fourteenth Amendment, argue that general moral principles underlie much of the text of the Constitution.[159] Thus, arguments about what the Constitution means based on moral reasoning produce "more candid opinions," as judges often rely upon moral arguments but disguise them as textual arguments or arguments based on precedent.[160] Some also argue that the Framers designed the Constitution as an instrument that would grow over time.[161] Thus, supporters of moral reasoning in constitutional

---

[153] *Id.* at 498–99 (citing Brown v. Bd. of Educ., 347 U.S. 483 (1954)).
[154] *Id.*
[155] *Id.*; *see also* U.S. Const. art. I, § 8, cl. 17.
[156] U.S. Const. amend. V; *Bolling*, 347 U.S. at 498–500.
[157] *Id.*
[158] *Id.* at 499–500.
[159] Hadley Arkes, *Beyond The Constitution* 19 (1990).
[160] Bobbitt, *supra* note 22, at 106.
[161] Barber, *supra* note 35, at 40 (discussing the view that the Constitution "marks out 'lines of growth' toward the real values of the framers and away from those of their views and

interpretation contend that its use appropriately leads to more flexibility for judges to incorporate contemporary values when deriving meaning from the Constitution.[162] Ethical arguments can also fill in gaps in the text to address situations unforeseen at the time of the Founding,[163] consistent with the understanding of the Bill of Rights as a starting point for individual rights.[164]

Critics of using moral reasoning in constitutional interpretation have argued that courts should not be "moral arbiters."[165] They argue that ethical arguments are based on principles that are not objectively verifiable[166] and may require a judge to choose between "competing moral conventions."[167] Courts may thus be ill-equipped to discern established moral principles. Judges using this mode of constitutional interpretation may therefore decide cases according to their own policy views, and opponents believe that overturning acts of the political branches based on such considerations is undemocratic.[168] Some opponents argue that moral considerations may be better left to the political branches.[169]

National Identity or "National Ethos"

Another approach to interpretation that is closely related to but conceptually distinct from moral reasoning is judicial reasoning that relies on the concept of a "national ethos." This national ethos is defined as the unique character of American institutions, the American people's distinct national identity, and "the role within [the nation's public institutions] of the American people."[170] An example of the "national ethos" approach to

attitudes that were inconsistent with their aspirations" (citing John Hart Ely, *Constitutional Interpretivism: Its Allure and Impossibility*, 53 IND. L.J. 399, 410–14 (1978))).

[162] Ely, *supra* note 78, at 1.

[163] Bobbitt, *supra* note 22, at 102.

[164] Arkes, *supra* note 159, at 60–62.

[165] Bobbitt, *supra* note 22, at 137.

[166] *Id.* at 138.

[167] *Id.* at 139; Ely, *supra* note 78, at 59.

[168] *Id.* at 5.

[169] *See id.*

[170] Bobbitt, *supra* note 22, at 94.

ethical reasoning is found in *Moore v. City of East Cleveland*, in which the Court struck down as unconstitutional a city zoning ordinance that prohibited a woman from living in a dwelling with her grandson.[171] In its decision, the Court surveyed the history of the family as an institution in American life and stated, "Our decisions establish that the Constitution protects the sanctity of the family precisely because the institution of the family is deeply rooted in this Nation's history and tradition. It is through the family that we inculcate and pass down many of our most cherished values, moral and cultural."[172] Thus, the Court struck down the zoning ordinance, at least in part, because it interfered with the American institution of the family by preventing a grandmother from living with her grandson.[173]

Another example of the Court's reliance on national ethos as a rationale is *West Virginia State Board of Education v. Barnette*.[174] In that case, the Court held that the First Amendment prohibited a state from enacting a law compelling students to salute the American flag.[175] Writing for the majority, Justice Robert Jackson noted that, in contrast to authoritarian regimes such as the Roman Empire, Spain, and Russia, the United States' unique form of constitutional government eschews the use of government coercion as a means of achieving national unity.[176] The Court invoked the nation's character as reflected in the Constitution, writing that, "If there is any fixed star in our constitutional constellation, it is that no official, high or petty, can prescribe what shall be orthodox in politics, nationalism, religion, or other matters of opinion or force citizens to confess by word or act their faith therein."[177]

Many of the arguments in the debate over reliance on the "national ethos" in constitutional interpretation share similarities with arguments made about the use of moral reasoning as a mode of interpretation. Some proponents of using the distinct character of the American national identity

---

[171] 431 U.S. 494, 506 (1977).
[172] *Id.* at 499–504.
[173] *Id.*
[174] 319 U.S. 624 (1943).
[175] *Id.* at 642.
[176] *Id.* at 640–41.
[177] Id.

and the nation's institutions as a method for elaborating on the Constitution's meaning argue that the "national ethos" underlies the text of the Constitution, and that the use of this method allows more flexibility for judges to incorporate contemporary American values when deriving meaning from the Constitution.[178] Moreover, unlike approaches that discern meaning from general moral or ethical principles, the "national ethos" approach arguably has added legitimacy as a mode of interpretation because it is specifically tied to the identity and values of the United States and those aspects of the Constitution that are distinctly American.[179] As noted, ethical arguments can also fill in gaps in the text to address situations unforeseen at the time of the Founding.[180]

On the other hand, as with moral reasoning, critics of an approach to constitutional interpretation based on the "national ethos" have argued that such an approach involves unelected judges determining the meaning of the Constitution based on principles that are not objectively verifiable—determinations that critics argue should be made by the political branches.[181]

STRUCTURALISM

One of the most common modes of constitutional interpretation is based on the structure of the Constitution. Indeed, drawing inferences from the design of the Constitution gives rise to some of the most important relationships that everyone agrees the Constitution establishes—the relationships among the three branches of the federal government (commonly called separation of powers or checks and balances); the relationship between the federal and state governments (known as

---

[178] Cf. supra notes 159, 162.

[179] Cf. Thompson v. Oklahoma, 487 U.S. 815, 869 n.4 (1988) (Scalia, J., dissenting) ("The plurality's reliance upon Amnesty International's account of what it pronounces to be civilized standards of decency in other countries...is totally inappropriate as a means of establishing the fundamental beliefs of this Nation....We must never forget that it is a Constitution for the United States of America that we are expounding.").

[180] See supra notes 163-64.

[181] Cf. supra notes 165-69.

federalism); and the relationship between the government and the people.[182] Two basic approaches seek to make sense of these relationships.

The first, known as formalism, posits that the Constitution sets forth all the ways in which federal power may be shared, allocated, or distributed.[183] An example of the use of this form of structuralism as a mode of interpretation is found in *Immigration and Naturalization Service v. Chadha*.[184] In that case, the Court held that one house of Congress could not by resolution unilaterally curtail the statutory authority of the executive branch to allow a deportable alien to remain in the United States.[185] The Court examined the structure of the Constitution and noted that under the Bicameralism and Presentment Clauses in Article I, Sections 1 and 7, laws with subject matter that is "legislative in character or effect" require passage by a majority in both houses and presentment to the President for his signature or veto.[186] Viewing the exercise of the one-house veto in *Chadha* to be of a legislative nature, the Court concluded that the structural relationships that the Constitution established between the legislative and executive branches forbid the "one-House legislative veto."[187]

An example of the Court's use of formalist structural reasoning in the context of federalism is *U.S. Term Limits, Inc. v. Thornton*.[188] In that case, the Court considered whether the State of Arkansas could prohibit the names of otherwise-qualified candidates for congressional office from appearing on the state's general election ballot if the candidates had served three terms

---

[182] Charles L. Black, Jr., *Structure and Relationship in Constitutional Law* 7 (1969) [hereinafter *Black, Structure and Relationship*].

[183] John F. Manning, *Separation of Powers as Ordinary Interpretation*, 124 Harv. L. Rev. 1939, 1942–44 (2011); Peter L. Strauss, *Formal and Functional Approaches to Separation-of-Powers Questions—A Foolish Inconsistency?*, 72 Cornell L. Rev. 488, 489 (1987) ("The Supreme Court has vacillated over the years between using a formalistic approach to separation-of-powers issues grounded in the perceived necessity of maintaining three distinct branches of government (and consequently appearing to draw rather sharp boundaries), and a functional approach that stresses core function and relationship, and permits a good deal of flexibility when these attributes are not threatened.").

[184] 462 U.S. 919 (1983).

[185] *Id.* at 923, 946.

[186] *Id.* at 952, 54–55.

[187] Id.

[188] 514 U.S. 779 (1995).

in the House of Representatives or two terms in the Senate.[189] In striking down an amendment to the Arkansas State Constitution, the Court relied heavily on its view of the formal structural relationships that the Constitution established among the people of the United States, the states, and the federal government.[190] In particular, the Court determined that the Founding Fathers established a single, national legislature representing "the people of the United States" rather than a "confederation of sovereign states."[191] Thus, allowing states to adopt a patchwork of distinct qualifications for congressional service would "erode the structure envisioned by the Framers."[192] Notably, the Court in *Thornton* adhered closely to its view of how the Constitution allocates power between the federal and state governments, and did not employ a balancing test to examine the degree to which the states' power to set qualifications for congressional office would interfere with the federal government's constitutional prerogatives.

A second form of structural reasoning, known as functionalism, treats the Constitution's text as having firmly spelled out the relationship among the three federal branches only at their apexes, but otherwise left it to be worked out in practice how power may be distributed or shared below the apexes.[193] Whereas formalism purports to hew closely to original meaning and regards historical practices as basically irrelevant or illegitimate, functionalism uses a balancing approach that weighs competing

---

[189] Id. at 783. The Constitution imposes qualifications regarding minimum age, citizenship, and residency of a Member of the House or Senate, but it does not contain language expressly imposing term limits on Members. U.S. Const. art. I, § 2, cl. 2 (qualifications for Members of the House of Representatives); id. art. I, § 3, cl. 3 (qualifications for Senators).

[190] U.S. Term Limits, 514 U.S. at 783.

[191] Id. at 783, 822, 837–38; Kathleen M. Sullivan, Comment, Dueling Sovereignties: U.S. Term Limits, Inc. v. Thornton, 109 *Harv. L. Rev.* 78, 88 (1995) ("The majority and the dissent deduced opposite formal structural axioms from the founding. To the majority, the founding was a 'revolutionary' act that replaced a confederation of sovereign states with a 'National Government' in which the 'representatives owe primary allegiance not to the people of a State, but to the people of the Nation.'").

[192] U.S. Term Limits, 514 U.S. at 783, 822, 837–38. The Court also determined that the sovereign powers possessed by the states prior to the American Revolution did not include the power to establish additional qualifications for congressional service. Id. at 802.

[193] Michael C. Dorf, *Interpretive Holism and the Structural Method*, 92 GEO. L.J. 833, 837 (2004); Strauss, *supra* note 183, at 489.

governmental interests as one of its principal methodologies.[194] One early example of functionalism is *McCulloch v. Maryland*.[195] In that case, the Court held that Congress had the power to create the Second Bank of the United States.[196] While Congress's enumerated powers in Article I, Section 8 of the Constitution do not specifically include the power to create a central bank, the Court considered whether Congress had such authority under its enumerated powers when viewed in conjunction with Article I, Section 8, Clause 18, which provides Congress the power "To make all Laws which shall be necessary and proper for carrying into Execution the foregoing Powers, and all other Powers vested by this Constitution in the Government of the United States."[197] The Court determined that Congress had an implied power to create the bank under the Necessary and Proper Clause in order to implement its express powers to tax and spend, concluding that the terms "necessary" and "proper" should not have a restrictive meaning on Congress's power.[198] In so holding, the Court examined the structure of the Constitution's text, noting that the Constitution located the Necessary and Proper Clause in the section of the Constitution that grants powers to Congress (Article I, Section 8), instead of the section of the Constitution that restricts the powers of the federal government (Article I, Section 9).[199] Moreover, the *McCulloch* Court noted that a more restrictive reading of Congress's powers would impair its ability to "perform[] its functions," as a narrow reading of the Necessary and Proper Clause would impose "some difficulty in sustaining the authority of Congress to pass other laws for the accomplishment of the same objects."[200]

As is evident, a threshold debate among structuralists is whether to use a formalist or functionalist approach when interpreting the Constitution. This debate is founded partly in concerns about which approach demonstrates greater fidelity to the Constitution, which is closest to the

---

[194] *See* Manning, *supra* note 183, at 1942–44.
[195] 17 U.S. (4 Wheat.) 316 (1819).
[196] *Id.* at 425.
[197] *Id.* at 411–12.
[198] *Id.* at 419–21.
[199] *Id.*
[200] *Id.* at 409.

original meaning of the Constitution, and which best protects liberty in cases raising questions about the proper allocation of power between the branches of the federal government; federal government and states; government institutions; or citizens and government.[201]

Formalism focuses on the structural divisions in the Constitution with the idea that close adherence to these rules is required in order to achieve the preservation of liberty.[202] An example is the Court's opinion in *Chadha*, which, as noted, held that structural relationships that the Constitution established between the legislative and executive branches forbid the "one-House legislative veto."[203] The Court rested its holding in part on a close adherence to the structural divisions established in the Constitution, stating, "It emerges clearly that the prescription for legislative action in [Article I, Sections 1 and 7 of the Constitution] represents the Framers' decision that the legislative power of the Federal Government be exercised in accord with a single, finely wrought and exhaustively considered, procedure."[204] As demonstrated in *Chadha*, a formalist approach to separation-of-powers questions rejects not only looking to postratification historical practices as a guide for determining constitutional meaning, but also eschews balancing tests that weigh the degree of interference with one branch's powers.

By contrast, *functionalism* takes a more flexible approach, emphasizing the core functions of each of the branches, and asking whether an overlap in these functions upsets the equilibrium that the Framers sought to maintain.[205] An example is the Court's opinion in *Zivotofsky v. Kerry*.[206] In that case, the Court held that the President has the exclusive power to recognize formally a foreign sovereign and its territorial boundaries, and that Congress could not effectively require the State Department to issue a

---

[201] *See* Manning, *supra* note 183, at 1942–44, 1950–52, 1958–60. *See also* Myers v. United States, 272 U.S. 52, 116 (1926).

[202] Manning, *supra* note 183, at 1958–60.

[203] 462 U.S. 919, 952, 54–55 (1983).

[204] *Id.* at 951.

[205] Manning, *supra* note 183, at 1950–52.

[206] 576 U.S. __, No. 13-628, slip op. at 1 (2015).

formal statement contradicting the President's policy on recognition.[207] In so holding, the Court stated that the President should have such an exclusive power because the nation must have a "single policy" on which governments are legitimate, and that additional pronouncements from Congress on the issue could result in confusion.[208] The Court thus adopted a functionalist approach by considering the practical consequences of allocating the power of recognition between the legislative and executive branches, ultimately concluding that the President alone should exercise that power.

A further illustration of the distinction between formalism and functionalism in a separation of powers case is *Morrison v. Olson*.[209] In *Morrison*, the Court upheld against constitutional challenge provisions in the Ethics in Government Act of 1978 that allowed for appointment of an "independent counsel to investigate and, if appropriate, prosecute certain high-ranking Government officials for violations of federal criminal laws."[210] The Attorney General could remove the independent counsel only for "good cause,"[211] a legal standard that provided the special prosecutor with significant independence from the President and his officers.[212] In a 7-1 decision, the Court employed a functionalist approach and held that the act did not violate constitutional separation-of-powers principles by sufficiently interfering with the President's executive authority under Article II.[213] The Court determined the limited nature of the special prosecutor's jurisdiction and authority meant that the position did not "interfere impermissibly with [the President's] constitutional obligation to ensure the faithful execution of the laws."[214] Justice Scalia, the sole dissenter, adopted a formalist approach, arguing that the majority failed to adhere to the strict allocations of power that the Constitution

---

207 *Id.* at 29.
208 *Id.* at 11.
209 487 U.S. 654 (1988).
210 *Id.* at 659–60.
211 *Id.* at 663.
212 *Cf.* Humphrey's Ex'r v. United States, 295 U.S. 602, 629 ("We think it plain under the Constitution that illimitable power of removal is not possessed by the President in respect of officers [subject to removal 'for cause'].")
213 *Id.* at 689–97.
214 *Id.*

establishes among the branches of government.[215] Justice Scalia wrote that the independent counsel provisions deprived the President of "exclusive control" over the exercise of "purely executive powers" (e.g., investigation and prosecution of crimes) by vesting them in the independent counsel, who was not removable at will by the President.[216]

Proponents of structuralism note that it is a method of interpretation that considers the entire text of the Constitution rather than a particular part of it.[217] As a consequence, some proponents argue that structuralist methods produce clearer justifications for decisions that require interpretation of vague provisions of the Constitution and their application to particular factual circumstances than textualism alone.[218] Some argue that structuralism provides a firmer basis for personal rights than other modes of interpretation like textualism or moral reasoning.[219] For example, in *Crandall v. Nevada*, the Court struck down a state law imposing a tax on people leaving or passing through the state.[220] The Court inferred an individual right to travel among the states from the structural relationship the Constitution establishes between citizens and the federal and state governments.[221] While the Constitution does not specifically provide for a right to travel among the states, because citizens of the United States might need to travel among the states to exercise other constitutional rights, the Court inferred a right to travel from the Constitution viewed in its entirety.[222] As a result, some structuralists argue that the method of interpretation provides a more firm basis to establish key constitutional rights, like the right to travel, than other modes of constitutional interpretation.[223]

Some scholars maintain, however, that structuralism does not always lead to a clear answer.[224] More specifically, critics argue that it is more difficult for judges to apply and for citizens to understand interpretations

---

215 *Id.* at 699, 703–04 (Scalia, J., dissenting).
216 *Id.* at 705–10.
217 Bobbitt, *supra* note 22, at 74.
218 *Black, Structure and Relationship*, *supra* note 182, at 13, 22.
219 *Id.* at 46.
220 73 U.S. 35, 39, 49 (1868).
221 *Id.*
222 *Black, Structure and Relationship*, *supra* note 182, at 27.
223 *Id.* at 13, 22.
224 Bobbitt, *supra* note 22, at 84; Sunstein, *supra* note 9, at 120.

based on structuralism than arguments based on other modes of interpretation.[225] In addition, many believe that determinations about the proper structure established by the Constitution are often subjective. While the eminent Professor Charles Black argued that structure was the most important mode of constitutional interpretation, at least one other prominent commentator has argued that the approach provides "no firm basis for personal rights" because personal rights are considered to derive from the "structure of citizenship" and are therefore "vulnerable to the [government's] desire for power and its ability to manipulate the relation between citizen and state."[226]

HISTORICAL PRACTICES

Judicial precedents are not the only type of precedents that are arguably relevant to constitutional interpretation. Prior decisions of the political branches, particularly their long-established, historical practices, are an important source of constitutional meaning to many judges, academics, and lawyers.[227] Indeed, courts have viewed historical practices as a source of the Constitution's meaning in cases involving questions about the separation of powers, federalism, and individual rights, particularly when the text provides no clear answer.[228]

An example of judicial reliance on historical practices—sometimes described as tradition—in constitutional interpretation is the Court's decision in *National Labor Relations Board v. Canning*.[229] When

---

[225] Bobbitt, *supra* note 22, at 85.

[226] *Id.* at 85–86; Alexander M. Bickel, *The Morality of Consent* 53 (1975).

[227] Brest et al., *supra* note 20, at 56.

[228] *E.g.*, McCulloch v. Maryland, 17 U.S. (4 Wheat.) 316, 401 (1819) ("[A] doubtful question, one on which human reason may pause, and the human judgment be suspended, in the decision of which the great principles of liberty are not concerned, but the respective powers of those who are equally the representatives of the people, are to be adjusted; if not put at rest by the practice of the government, ought to receive a considerable impression from that practice."); *see also* PHH Corp. v. Consumer Fin. Prot. Bureau, 839 F.3d 1, 21–25 (D.C. Cir. 2016) (summarizing Supreme Court cases using historical practices as a method of constitutional interpretation in separation-of-powers cases).

[229] 573 U.S. __, No. 12-1281, slip op. at 1 (2014).

determining, among other things, that the President lacked authority to make a recess appointment during a Senate recess of fewer than ten days, the Court cited long-settled historical practices showing an absence of a settled tradition of such recess appointments as being relevant to the resolution of a separation-of-powers question not squarely addressed by the Constitution.[230] Another example of the influence of historical practices on constitutional interpretation is the Court's decision in *Zivotofsky v. Kerry*.[231] As noted above, in that case the Court held that the President had the exclusive power to recognize formally a foreign sovereign and its territorial boundaries, and that Congress could not effectively require the State Department to issue a formal statement contradicting the President's policy on recognition.[232] In deciding the case, the Court relied in part on the long-standing historical practice of the President in recognizing foreign sovereigns without congressional consent.[233]

An example of the use of historical practices as a method of constitutional interpretation in a case involving the limits of government power is *Marsh v. Chambers*.[234] In *Marsh*, the Court considered whether the First Amendment's Establishment Clause, which prohibits laws "respecting an establishment of religion," forbade the State of Nebraska from paying a chaplain with public funds to open each legislative session with a prayer in the Judeo-Christian tradition.[235] The Court held that the state's chaplaincy practice did not violate the Establishment Clause, attaching significance to the long-standing practices of Congress (including the Congress that adopted the First Amendment as part of the Bill of Rights) and some states in funding chaplains to open legislative sessions with a prayer.[236] The Court wrote, "The opening of sessions of legislative and other deliberative public bodies with prayer is deeply embedded in the history and tradition of this country. From colonial times through the founding of the Republic and ever since, the practice of legislative prayer

---

230 *Id.* at 21.
231 576 U.S. __, No. 13-628, slip op. at 1 (2015).
232 *Id.* at 29.
233 *Id.* at 20–21.
234 463 U.S. 783 (1983).
235 *Id.* at 784.
236 *Id.* at 788–89.

has coexisted with the principles of disestablishment and religious freedom."[237]

The debate over historical practices as a mode of interpretation echoes many of the elements of debates over original meaning, judicial precedent, and arguments based on a "national ethos."[238] Functionalists, for example, attach considerable importance to historical practices as a source of constitutional meaning, while formalists generally regard them as irrelevant.[239] Those employing this method often argue that, when the text of the Constitution is ambiguous, the use of historical practices has legitimacy as an interpretive tool.[240] They also contend that such an approach provides an objective and neutral basis for decisionmaking, leading to more predictability and stability in the law upon which parties can rely.[241] Moreover, according interpretive significance to historical practices in cases concerning the allocation of power among the branches of government may help to preserve settled expectations that have resulted from long-standing compromises among the branches regarding such allocations.[242]

Those opposing reliance on historical practices as a source of constitutional meaning argue that it may be difficult to establish definitively what the relevant historical practices are in order to interpret

---

[237] *Id.* at 786.

[238] The arguments in the following three paragraphs draw heavily from the sections *supra* on "Original Meaning," "Judicial Precedent," and "Moral Reasoning."

[239] Jonathan Turley, *Constitutional Adverse Possession: Recess Appointments and the Role of Historical Practice in Constitutional Interpretation*, 2013 WIS. L. REV. 965, 969 ("[Functionalism] is a model of interpretation that invites the use of historical practice as self-affirming support for meaning.").

[240] *Cf.* Youngstown Sheet & Tube Co. v. Sawyer, 343 U.S. 579, 610 (1952) (Frankfurter, J., concurring) ("The Constitution is a framework for government. Therefore the way the framework has consistently operated fairly establishes that it has operated according to its true nature. Deeply embedded traditional ways of conducting government cannot supplant the Constitution or legislation, but they give meaning to the words of a text or supply them."); *see also* Turley, *supra* note 239, at 969.

[241] *Cf.* Gerhardt, *supra* note 94, at 70–71, 86–87 (discussing similar arguments in support of the use of judicial precedent in constitutional interpretation).

[242] Curtis A. Bradley & Neil S. Siegel, *After Recess: Historical Practice, Textual Ambiguity, and Constitutional Adverse Possession*, 2014 SUP. CT. REV. 1, 40 ("[I]nterests in stability and related rule-of-law considerations, such as consistency, predictability, reliance, and transparency, also can be advanced by adhering to long-standing practices, regardless of whether they date to the early post-Founding period.").

the Constitution properly.[243] They suggest that not all practices are authorized by the written text and that historical sources may differ and thus might not be helpful in illuminating patterns in historical practices.[244] They also warn that this methodology could allow judges to engage in a form of what is called "law office history"—simply choosing the sources that support the historical practices they wish to ratify or reject.[245] Thus, it could be argued that historical practices may not lend themselves to easy or clear interpretation. Moreover, they can lead to results inconsistent with the original meaning of the Constitution.[246] Another possible problem with reliance on historical practices in constitutional interpretation, according to its critics, is that courts could end up legitimizing long-standing historical practices, such as slavery or segregation, that offend modern moral principles. Indeed, giving historical practices special place in constitutional interpretation could lead courts to fail to protect minority rights[247] or to preserve the basic structure of government established by the Constitution.[248] At the same time, reliance on historical practices might undermine the political branches when they are attempting to be innovative or opt for novel solutions to old problems.[249]

---

[243] *Cf.* Epstein & Walker, *supra* note 22, at 28 (reciting arguments made against original meaning as a method of constitutional interpretation).

[244] Bradley & Siegel, *supra* note 242, at 41–44; Bobbitt, *supra* note 22, at 11 (summarizing arguments made against original meaning).

[245] Alfred H. Kelly, *Clio and the Court: An Illicit Love Affair*, 1965 Sup. Ct. Rev. 119, 122 & n.13 (defining "law office history" as "the selection of data favorable to the position being advanced without regard to or concern for contradictory data or proper evaluation of the relevance of the data proffered").

[246] Bradley & Siegel, *supra* note 242, at 27–29.

[247] *Cf.* Brennan, *supra* note 20, at 436–37.

[248] NLRB v. Canning, 573 U.S. __, No. 12-1281, slip op. at 4–5 (2014) (Scalia, J., concurring in the judgment) ("[P]olicing the 'enduring structure' of constitutional government when the political branches fail to do so is 'one of the most vital functions of this Court.'") (citation omitted); *id.* at 47–48 ("Even if the Executive could accumulate power through adverse possession by engaging in a *consistent* and *unchallenged* practice over a long period of time, the oft-disputed practices at issue here would not meet that standard. Nor have those practices created any justifiable expectations that could be disappointed by enforcing the Constitution's original meaning. There is thus no ground for the majority's deference to the unconstitutional recess-appointment practices of the Executive Branch.").

[249] *See* Manning, *supra* note 183, at 1943 ("[F]unctionalists believe that Congress has substantially free rein to innovate, as long as a particular scheme satisfies the functional aims of the constitutional structure, taken as a whole.").

Deriving the Constitution's meaning from long-established, historical practices of the political branches is one of several methods of constitutional interpretation the Court has relied upon when exercising the power of judicial review. In explaining the meaning of the provisions of the Constitution, courts and commentators often refer to these modes of interpretation. An understanding of these methods, which are not mutually exclusive, will aid congressional staff in understanding the development of the constitutional doctrines that guide the Justices, government officials, and other individuals when they interpret the Constitution.

In: Constitution
Editor: Jackelyn Haggerty
ISBN: 978-1-53614-198-6

Chapter 2

UNDERSTANDING THE SPEECH OR DEBATE CLAUSE*

Todd Garvey

SUMMARY

The Speech or Debate Clause (Clause) of the U.S. Constitution states that "[F]or any Speech or Debate in either House," Members of Congress (Members) "shall not be questioned in any other Place." The Clause serves various purposes: principally to protect the independence and integrity of the legislative branch by protecting against executive or judicial intrusions into the protected legislative sphere, but also to bar judicial or executive processes that may constitute a "distraction" or "disruption" to a Member's representative or legislative role. Despite the literal text, protected acts under the Clause extend beyond "speeches" or "debates" undertaken by Members of Congress, and have also been interpreted to include all "legislative acts" undertaken by Members or their aides.

Judicial interpretations of the Clause have developed along several strains. First and foremost, the Clause has been interpreted as providing

* This is an edited, reformatted and augmented version of Congressional Research Service report 7-5700, R45043, www.crs.gov, dated December 1, 2017.

Members with general criminal and civil immunity for all "legislative acts" taken in the course of their official responsibilities. This immunity principle protects Members from "intimidation by the executive" or a "hostile judiciary" by prohibiting both the executive and judicial powers from being used to improperly influence or harass legislators. Second, the Clause appears to provide complementary evidentiary and testimonial privileges. Although not explicitly articulated by the Supreme Court, lower federal courts have generally viewed these component privileges as a means of effectuating the purposes of the Clause by barring evidence of protected legislative acts from being used against a Member, and protecting a Member from compelled questioning about such acts.

The testimonial privilege component of the Clause has given rise to significant disagreement in the lower courts. The U.S. Court of Appeals for the District of Columbia Circuit (D.C. Circuit) has held that the Clause's testimonial privilege encompasses a general documentary nondisclosure privilege that applies regardless of the purposes for which disclosure is sought. To the contrary, the U.S. Court of Appeals for the Third Circuit and the U.S. Court of Appeals for the Ninth Circuit have rejected that position, holding instead that, at least in criminal cases, the Clause prohibits only the evidentiary use of privileged documents, not their mere disclosure to the government for review as part of an investigation.

[F]or any Speech or Debate in either House, [The Senators and Representatives] shall not be questioned in any other Place.

U.S. CONST. Art I, § 6 cl. 1

INTRODUCTION

The Constitution's Speech or Debate Clause (Clause) represents a key pillar in the American separation of powers.[1] The Clause, which derives its form from the language of the English Bill of Rights and has deep roots in

[1] United States v. Helstoski, 442 U.S. 477, 491 (1979) (noting that the Clause's "purpose was to preserve the constitutional structure of separate, coequal, and independent branches of government."); United States v. Johnson, 383 U.S. 169, 178 (1966) (holding that the Clause "reinforc[es] the separation of powers so deliberately established by the Founders."); United States v. Renzi, 651 F.3d 1012, 1037 (9th Cir. 2011) (noting that the "Speech or Debate Clause is a creature born of separation of powers concerns"); Fields v. Office of Johnson, 459 F.3d 1, 8 (D.C. Cir. 2006) (en banc) ("The Speech or Debate Clause reinforces the separation of powers and protects legislative independence.").

the historic struggles between King and Parliament,[2] serves chiefly to protect the independence, integrity, and effectiveness of the legislative branch by barring executive or judicial intrusions into the protected sphere of the legislative process.[3] These prohibited intrusions may take various forms, and, judicial interpretation of the Clause's relatively ambiguous language has developed along several related lines of cases.[4]

First and foremost, the Clause has been interpreted as providing Members of Congress (Members)[5] with general immunity from liability for all "legislative acts"[6] taken in the course of their official responsibilities.[7] This "cloak of protection"[8] shields Members from "intimidation by the executive" or a "hostile judiciary" by protecting against either the executive or judicial powers from being used to improperly influence or harass legislators through retaliatory litigation.[9] This overarching immunity principle has traditionally been viewed as advancing the primary purpose of the Clause: that of preserving the independence of the legislative branch.

The Clause has also been said to serve a good governance role, barring judicial or executive processes that may constitute a "distraction" or

---

[2] *Johnson*, 383 U.S. at 178 (describing the Clause as "the culmination of a long struggle for parliamentary supremacy" in which "successive monarchs utilized the criminal and civil law to suppress and intimidate critical legislators."). For a thorough discussion of the historical evolution of the legislative privilege associated with the Clause, *see* Josh Chafetz, *Congress's Constitution: Legislative Authority and the Separation of Powers* 201-10 (2017).

[3] *See Helstoski*, 442 U.S. at 491("This Court has reiterated the central importance of the Clause for preventing intrusion by [the] Executive and Judiciary into the legislative sphere."); *Johnson*, 383 U.S. at 181 (noting that the primary purpose of the Clause is to "prevent intimidation by the executive and accountability before a possibly hostile judiciary").

[4] Brown & Williamson Tobacco Corp. v. Williams, 62 F.3d 408, 415 (D.C. Cir. 1995) ("From this terse prohibition has emerged a somewhat complicated privilege, with several strands.").

[5] This report will refer generally to "Members," but as discussed infra, the privilege applies to Members and their aides. *See* "Who Is Protected?" *infra.*

[6] *See* "What Constitutes a Legislative Act?" *infra.*

[7] Eastland v. United States Servicemen's Fund, 421 U.S. 491, 502-03 (1975) ("Thus we have long held that, when it applies, the Clause provides protection against civil as well as criminal actions, and against actions brought by private individuals as well as those initiated by the Executive Branch."); Gravel v. United States, 408 U.S. 606, 615-17 (1972).

[8] Senate Permanent Subcomm. on Investigations v. Ferrer, 856 F.3d 1080, 1085 (D.C. Cir. 2017).

[9] *See Johnson*, 383 U.S. at 181; *Gravel*, 408 U.S. at 617; Miller v. Transamerican Press, Inc., 709 F.2d 524, 528 (9th Cir. 1983).

"disruption" to a Member's representative or legislative role.[10] The Court has cited this "distraction" principle, and the Clause's broad proscription that Members not be "questioned in *any* other place," as justification for extending the Clause's immunity protection beyond criminal actions initiated by the executive branch— which clearly implicate the separation of powers—to private civil suits initiated by members of the public—which generally implicate the separation of powers only to a lesser degree.[11]

Even when absolute immunity is not appropriate—for example, when a charge or claim does not arise directly out of a legislative act but is rather entangled with protected and unprotected acts— the Clause appears to provide Members with complementary evidentiary and testimonial privileges which may be invoked by a Member to protect against the introduction of specific "legislative act" evidence. Although not explicitly articulated by the Supreme Court,[12] lower federal courts have generally viewed these component privileges as a means of effectuating the protections afforded by the Clause by barring the introduction of specific documentary evidence of protected legislative acts for use against a

---

[10] Eastland, 421 U.S. at 503 ("Just as a criminal prosecution infringes upon the independence which the Clause is designed to preserve, a private civil action, whether for an injunction or damages, creates a distraction and forces Members to divert their time, energy, and attention from their legislative tasks to defend the litigation. Private civil actions also may be used to delay and disrupt the legislative function."); United States v. Brewster, 408 U.S. 501, 507 (1972) (noting that the Clause exists to "protect the integrity of the legislative process"); Powell v. McCormack, 395 U.S. 486, 505 (1969) (stating that "[t]he purpose of the protection afforded legislators is... to insure that legislators are not distracted from or hindered in the performance of their legislative tasks by being called into court to defend their actions"); Tenney v. Brandhove, 341 U.S. 367, 377 (1951) ("Legislators are immune from deterrents to the uninhibited discharge of their legislative duty, not for their private indulgence but for the public good... The privilege would be of little value if they could be subjected to the cost and inconvenience and distractions of trial ...").

[11] *Eastland*, 421 U.S. at 503; Brown & Williamson, 62 F.3d 408, 416 (1995) ("The Clause states, after all, that Members shall not be called to account 'in any other Place'—not just a criminal court."). Even civil suits may arguably implicate the separation-of-powers principles that underlie the Clause. Any court order directed at a Member could be viewed as a clash between the judicial and legislative powers. *See Eastland*, 421 U.S. at 503 ("[W]hether a criminal action is instituted by the Executive Branch, or a civil action is brought by private parties, judicial power is still brought to bear on Members of Congress and legislative independence is imperiled.").

[12] *See infra* notes 29-36.

Member and protecting a Member from being questioned[13] regarding those same acts.[14]

Some appellate opinions have recognized that the Clause must also include a broad documentary nondisclosure privilege to protect Members from the perils and burdens of revealing written legislative materials, even when the documents are not used as evidence against the Member.[15] Although this nondisclosure privilege has not been adopted by the Supreme Court, it has been utilized to extend the protections of the Clause to prohibit the compelled disclosure of documents in various circumstances, including during searches conducted as a part of a criminal investigation.[16] Some courts, however, have rejected this reasoning, considering it an undue expansion of the Clause.[17] These courts have instead held that, at least in criminal cases, the Clause prohibits only the evidentiary *use* of privileged documents, not their mere disclosure to the government for review as part of an investigation.[18]

The Clause has also been interpreted to protect Congress's ability to obtain and use information without interference from the judiciary.[19] These cases tend to emphasize the structural aspects of the Clause's role in the separation of powers and, more specifically, the proper relationship

---

[13] This component of the Clause would appear to apply to questioning that occurs at trial, before the grand jury, or in a deposition. *See* Fields, 459 F.3d at 14.

[14] *See Gravel*, 408 U.S. at 616, 622, 628-29 (reasoning that a Senator "may not be made to answer—either in terms of questions or in terms of defending himself" for legislative acts); *Helstoski*, 442 U.S. at 490 (holding that "[r]evealing information as to a legislative act" to a jury violates the Clause"). Perhaps the chief distinction between the immunity principle and the evidentiary and testimonial components of the Clause is that when a claim is predicated on a legislative act, and therefore triggers immunity, the Clause operates as a "jurisdictional bar." *See* Fields, 459 F.3d at 13 (2006).

[15] *See, e.g.*, United States v. Rayburn House Office Bldg., 497 F.3d 654 (D.C. Cir. 2007); MINPECO, S.A. v. Conticommodity Serv. Inc., 844 F.2d 856 (D.C. Cir. 1988). The D.C. Circuit's jurisprudence holds that the documentary nondisclosure privilege is part of the testimonial privilege. *Rayburn*, 497 F.3d at 655 ("Our precedent establishes that the testimonial privilege under the Clause extends to non-disclosure of written legislative materials.").

[16] *Rayburn*, 497 F.3d at 655.

[17] *See, e.g.*, In re *Fattah*, 802 F.3d 516, 529 (3rd Cir. 2015); *Renzi*, 651 F.3d at 1034 ("We disagree with both *Rayburn*'s premise and its effect and thus decline to adopt its rationale.").

[18] *Fattah*, 802 F.3d at 529 ("The Speech or Debate Clause does not prohibit the disclosure of privileged documents. Rather, it forbids the evidentiary use of such documents.").

[19] *Eastland*, 421 U.S. at 501.

between Congress and the courts.[20] For example, courts have generally read the Clause as prohibiting the judicial branch from invalidating or blocking a congressional subpoena, or from interfering with how Congress, and its Members, choose to use information within the legislative sphere.[21]

THE CORE OF THE CLAUSE: MEMBER IMMUNITY AND COMPONENT PRIVILEGES

In fashioning an evolving interpretation, the Supreme Court has described the Clause as a provision in which the text simply cannot be interpreted literally.[22] "Deceptively simple" phrases such as "shall not be questioned," "Speech or Debate," and even "Senators and Representatives" have been the subject of significant debate.[23] While there appears to be much about the Clause that is unclear, it is well established that the Clause seeks to secure the independence of legislators by providing Members with immunity from criminal prosecutions or civil suits that stem from acts taken within the legislative sphere.[24] This general immunity principle forms the core of the protections afforded by the Clause.

The Supreme Court has consistently and repeatedly suggested the Clause's immunity principle should be interpreted "broadly" to effectuate

---

[20] *Id.* at 509 n.16 ("Where we are presented with an attempt to interfere with an ongoing activity by Congress, and that activity is found to be within the legitimate legislative sphere, balancing plays no part. The speech or debate protection provides an absolute immunity from judicial interference.").

[21] *See Ferrer*, 856 F.3d at 1086 ("To circumscribe the committee's use of material in its physical possession would... 'destroy[]' the independence of the Legislature and 'invade[]' the constitutional separation of powers.") (citations omitted).

[22] Hutchinson v. Proxmire, 443 U.S. 111, 124 (1979) (noting that the "Court has given the Clause a practical rather than a strictly literal reading ..."). *See also*, Bastien v. Office of Campbell, 390 F.3d 1301, 1305 (10th Cir. 2004) ("[T]he Supreme Court has long treated the Clause as constitutional shorthand for a more extensive protection.").

[23] *Brown & Williamson*, 62 F.3d at 415.

[24] *Eastland*, 421 U.S. at 510-11 (noting that the Clause should be "construed to provide the independence which is its central purpose"); *Johnson*, 383 U.S. at 182 ("There is little doubt that the instigation of criminal charges against critical or disfavored legislators by the executive in a judicial forum was the chief fear prompting the long struggle for parliamentary privilege in England and, in the context of the American system of separation of powers, is the predominate thrust of the Speech or Debate Clause.").

the purpose of maintaining an independent legislature.[25] Once it is determined that the Clause applies to a given action, the resulting protections from liability are "absolute,"[26] and the action "may not be made the basis for a civil or criminal judgment against a Member."[27] Unlike some constitutional provisions, the Clause does not require a court to engage in a balancing of interests.[28]

The Clause's general immunity principle is perhaps best understood as complemented—and effectuated—by two component privileges that courts have viewed as emanating from the Clause. The evidentiary component of the Clause prohibits evidence of legislative acts from being introduced for use against a Member.[29] Similarly, the testimonial component of the Clause generally may be invoked when a Member is questioned about his legislative acts, either in a trial, before the grand jury, or in a deposition, and, in some courts, to block the compelled disclosure of documents pursuant to a subpoena or a warrant.[30] The Supreme Court has not explicitly framed the protections of the Clause by reference to these two independent component privileges, but has instead used language that implies only their existence.[31] As such, these privileges are neither clearly

[25] *Eastland*, 421 U.S. at 501 ("Without exception, our cases have read the Speech or Debate Clause broadly to effectuate its purposes.").

[26] *Id.* at 503 ("[O]nce it is determined that Members are acting within the 'legitimate legislative sphere' the Speech or Debate Clause is an absolute bar to interference."); Doe v. McMillan, 412 U.S. 306, 324 (1973) ("The business of *Congress* is to legislate; Congressmen and aides are absolutely immune when they are legislating."). Indeed, the Court has gone so far as to say that legislative acts may not even be the subject of "inquiry" by either the executive or judicial branches. *Brewster*, 408 U.S. at 509 ("The privilege protect[s] Members from inquiry into legislative acts or the motivation for actual performance of legislative acts.").

[27] *McMillan*, 412 U.S. at 312.

[28] *Eastland*, 421 U.S. at 508 n.16 ("Where we are presented with an attempt to interfere with an ongoing activity by Congress, and that activity is found to be within the legitimate legislative sphere, balancing plays no part.").

[29] *Helstoski*, 442 U.S. at 487 (noting that the Court's previous holdings "leave no doubt that evidence of a legislative act of a Member may not be introduced by the Government"); *Brewster*, 408 U.S. at 527 (holding that "evidence of acts protected by the Clause is inadmissible").

[30] *Gravel*, 408 U.S. at 616 (holding that Members "may not be made to answer—either in terms of questions or in terms of defending himself from prosecution" for legislative acts).

[31] Indeed, the Supreme Court has never used the phrase "testimonial privilege" or "evidentiary privilege" in discussing the Speech or Debate Clause. In *United States v. Gillock*, the Court

established nor described, and, especially in regard to the testimonial privilege, relatively unsettled. Nevertheless, in understanding the Speech or Debate Clause, it would seem prudent to describe the Clause as composed of a general immunity principle, complemented by component evidentiary and testimonial privileges.[32]

Although there appears to be some agreement on the existence of the immunity principle and the evidentiary and testimonial privileges, the Supreme Court's relatively ambiguous treatment of the interactions between the different aspects of the Clause has led to significant disagreement among the lower courts.[33] For example, the Court's silence on the scope of the testimonial component of the Clause, combined with the inherent confusion[34] surrounding what constitutes a "testimonial" disclosure in other areas of federal law, has led to a deep split among the federal appellate courts as to whether the Clause protects against nonevidentiary disclosures of written legislative materials—for example, disclosures made in response

---

referenced an evidentiary privilege for state legislators "similar in scope" to the Clause. 445 U.S. 360, 366 (1980).

[32] *See, e.g., Renzi*, 651 F.3d at 1035 n. 27 ("To reiterate, the Court has identified three distinct privileges in the Clause: a testimonial privilege, an evidentiary privilege, and a privilege against liability."); Howard v. Office of the Chief Admin. Officer of the United States House of Representatives, 720 F.3d 939, 946 (2013) ("As a general matter, the Speech or Debate Clause affords three distinct protections: (a) an immunity from 'a civil or criminal judgment ...' (b) an evidentiary privilege ... and (c) a testimonial and non-disclosure privilege ...") (citations omitted).

[33] *See Brown & Williamson*, 62 F.3d at 418 ("Based on the text of the Constitution, it would seem that the immunity from suit derives from the testimonial privilege, not the other way around.")

[34] *See, e.g.*, Crawford v Washington, 541 U.S. 36, 51-61 (2004) (addressing the meaning of "testimonial" for purposes of the Confrontation Clause); United States v. Hubbell, 530 U.S. 27, 34-46 (2000) (discussing the act of production doctrine and the testimonial privilege arising from the Fifth Amendment privilege against self-incrimination). In a Fifth Amendment case, the Court held that "to be testimonial, an accused's communication must itself, explicitly or implicitly, relate a factual assertion or disclose information." Doe v. United States, 487 U.S. 201, 210 (1988). As previously mentioned, the Supreme Court has never directly addressed the testimonial privilege arising from the Clause. Lower federal courts have adopted very different descriptions of what is meant by testimonial, and, in fact, no circuit court has explicitly defined the term "testimonial." *Compare Brown & Williamson*, 62 F.3d at 421 (describing "testimonial purposes" as "not for use as evidence against Congress or any of its Members.") *with* In re Grand Jury Investigation into Possible Violations of Title 18, 587 F.2d 589, 596 (3d Cir. 1978) (equating the testimonial privilege to "hostile questioning").

to discovery subpoenas or search warrants[35]—or, to the contrary, whether such disclosures are covered only by the evidentiary component of the Clause, and therefore disclosure of such documents is protected only when used for evidentiary purposes.[36]

Despite the doctrinal uncertainty, it would appear that the different aspects of the Clause may be best summarized in the following way. First, the immunity principle of the Clause acts as a jurisdictional bar to legal actions seeking to hold a Member liable, either civilly or criminally, for protected legislative acts.[37] When the claim itself does not require proof of a legislative act, but rather arises from nonlegislative or unprotected activity, the Member is not immune, and the criminal or civil action may go forward.[38] Second, during the course of the litigation, the Member may nonetheless assert the evidentiary privilege to block the introduction of specific evidence reflecting protected legislative acts.[39] Third, the testimonial privilege may be invoked in a variety of circumstances in order to protect the Member from compelled testimony, or in some courts from disclosing documents, about those acts.[40]

Viewing the Clause holistically, it becomes apparent that whether a court chooses to address a Speech or Debate case by reference to the general immunity principle, or the evidentiary and testimonial privileges, in some cases the ultimate result may be the same. For example, a Member may avoid liability that may have otherwise attached to his actions either

---

[35] *Compare Rayburn*, 497 F.3d at 655 (holding that the testimonial component of the Clause includes a documentary nondisclosure privilege), with *Renzi*, 651 F.3d at 1034 (holding that the testimonial component of the Clause does not create the documentary nondisclosure privilege outlined in *Rayburn*).

[36] *Fattah*, 802 F.3d at 529 ("The Speech or Debate Clause does not prohibit the disclosure of privileged documents. Rather, it forbids the evidentiary use of such documents.").

[37] *Eastland*, 421 U.S. at 502-03 ([W]e have long held that, when it applies, the Clause provides protection against civil as well as criminal actions, and against actions brought by private individuals as well as those initiated by the Executive Branch."); Fields v. Office of Eddie Bernice Johnson, 459 F.3d 1, 13 (D.C. Cir. 2006) ("The Speech or Debate Clause operates as a jurisdictional bar when 'the actions upon which [a plaintiff] sought to predicate liability were "legislative acts."'") (citing *McMillan* 412 U.S. at 318) (quoting *Gravel*, 408 U.S. at 618).

[38] *Brewster*, 408 U.S. at 525.

[39] *Helstoski*, 442 U.S. at 487 (holding that "evidence of a legislative act of a Member may not be introduced by the Government ...").

[40] See "Nondisclosure Privilege: A Continued Circuit Split" *infra*.

because the court relies on the Clause's immunity principle, or because the party initiating the legal action is unable to prove his case without resort to evidence and testimony that is protected by the evidentiary and testimonial privilege components of the Clause.[41]

As a result of the breadth of these protections, the Clause seemingly makes it more difficult for the executive branch to prosecute Members for unlawful acts committed in the context of legislative activity, including those offenses directly related to corruption.[42] This impact on executive enforcement of the law was fully understood at the time the Clause was adopted, and considered a necessary consequence of protecting legislators from undue influence or intimidation.[43]

The Clause does not, however, turn Members into "supercitizens" by providing them with a blanket exemption from legal liability for any and all illegal acts.[44] Rather, the Clause immunizes or protects only a certain class of actions, known as "legislative acts," that are undertaken as part of the legislative process.[45] Not all actions taken by a Member in the course of his congressional duties are considered legislative acts. In fact, many acts that may otherwise be considered "official," in that they relate to

---

[41] *See* Jay Rothrock, *Striking a Balance: The Speech or Debate Clause's Testimonial Privilege and Policing Government Corruption*, 24 Touro L. Rev. 739, 751 n. 45 (2008). In this sense, an analogy may arguably be drawn to judicial implementation of the state secrets privilege, an evidentiary privilege that allows the federal government to resist disclosure of information during litigation if there is a reasonable danger that disclosure would harm the national security of the United States. *See* U.S. v. Reynolds, 345 U.S. 1, 7-8 (1953). Dismissal of a claim based on a valid assertion of the state secrets privilege can either result in an outright bar to the claim, for example when the "very subject matter of the case is a state secret," Mohamed v. Jeppesen Dataplan, Inc., 614 F.3d 1070, 1083 (9th Cir. 2010), or after it becomes clear that a plaintiff cannot establish a *prima facie* case without privileged evidence. Kasza v. Browner, 133 F.3d 1159 (9th Cir. 1998).

[42] *Helstoski*, 442 U.S. at 488 ("[W]ithout doubt the exclusion of such evidence will make prosecutions more difficult."); *Brewster* 408 U.S. at 516.

[43] *Brewster*, 408 U.S. at 516-17 ("In its narrowest scope, the Clause is a very large, albeit essential, grant of privilege. It has enabled reckless men to slander and even destroy others with impunity, but that was the conscious choice of the Framers ... The authors of our Constitution were well aware of the history of both the need for the privilege and the abuses that could flow from too sweeping safeguards.").

[44] *Id.* at 516 (noting that the purpose of the Clause was not "to make Members of Congress super-citizens, immune from criminal responsibility").

[45] *Gravel*, 408 U.S. at 625.

governmental duties, are not covered by the protections of the Clause.[46] The Clause protects only those acts that are an "integral part of the deliberative and communicative processes" through which Members engage either in "the consideration and passage or rejection of proposed legislation" or "other matters which the Constitution places within the jurisdiction of either House."[47] The legislative act limitation and other aspects of the Clause are discussed in greater detail below.[48]

Supreme Court Interpretations

A series of decisions from the Supreme Court address the general scope of the Clause and elucidate the distinction between legislative acts, such as voting or debating, which are accorded protection under the Clause and are not subject to "inquiry,"[49] and political or other nonlegislative acts, which are not protected by the Clause and therefore may serve as the basis for a legal action.[50] These cases suggest at least three noteworthy themes. First, despite the text, the protections afforded by the Clause extend well beyond "speeches" or "debates" undertaken by "Senators and Representatives."[51] Second, otherwise legitimate political interactions external to the legislative sphere—for example, disseminating information outside of Congress—are generally not considered protected legislative

[46] *McMillan*, 412 U.S. at 313 ("Our cases make perfectly apparent [] that everything a Member of Congress may regularly do is not a legislative act within the protection of the Speech or Debate Clause."); United States v. McDade, 28 F.3d 283, 295 (3rd Cir. 1994) ("The Speech or Debate Clause does not immunize every official act performed by a member of Congress.").

[47] *Gravel*, 408 U.S. at 625.

[48] *See* "What Constitutes a Legislative Act?" *infra*.

[49] Gravel, 408 U.S. at 616.

[50] *See, e.g., Id.* at 613-29; *Brewster*, 408 U.S. at 507-29; *Johnson*, 383 U.S. 174-85; Kilbourn v. Thompson, 103 U.S. 168, 201-05 (1881). Additional Supreme Court cases significantly addressing the Clause include Harlow v. Fitzgerald, 457 U.S. 800, 810-12 (1982); Hutchinson v. Proxmire, 443 U.S. 111, 124-33 (1979); *Helstoski*, 442 U.S. at 484-94 (1979); *Eastland*, 421 U.S. at 501-11 (1975); *McMillan*, 412 U.S. at 311-19 (1973); *Powell*, 395 U.S. at 501-06 (1969); Tenney v. Brandhove, 341 U.S. 367, 372-79 (1951).

[51] *Kilbourn*, 103 U.S. at 204 (extending the protections of the Clause beyond speeches and debates); *Gravel*, 408 U.S at 616-17 (extending the protections of the Clause to acts of aides).

acts.[52] Third, the Clause does not immunize criminal conduct that is clearly no part of the "due functioning" of the legislative process.[53]

The Supreme Court adopted a broad interpretation of "Speech or Debate" from its first assessment of the Clause in the 1881 case *Kilbourn v. Thompson*.[54] In *Kilbourn*, the Court considered whether a civil action could be maintained against Members who were responsible for initiating and approving a contempt resolution ordering an unlawful arrest.[55] The Members defended themselves on the ground that their acts were protected by the Clause.[56] The Court agreed, determining that the Members were not subject to suit for their actions.[57] The Court adopted an interpretation of the Clause that extended protections beyond mere legislative deliberation and argument, holding that "it would be a narrow view of the constitutional provision to limit it to words spoken in debate."[58] Instead, the Court determined that the Clause applied to "things generally done in a session of the House by one of its members in relation to the business before it," including the presentation of reports, the offering of resolutions, and the act of voting.[59] Accordingly, the Court concluded that although the arrest itself may have been unlawful, the Members were immune from suit and could not be "brought in question" for their role in approving the resolution "in a court of justice or in any other place," as that act was protected by the Clause.[60]

The Court only rarely addressed the Clause after *Kilbourn*.[61] It was not until the 1966 case *United States v. Johnson* that the Court embarked on an

---

[52] *See Gravel*, 408 U.S. at 625-26.
[53] *See Johnson*, 383 U.S. at 172.
[54] *Kilbourn*, 103 U.S. at 200-05.
[55] *Id.* at 200.
[56] *Id.* at 201.
[57] In reaching its holding, the Court noted that if the Members had ordered the unlawful arrest "in any ordinary tribunal" they would have been liable for the act. *Id.* The Court concluded, however, that the Constitution and the Clause make clear that Congress "is not an ordinary tribunal." *Id.*
[58] *Id.* at 204.
[59] *Id.*
[60] *Id.* 201.
[61] See Philip Mayer, An Uncertain Privilege: Reexamining the Scope and Protections of the Speech or Debate Clause, 50 Colum. J.L. & Soc. Probs. 229, 233 (2017) ("After Kilbourn, the Supreme Court did not substantively address the Clause until almost a century later.").

early attempt to define the protections afforded by the Clause in the context of a criminal prosecution of a Member.[62] In *Johnson*, a former Member challenged his conviction for conspiracy to defraud the United States that arose from allegations he had agreed to give a speech defending certain banking interests in exchange for payment.[63] In prosecuting the case, the government relied heavily on the former Member's motive for giving the speech, introducing evidence that the speech had been made solely to serve private, rather than public, interests.[64] Focusing on the *admission* of this protected evidence, the Court overturned the conviction. "However reprehensible such conduct may be," the Court concluded that a criminal prosecution, the "essence" of which requires proof that "the Congressman's conduct was improperly motivated," was "precisely what the Speech or Debate Clause generally forecloses from executive and judicial inquiry."[65] The opinion noted that thc Clausc must be "read broadly to effectuate its purposes," ultimately concluding that the Clause prohibits a prosecution that is "dependent" upon the introduction of evidence of "the legislative acts" of a Member *or* "his motives for performing them."[66]

Although overturning the conviction, the Court remanded the case to the district court for further proceedings, holding that the government should not be precluded from bringing a prosecution "purged of elements offensive to the Speech or Debate clause" through the elimination of all references to the making of the speech.[67] The *Johnson* case therefore stands for at least two important propositions. First, the opinion demonstrated that the government is not prohibited from prosecuting conduct that merely relates to legislative duties, but is not itself a legislative act.[68] When a legislative act is not an element of the offense, the government may

---

[62] *Johnson*, 383 U.S. at 170-85.

[63] *Id.* at 170-73. The Member also allegedly agreed to "exert influence" over Department of Justice enforcement decisions. *Id.* at 171. With regard to that aspect of the claim, the Court suggested that an "attempt to influence the Department of Justice" was not legislative. *Id* at 172.

[64] *Id.* at 177.

[65] *Id.* at 180.

[66] *Id.* at 185.

[67] *Johnson*, 383 U.S. at 185.

[68] *Id.* at 185.

proceed with its case by effectively "purg[ing]" the introduction of evidence offensive to the Clause.[69] Second, though not explicitly articulating such a privilege, the opinion impliedly introduced the evidentiary component of the Clause by holding that even though a case may go forward, the Clause may be invoked by Members to bar admission of specific protected evidence.[70]

Less than a decade after *Johnson*, the Supreme Court issued two decisions on the same day in 1972 that established important limitations on the types of actions that are protected by the Clause. In *United States v. Brewster*, which involved a Member's challenge to his indictment on a bribery charge, the Court reaffirmed *Johnson* and clarified that "a Member of Congress may be prosecuted under a criminal statute provided that the Government's case does not rely on legislative acts or the motivation for legislative acts."[71] The Court made clear that the Clause does not prohibit inquiry into illegal conduct simply because it is "related" to the legislative process or has a "nexus to legislative functions," but rather, the Clause protects only the legislative acts themselves.[72] By adhering to such a limitation, the Court reasoned that the result would be a Clause that was "broad enough to insure the historic independence of the Legislative Branch, essential to our separation of powers, but narrow enough to guard against the excesses of those who would corrupt the process by corrupting its Members."[73]

Brewster also drew an important distinction between legislative and political acts. The opinion labeled a wide array of constituent services,[74]

---

[69] *Id.*

[70] *Id.* at 173 ("The language of the Speech or Debate Clause clearly proscribes at least some of the evidence taken during trial.").

[71] *Brewster*, 408 U.S. at 512.

[72] *Id.* at 513, 528.

[73] *Id.* at 525.

[74] These unprotected activities include "a wide range of legitimate 'errands' performed for constituents, the making of appointments with Government agencies, assistance in securing Government contracts, preparing so-called 'news letters' to constituents, news releases, and speeches delivered outside the Congress." *Id.* at 512. Similarly, in *Hutchinson v. Proxmire*, the Court held that informing the public of legislative activities is not protected by the Clause. 443 U.S. 111, 133 (1979) ("Valuable and desirable as it may be in broad terms, the transmittal of such information by individual Members in order to inform the public and other Members is not a part of the legislative function or the deliberations that make up the

though "entirely legitimate," as "political in nature" rather than legislative.[75] As a result, the Court suggested that "it has never been seriously contended that these political matters ... have the protection afforded by the Speech or Debate Clause."[76]

Turning to the terms of the bribery indictment, the Court framed the fundamental threshold question for any prosecution of a Member of Congress as: "whether it is necessary to inquire into how [the Member] spoke, how he debated, how he voted, or anything he did in the chamber or in committee in order to make out a violation of this statute."[77] With regard to bribery, the Court reasoned that because acceptance of the bribe is enough to prove a violation of the statute, there was no need for the government to present evidence that the Member had later *voted* in accordance with the illegal promise, "[f]or it is *taking* the bribe, not performance of the illicit compact, that is a criminal act."[78] Because "taking the bribe is, obviously, no part of the legislative function" and was therefore "not a legislative act," the government would not be required to present any protected legislative evidence in order to "make out a prima facie case."[79] In that sense, the Court distinguished the case before it from *Johnson*. Whereas the prosecution in *Johnson* relied heavily on showing the motive for Johnson's floor speech, the prosecution in *Brewster* need not prove any legislative act, but only that money was accepted in return for a promise.

Finally, *Gravel v. United States* exemplifies that communications outside of the legislative process are generally not protected by the Clause.[80] *Gravel* involved a Speech or Debate challenge to a grand jury investigation into the disclosure of classified documents by a Senator and

---

legislative process. As a result, transmittal of such information by press releases and newsletters is not protected by the Speech or Debate Clause.").

[75] *Brewster,* 408 U.S. at 512.

[76] *Id.*

[77] *Id.* at 526.

[78] *Id.*

[79] *Id.* at 525.

[80] *Gravel*, 408 U.S. at 622-27. *Gravel* also exemplifies that the Speech or Debate protections can extend to a Member's personal aides. *Id.* at 616-22.

his aides.[81] After coming into possession of the "Pentagon Papers"—a classified Defense Department study addressing U.S. involvement in the Vietnam War—Senator Mike Gravel disclosed portions of the document at a subcommittee hearing and submitted the entire study into the record.[82] The Senator and his staff had also allegedly arranged for the study to be published by a private publisher.[83] A grand jury subsequently issued a subpoena for testimony from one of Senator Gravel's aides and the private publisher.[84] Senator Gravel intervened to quash the subpoenas.[85]

The *Gravel* opinion began by reasoning that "[b]ecause the claim is that a Member's aide shares the Member's constitutional privilege, we consider first whether and to what extent Senator Gravel himself is exempt from process or inquiry by a grand jury investigating the commission of a crime."[86] In addressing the scope of the Senator's protections, the Court implied the existence of the testimonial component of the Clause, noting that the protections of the Clause protect a Member from compelled questioning.[87] The Court did so by stating, without further discussion, that it had "no doubt" that "Senator Gravel may not be made to answer—either in terms of questions or in terms of defending himself from prosecution—for the events that occurred at the subcommittee meeting."

The *Gravel* opinion also drew a clear line of demarcation between protected legislative acts and other unprotected acts not "essential to the deliberations" of Congress.[88] Although the Senator was protected for his actions at the hearing, the Senator's alleged arrangement for private publication of the Pentagon Papers was not "part and parcel of the

---

[81] *Id.* at 608-10.

[82] *Id.* at 608.

[83] *Id.* at 610.

[84] *Id.* at 608.

[85] *Id.* at 609.

[86] *Gravel*, 408 U.S. at 613. Speech or Debate Clause protections for aides are discussed below.

[87] *Id.* at 626. *Brown & Williamson*, 62 F.3d at 418 (holding that "the Supreme Court recognized the testimonial privilege in *Gravel v. United States*"). *Gravel* involved questioning before a grand jury. 408 U.S. at 613. The D.C. Circuit has suggested, however, that the prohibition extends to questions asked "in a deposition, on the witness stand, and so forth ..." Fields v. Office of Johnson, 459 F.3d 1, 14 (D.C. Cir. 2006).

[88] *Gravel*, 408 U.S. at 625.

legislative process" and was therefore not protected by the Clause.[89] In reaching this determination, the Court established a working definition of "legislative act" that remains applicable today, holding that a legislative act is an:

> integral part of the deliberative and communicative processes by which Members participate in committee and House proceedings with respect to the consideration and passage or rejection of proposed legislation or with respect to other matters which the Constitution places within the jurisdiction of either House.[90]

Private publication, as opposed to publication in the record, was "in no way essential to the deliberations of the Senate."[91] Thus, the Clause provided no immunity from testifying before the grand jury relating to that arrangement.[92]

Who Is Protected?

Although the text of the Speech or Debate Clause refers only to "Senators and Representatives," and therefore clearly applies to actions by any Member of Congress,[93] it is well established that protections of the Clause generally apply equally to congressional staff.[94] In *Gravel*, the Court held that the Clause protects an aide's action when the Clause would have protected the same action if it were done by a Member.[95] An aide, the Court reasoned, should be viewed as the "alter ego" of the Member he

---

[89] *Id.*
[90] *Id.* at 625.
[91] *Gravel*, 408 U.S. at 625.
[92] *Id.* at 626.
[93] The Clause may be asserted not only by a current Member, but also by a former Member in an action implicating his conduct while in Congress. *See Brewster*, 408 U.S. at 502.
[94] *Gravel*, 408 U.S. at 616-17.
[95] *Id.* at 628 (holding that an aide's "immunity, testimonial or otherwise, extends only to legislative acts as to which the Senator himself would be immune").

serves.[96] The *Gravel* Court recognized that the Member and his aide must be "treated as one,"[97] noting:

> [I]t is literally impossible, in view of the complexities of the modern legislative process, with Congress almost constantly in session and matters of legislative concern constantly proliferating, for Members of Congress to perform their legislative tasks without the help of aides and assistants; that the day-to-day work of such aides is so critical to the Members' performance that they must be treated as the latter's alter egos; and that if they are not so recognized, the central role of the Speech or Debate Clause—to prevent intimidation of legislators by the Executive and accountability before a possibly hostile judiciary—will inevitably be diminished and frustrated.[98]

At issue in *Gravel* were the actions of a Member's *personal* staff. Other decisions of the Court have extended the protections of the Clause to *committee* staff, including those in the position of chief counsel, clerk, staff director, and investigator.[99]

However, it should be noted that any protections under the Clause that are enjoyed by congressional staff flow from the Member.[100] They do not inhere personally to the individual. As a result, an "aide's claim of privilege can be repudiated and thus waived by the [Member]."[101]

What Constitutes a Legislative Act?

It is apparent that the key determination in Speech or Debate Clause cases is whether the conduct directly in question, or on which evidence or

---

[96] *Id.* at 617.

[97] *Id.* at 616 (quoting United States v. Doe, 455 F.2d 753, 761 (1972)).

[98] *Id.* at 616-17 (internal citations omitted).

[99] *See Eastland*, 421 U.S. at 507; *McMillan*, 412 U.S. at 309. *See also*, Rangel v. Boehner, 785 F.3d 19, 24-5 (D.C. Cir. 2015).

[100] *Gravel*, 408 U.S. at 621 (noting that the "privilege applicable to the aide is viewed, as it must be, as the privilege of the Senator, and invocable only by the Senator or by the aide on the Senator's behalf ...").

[101] *Id.* at 622 n.13.

testimony is sought, constitutes a legislative act.[102] If legislative, the Member is exempt from criminal or civil liability that may otherwise have attached to that act, and evidence of the act may not be introduced or testimony by the Member compelled.[103] As the Court has repeatedly stated, Members are "immune from liability for their actions within the 'legislative sphere,' even though their conduct, if performed in other than legislative contexts, would in itself be unconstitutional or otherwise contrary to criminal or civil statutes."[104] If the underlying conduct is not legislative, however, the prosecution or civil claim is not barred by the Clause, and evidence of the act is not privileged.[105]

Examining judicial precedent regarding acts that are "legislative," it would appear that Members enjoy protection under the Clause when:

- speaking or acting on the House or Senate floor;[106]
- introducing and voting on bills and resolutions;[107]
- preparing and submitting committee reports;[108]
- speaking or acting at committee meetings and hearings;[109]
- conducting official investigations and issuing subpoenas;[110] and
- engaging in fact-finding and information-gathering for legislative purposes.[111]

---

[102] *Johnson*, 383 U.S. at 185; *Brewster*, 408 U.S. at 512; *Gravel*, 408 U.S. at 625. *See also*, *Renzi*, 651 F.3d at 1021 (describing the question of what constitutes a legislative act as "of fundamental importance").

[103] See *Gravel*, 408 U.S. at 626 (noting that the Clause "recognizes speech, voting and other legislative acts as exempt from liability that might otherwise attach ...").

[104] *McMillan*, 412 U.S. at 312-13.

[105] *See Brewster*, 408 U.S. at 512.

[106] *Johnson*, 383 U.S. at 184-85; *Gravel*, 408 U.S. at 616.

[107] *Kilbourn*, 103 U.S. at 204 (holding that the Clause protects "resolutions offered ... and ... the act of voting ...").

[108] *McMillan*, 412 U.S. at 311; *Kilbourn*, 103 U.S. at 204.

[109] *See McMillan*, 412 U.S. at 311; *see also*, *Gravel*, 408 U.S. at 628-29. In addition, some lower federal courts have held that the Clause bars the use of evidence of a Member's committee membership. *Compare* United States v. Swindall, 971 F.2d 1531, 1543 (11th Cir. 1991), *rehearing denied*, 980 F.2d 1449 (11th Cir. 1992), *with* United States v. McDade, 28 F.3d 283, 291 (3rd Cir. 1994), *cert. denied*, 514 U.S. 1003 (1995).

[110] *See Eastland*, 421 U.S. at 507; *Tenney*, 341 U.S. at 377 (refusing to examine motives of state legislator in summoning witness to hearing).

Conversely, actions that have not been viewed as "integral" to the legislative process and, therefore, have not been interpreted to be protected legislative acts include:

- speaking outside of Congress;[112]
- writing newsletters and issuing press releases;[113]
- privately publishing a book;[114]
- distributing official committee reports outside the legislative sphere;[115]
- engaging in political activities;[116]
- engaging in constituent services, including acting as a conduit between a constituent and the executive branch;[117]
- promising to perform a future legislative act;[118] and
- accepting a bribe.[119]

The general legal guidance provided by the Court in *Gravel* and other cases does not clearly categorize every type of action in which Members may regularly engage. As a result, determining whether novel conduct, not analogous to past precedent, should be viewed as a legislative act may sometimes be difficult.

One federal appellate court, however, has adopted a two-step analysis for identifying whether certain conduct is protected by the Clause.[120] In *United States v. Menendez*, Senator Robert Menendez challenged, on Speech or Debate grounds, an indictment alleging that he solicited and

---

[111] Gov't of V.I. v. Lee, 775 F.2d 514, 521 (3rd Cir. 1985); Miller v. Transamerican Press, Inc., 709 F.2d 524, 530 (9th Cir. 1983); McSurely v. McClellan, 553 F.2d 1277, 1286-87 (D.C. Cir. 1976).

[112] *Brewster*, 408 U.S. at 512.

[113] *Proxmire*, 443 U.S. at 130.

[114] *Gravel*, 408 U.S. at 625-26.

[115] *McMillan*, 412 U.S. at 315-16.

[116] *Brewster*, 408 U.S. at 512.

[117] *Id.* (excluding "the making of appointments with Government agencies [and] assistance in securing Government contracts" from the Clause's protections).

[118] *Helstoski*, 442 U.S. at 489.

[119] *Brewster*, 408 U.S. at 525.

[120] United States v. Menendez, 831 F.3d 155, 166-67 (3rd Cir. 2016).

accepted gifts in exchange for his efforts to influence executive branch action for the benefit of a friend.[121] In rejecting the Senator's claim, the U.S. Court of Appeals for the Third Circuit (Third Circuit) laid out its analytical framework, noting that first "we look to the form of the act to determine whether it is inherently legislative or non-legislative."[122] Some acts, the court reasoned, are "so clearly legislative" that "no further examination has to be made."[123] These "manifestly legislative acts" are entitled to absolute protection under the Clause, even if undertaken for an "unworthy purpose."[124] Other acts, the court suggested, are just as clearly nonlegislative, and receive no protection under the Clause.[125] If an act is either clearly legislative or clearly nonlegislative, the Third Circuit has suggested that a court should, at step one, give effect to that clear categorization.[126] If, however, an act does not fall neatly into either category, the court may proceed to the second step of the inquiry where it may consider "the content, purpose, and motive of the act to assess its legislative or non-legislative character."[127] These so-called "ambiguously legislative" acts, the court reasoned, "will be protected or unprotected based on their particular circumstances."[128] In this instance, the court determined that the alleged acts were "outside the constitutional safe harbor" because the Senator was "essentially lobbying on behalf of a particular party...."[129]

This approach may be subject to criticism in light of the Supreme Court's repeated warning that inquiries into the motive or purpose underlying actions of Members are generally not permitted by the Clause.[130] The Court has expressly held that "in determining the legitimacy of a congressional act we do not look to the motives alleged to

---

[121] *Id.* at 159.
[122] *Id.* at 166.
[123] *Id.*
[124] *Id.*
[125] *Id.*
[126] *Menendez*, 831 F.3d at 166.
[127] *Id.*
[128] *Id.* at 166-67. For example, in *Lee*, the Third Circuit court suggested that it is the content of the conversation, not the purpose that is determinative. 775 F.2d at 522-24.
[129] *Id.* at 169.
[130] *Johnson*, 383 U.S. at 185.

have prompted it."[131] Other courts have rejected an analytical approach that would empower a court to look beneath an act that appears legislative. For example, the U.S. Court of Appeals for the Fourth Circuit (Fourth Circuit) has held that the Clause not only protects "acts which are manifestly legislative,"[132] but "also forbids inquiry into acts which are purportedly or apparently legislative, even to determine if they are legislative in fact."[133]

While the Menendez opinion acknowledged Supreme Court precedent, it nonetheless determined that "only after we conclude that that an act is in fact legislative must we refrain from inquiring into a legislator's purpose or motive."[134] Prior to such a determination, the Third Circuit suggested, a court should—and at times must—make such an inquiry to prevent nonlegislative acts from being "misrepresented" as legislative acts.[135]

Member Interactions with the Executive Branch

A closer look at judicial treatment of Member interactions with the executive branch reveals some of the difficulty in determining whether certain conduct qualifies as a legislative act. While interactions with the executive branch may be viewed as "official" and "legitimate," they are not always "legislative."[136] It seems from *Brewster* and *Johnson*, for example, that communicating with an executive branch agency on behalf of a constituent is not a protected legislative act.[137] Interactions with the executive branch intended to "influence" executive policy for nonlegislative reasons are similarly not legislative acts.[138] The *Gravel* opinion further narrowed the class of interactions with the executive branch that could be deemed legislative, holding that:

---

[131] *Eastland*, 421 U.S. at 508.
[132] United States v. Dowdy, 479 F.2d 213, 226 (4th Cir. 1973).
[133] *Id.*
[134] *Menendez*, 831 F.3d at 167.
[135] *Id.* at 167.
[136] *See Brewster*, 408 U.S. at 512.
[137] *Id.*; *Johnson*, 383 U.S. at 172.
[138] *See Gravel*, 408 U.S. at 625; *Johnson*, 383 U.S. at 172.

> Members of Congress are constantly in touch with the Executive Branch of the Government and with administrative agencies—they may cajole, and exhort with respect to the administration of a federal statute—but such conduct, though generally done, is not protected legislative activity.[139]

This passage suggests that even communications and interactions with the executive branch pertaining to an agency's administration and execution of a federal statute, though wholly unrelated to constituent services, are similarly unprotected.

Yet, when the interaction is connected to the conduct of "oversight," the action may be more likely to be viewed as legislative and subject to the protections of the Clause. For example, in *Eastland v. United States Serviceman's Fund*, the Supreme Court held that "the power to investigate ... plainly falls" within the definition of legislative.[140] Thus, interactions with the executive branch taken pursuant to an authorized congressional investigation, including those actions taken at hearings, in issuing subpoenas, or pursuing contempt, have all been interpreted to be protected legislative acts.[141]

Less formal oversight contacts with the executive branch (for example, actions taken by individual Members not pursuant to an official committee investigation) have not always received protections under the Clause.[142] In *Menendez*, the Third Circuit held that a claim of conducting "'oversight' does not automatically result in Speech or Debate protections."[143] Instead, the court reasoned that "oversight activities exist along a spectrum" in which some informal actions are unprotected, but other "informal attempts to influence the Executive Branch on policy, for actual legislative purposes,

---

139 *Gravel*, 408 U.S. at 625.

140 *Eastland*, 421 U.S. at 504.

141 *Id.*

142 *See McDade*, 28 F.3d at 299-300. Confusion among the courts on this topic may be highlighted by comparing McSurely v. McClellan, 553 F.2d 1277, 1287 (D.C. Cir. 1976) (suggesting a "requirement of congressional authorization of the inquiry" for oversight activity to be protected by the Clause) with Miller v. Transamerican Press, Inc., 709 F.2d 524, 530 (9th Cir. 1983) (holding that actions during an unofficial investigation by an individual Member are protected by the Clause).

143 *Menendez*, 831 F.3d at 166.

may qualify as 'true legislative oversight' and merit Speech or Debate immunity."[144] Lobbying on behalf of a particular party, the court held, was an action "outside the constitutional safe harbor" created by the Clause.[145]

To the contrary, other courts have held that "the applicability of the Speech or Debate Clause's protections does not hinge on the formality of the investigation."[146] "The controlling principle," one court has asserted, is "whether information is acquired in connection with or in aid of an activity that qualifies as 'legislative' in nature."[147] Consistent with this reasoning, federal courts have found "fact finding," "field investigations," and "information gathering" by individual Members to be protected legislative acts.[148]

One way to harmonize these "informal contacts" cases is perhaps that when a Member is seeking to obtain information from the executive branch, the act is "legislative," but when the Member is attempting to "influence" executive branch policy, the act is not legislative, at least generally.[149] It would appear difficult, however, to draw a distinction between "cajoling" executive branch officials on the "administration of a federal statute," which is unprotected, and "true legislative oversight."[150] Oversight often serves many purposes, including a desire to influence executive branch operations. For example, a committee may solely be seeking information, or it may be conducting an investigation for the purposes of pushing the agency to

---

[144] *Id.* at 168.

[145] *Id.* at 169.

[146] SEC v. Comm. on Ways & Means of the United States House of Representatives, 161 F. Supp. 3d 199, 236 (S.D.N.Y. 2015).

[147] Jewish War Veterans of the United States of Am., Inc. v. Gates, 506 F. Supp. 2d 30, 57 (D.D.C. 2007).

[148] United States v. Biaggi, 853 F.2d 89, 103 (2nd Cir. 1988); *Lee*, 775 F.2d at 521; *Miller*, 709 F.2d at 530; *McSurely*, 553 F.2d at 1286-87.

[149] *See* Comm. on Ways & Means, 161 F. Supp. 3d at 246 (noting that documents that reflect a Member "'cajol[ing]' or 'exhort[ing] with respect to the administration of a federal statute,' they must be produced," but documents that "reflect the Committee's or the Subcommittee's gathering of information to aid in legislating on the issue of Medicare reimbursement rates—whether according to formal congressional processes, [] or informal efforts []—they are protected under the Clause and need not be produced") (citations omitted).

[150] *Gravel*, 408 U.S. at 625; *Menendez*, 831 F.3d at 168.

implement the law in the manner that Congress desires.[151] Nevertheless, there remains significant uncertainty concerning what types of Member communications with the executive branch are protected by the Clause.

Application of the Clause to Employment and Personnel Actions

The Speech or Debate Clause plays a key role in civil actions challenging Members' employment and personnel actions. These cases generally arise under the Congressional Accountability Act (CAA), which made several civil rights, labor and employment, and workplace safety laws applicable to congressional offices.[152] After seeking confidential[153] counseling and mediation, the CAA expressly authorizes "covered employees" to bring a civil action for violations of the incorporated laws, not against an individual Member, but against the "employing office."[154] The CAA also prohibits any employing office from retaliating against an employee for alleging a CAA violation.[155] Settlements and judgments reached under a CAA authorized action are paid out of funds appropriated to the legislative branch.[156] The law, it appears, was "intended to subject the *legislative branch* to liability for violation of federal employment laws, not to subject its [M]embers personally to such liability."[157] Moreover, the law expressly provides that the authorization to bring a civil suit under the CAA "shall not constitute a waiver ... of the privileges of any Senator or

[151] *See* CRS Report RL30240, *Congressional Oversight Manual*, by L. Elaine Halchin et al. (describing the various purposes of oversight). *See also*, United States v. McDade, 28 F.3d 283, 299-300 (3rd Cir. 1994) (discussing the broad meaning of the term "oversight").

[152] P.L. 104-1 (1995) (codified at 2 U.S.C. §§ 1301-1438). 2 U.S.C. § 1302(a) provides a list of 11 laws that the CAA makes applicable to the legislative branch.

[153] 2 U.S.C. § 1416.

[154] *Id.* at §§ 1301, 1401-08. A "covered employee" includes employees of the House, Senate, and a number of other legislative branch offices. *Id.* at § 1301(3). "Employing office" includes "the personal office of a Member of the House of Representatives or of a Senator [or] ... a committee of the House of Representatives or the Senate or a joint committee ...," and other legislative branch offices such as the Congressional Budget Office and the Architect of the Capitol. *Id.* at § 1301(9).

[155] *Id.* at § 1317(a).

[156] *Id.* at § 1415(a).

[157] *Fields*, 459 F.3d at 28 (emphasis in original).

Member of the House of Representatives under [the Clause]."[158] The Supreme Court has held that "[t]his provision demonstrates that Congress did not intend the Act to be interpreted to permit suits that would otherwise be prohibited under the Speech or Debate Clause."[159]

The judicial framework for analyzing the Clause's application to Member employment and personnel decisions has evolved over time. Prior to enactment of the CAA,[160] the U.S. Court of Appeals for the District of Columbia Circuit (D.C. Circuit) had determined that the Clause immunized Members from claims challenging personnel decisions concerning most of their staff.[161] In *Browning v. Clerk of the United States House of Representatives*, the D.C. Circuit broadly held that "personnel decisions are an integral part of the legislative process to the same extent that the affected employee's duties are an integral part of the legislative process."[162] The court, therefore, held that the Clause protected personnel actions taken by Members that impacted any employee whose "duties were directly related to the due functioning of the legislative process."[163] Thus, the Clause's application depended on the functions and duties of the impacted employee.

The *Browning* holding, however, was subsequently called into question by two later decisions outside the Speech or Debate Clause context that addressed the "administrative" nature of personnel decisions. First, in *Forrester v. White*, the Supreme Court held that judicial immunity for "judicial acts" did not extend to an employment decision, which the court

---

[158] 2 U.S.C. § 1413. *See Fields*, 459 F.3d at 8 ("The [CAA] therefore does nothing to a Member's Speech or Debate Clause immunity....").

[159] Office of Senator Dayton v. Hanson, 550 U.S. 511, 514, (2007).

[160] Prior to the CAA, an employment-related claim arising from a personnel action that allegedly violated the Constitution could still be brought pursuant to an implied cause of action. *See, e.g.*, Davis v. Passman, 442 U.S. 228, 244 (1979) (implying a cause of action for sex discrimination under the Fifth Amendment); Walker v. Jones, 733 F.2d 923, 933 (D.C. Cir. 1984) (implying a cause of action for sex discrimination under the Fifth Amendment).

[161] Browning v. Clerk of the United States House of Representatives, 789 F.2d 923, 928-29 (D.C. Cir. 1986). *See also*, Niedermeier v. Office of Max S. Baucus, 153 F. Supp. 2d 23, 31 n.5 (D.D.C. 2001) ("It also appears that this [c]ourt lacks subject matter jurisdiction over plaintiff's amended claim, because the Speech or Debate Clause provides defendant immunity for his legislative acts and this Circuit has defined legislative acts to include personnel actions of members of Congress.") (citing *Browning*, 789 F.2d at 929).

[162] *Id.* at 928.

[163] *Id.* at 929.

categorized as an administrative act rather than a judicial act.[164] Second, in *Gross v. Winter*, the D.C. Circuit extended that reasoning to the legislative sphere.[165] In an opinion addressing common law legislative immunity enjoyed by members of the D.C. City Council, rather than Speech or Debate Clause protections enjoyed by Members, the court relied on *Forrester* to hold that the "functions ... legislators exercise in making personnel decisions ... are administrative, not [] legislative."[166] These cases arguably implied that a Member's personnel decision should be viewed as nonlegislative, and, therefore, not protected by the Clause.

Forrester and *Gross* suggest that the initial shift away from *Browning*'s reasoning predated the enactment of the CAA in 1995. Moreover, the courts have explained that the CAA "does nothing to a Member's Speech or Debate Clause immunity."[167] Therefore, it does not appear that the CAA compelled the courts to alter their approach to these types of claims. Yet, after enactment of the CAA, the courts continued to diverge from the course charted by *Browning*, ultimately leading to a rejection of that decision's determination that the Clause generally acts as a bar to employment-related claims.[168] In the 2004 decision of *Bastien v. Office of Campbell*, the first case addressing how the Clause applies to the CAA, the U.S. Court of Appeals for the Tenth Circuit (Tenth Circuit) "hesitate[d] to embrace" the D.C. Circuit's reasoning in *Browning*, finding instead that "a personnel decision is not a 'legislative act,' ... and is therefore not entitled to immunity."[169] The Clause provided protections in CAA-related claims, according to the court, only to the extent that other "legislative acts must be proved to establish the claim ..."[170]

Two years later, the D.C. Circuit reconsidered *Browning* in *Fields v. Office of Johnson*.[171] That consolidated case involved CAA claims for

---

[164] Forrester v. White, 484 U.S. 219, 220 (1988).
[165] Gross v. Winter, 876 F.2d 165, 170-72 (D.C. Cir. 1989).
[166] *Id.* at 172.
[167] *Fields*, 459 F.3d at 8. *See also*, 2 U.S.C. § 1413.
[168] *See Fields*, 459 F.3d at 11-13; Bastien v. Office of Campbell, 390 F.3d 1301, 1318-19 (10th Cir. 2004).
[169] *Bastien*, 390 F.3d at 1318.
[170] *Id.*
[171] *Fields*, 459 F.3d at 11-13.

racial, gender, and disability discrimination and retaliation brought by a pair of House and Senate staffers.[172] There was no clear majority opinion in *Fields*, but the en banc court was unanimous in deciding both that the Clause does not require automatic dismissal of CAA claims and that the *Browning* framework was no longer consistent with Supreme Court precedent and should be abandoned.[173] The plurality opinion[174] explicitly rejected *Browning*'s test for determining when the Clause protects a Member's personnel decisions, holding that regardless of the role of the given employee, "many personnel decisions" lack any "nexus" to legislative acts and are, therefore, not protected by the Clause.[175]

The *Fields* plurality, which has been relied upon in subsequent opinions,[176] articulated a new framework for evaluating CAA claims that highlights the distinction between the Clause's general immunity principle and the component evidentiary and testimonial privileges.[177] The plurality determined that the general immunity principle did not "bar" the suit because the personnel actions in question were not themselves legislative acts.[178] However, the plurality reasoned that "when the Clause does not preclude suit altogether, it still 'protect[s] Members from inquiry into legislative acts or the motivation for actual performance of legislative acts'" through the component evidentiary and testimonial privileges.[179] Thus, although generally not barring a CAA suit altogether, the Clause may "hinder" the suit by "preclud[ing] some relevant evidence."[180] This

---

[172] *Id.* at 4.

[173] *Id.* at 17; *Id.* at 17 (Rodgers, J., concurring); *Id.* at 25-26 (Brown, J., concurring); *id.* at 18 (Tatel, J., concurring).

[174] Judge Brown's concurring opinion took a narrower view, suggesting that the CAA creates a "legal fiction" by holding the Member's office liable for employment discrimination, not the Member or his aides individually. *Id.* at 26 (Brown, J., concurring) The employing office, Judge Brown asserted, should not enjoy the protections of the Clause, only the Member and covered aides if personally implicated. *Id.* at 26-7.

[175] *Fields*, 459 F.3d at 11.

[176] *See Howard*, 720 F.3d at 947 ("Our discussion of *Fields* focuses on Judge Randolph's plurality opinion because ... it reflects the broadest view of the Speech or Debate Clause."); Floyd v. Lee, 968 F. Supp. 2d 308, 318 (D.D.C. 2013) (applying the *Fields* plurality opinion).

[177] *Id.* at 13-15.

[178] *Id.* at 13. Nor did the claims seek "to predicate liability on protected conduct." *Id.*

[179] *Id.* at 14 (citing *Brewster*, 408 U.S. at 508).

[180] *Id.* at 14.

was especially so in a claim for discrimination that "rests not on the fact that action was taken ... but on the *reason* that action was taken," which would likely require the plaintiff to disprove the Member's proffered motivation for taking the challenged personnel action.[181]

The *Fields* plurality opinion was relied upon in *Howard v. Office of the Chief Administrative Officer of the United States House of Representatives*.[182] That case involved a CAA claim for racial discrimination and retaliation brought by a former House employee.[183] As in the *Fields* plurality, the court determined that the claim itself was not barred, as the personnel action in question was not a "legislative act."[184] But the court highlighted that "in many employment discrimination cases, proof of 'pretext' will be crucial to the success of the claimant's case,"[185] and those allegations of pretext, the court reasoned, must be proven "using evidence that does not implicate protected legislative matters."[186] In somc cases, the court warned, a plaintiff may not be able to meet the required burden of proof because the Clause bars him "from inquiring into legislative motives ... or conduct part of or integral to the legislative process...."[187] In the instant case, the court remanded to the district court with directions that the plaintiff's claims be allowed to proceed, under the caveat that "it remain[ed] to be seen" whether, due to the "strictures" of the

---

[181] *Id.* at 15-16 (emphasis in original) ("For example, if a Senator claimed to have fired an employee because speeches the employee wrote did not accurately reflect the Senator's legislative objectives, the Speech or Debate Clause would preclude the employee from proving her case by demonstrating that the speeches she wrote did in fact accurately reflect the Senator's legislative objectives. In such a case, if the evidence ultimately bore out the affiant's account of the plaintiff's discharge, then the very inquiry leading to that conclusion would be unconstitutional."). The Senate office appealed the D.C. Circuit's decision directly to the Supreme Court. *Office of Senator Dayton*, 550 U.S. at 511. The Court denied certiorari, while also determining that it lacked jurisdiction under the CAA to hear an appeal of the interlocutory order. *Id.* at 515.

[182] *Howard*, 720 F.3d at 947.

[183] *Id.* at 941.

[184] *Id.* at 949.

[185] *Id.* at 947. In *McDonnell Douglas Corp. v. Green*, the Supreme Court established a framework for certain types of employment discrimination claims in which after a plaintiff proves a prima facie case for discrimination, the employer rebuts by producing evidence of a nondiscriminatory purpose, which the plaintiff then attempts to demonstrate is pretextual. 411 U.S. 792, 802-804 (1973).

[186] *Id.* at 949.

[187] *Id.* at 950.

Clause, the plaintiff would be able to produce sufficient evidence to prove her claim.[188] Indeed, it was ultimately determined that the employee failed to produce sufficient evidence showing the asserted reason for her termination was pretextual.[189]

The CAA also authorizes congressional employees to bring sexual harassment claims for violations of Title VII of the Civil Rights Act of 1964,[190] although such claims appear to have only rarely been evaluated by federal courts. In *Scott v. Office of Alexander*, the former scheduler for a Member brought a CAA claim that included counts alleging sexual harassment and retaliation for reporting that harassment in the form of a demotion.[191] The majority of the district court decision focused on the plaintiff's retaliation claim.[192] Applying *Fields*, the court determined first that the demotion itself was not a legislative act, and thus the claim was not barred by the Clause's general immunity principle.[193]

However, the court also held that a retaliation claim "operates in the same way" as the discrimination claims brought in *Fields* and *Howard*.[194] Thus, the plaintiff would be required to rebut the Member's assertion of nonretaliatory reasons for her demotion in order to show that it was pretextual.[195] Through an affidavit, the Member had asserted that Scott was demoted because of scheduling errors that caused him to miss votes and committee hearings.[196] The court concluded that:

> Although Plaintiff argues that her "case would not require impermissibly questioning anything that Defendant may have done

---

[188] *Howard*, 720 F.3d at 950.

[189] Howard v. Office of the Chief Admin. Officer of the United States House of Representatives, No. 15-5243, 2015 U.S. App. LEXIS 22290, at *2 (D.C. Cir. 2015) ("Nor has appellant produced sufficient evidence for a reasonable jury to find that the appellee's asserted non-discriminatory reason for her termination—that she was insubordinate—was pretextual and that the appellee discriminated against her on the basis of race.").

[190] 2 U.S.C. § 1302(a)(2); 42 U.S.C. §§ 2000e-2000e-17.

[191] Scott v. Office of Alexander, 522 F. Supp. 2d 262, 265 (D.D.C. 2007).

[192] *Id.* at 267-72.

[193] *Id.* at 269 ("Plaintiff's retaliation claim predicates liability on conduct that does not constitute core legislative activities.").

[194] *Id.* at 270.

[195] *Id.*

[196] *Id.* at 270-71.

> during the course of an actual vote or hearing," whether the Congressman missed or attended an actual vote or hearing, and the reasons why he may have attended or missed an actual vote or hearing, are inquiries that impermissibly relate to the legislative process. Accordingly, the Court finds that Defendant has asserted, through the Congressman's affidavit, legitimate, non-retaliatory reasons for Plaintiff's demotion that are protected from inquiry by the Speech or Debate Clause.[197]

As a result, the court held that "the evidentiary privilege of the Clause prevents Plaintiff from refuting the Member's stated reasons for her demotion."[198] Because the plaintiff had not presented any evidence "unrelated to the Congressman's stated reasons for Plaintiff's demotion that would not require an inquiry into [] legislative acts," the court dismissed the retaliation claim.[199]

With respect to the sexual harassment claim, the court held that the defendant's argument that the claim was barred by the Clause was not properly before the court.[200] Nevertheless, the court provided some insight into how the Clause may apply to evidence supporting alleged sexual harassment, as opposed to alleged retaliation. Whereas the plaintiff was "precluded from seeking discovery or otherwise inquiring about the Congressman's reasons for removing Plaintiff as Scheduler," the court suggested that "[t]he proper focus of the remaining discovery ... appears to be the conduct that other individuals may have observed at times relevant to the Complaint, and what Plaintiff may have told others about such conduct."[201] That evidence, it would appear, would not be protected by the Clause's component privileges.

In sum, the Clause's general immunity principle does not typically act as an absolute bar to employment-related claims brought under the CAA.[202] However, it would appear that there may be cases in which a CAA claim fails as a result of the application of the Clause's evidentiary

---

[197] *Scott*, 522 F. Supp. 2d at 271.
[198] *Id.* at 272.
[199] *Id.*
[200] *Id.* at 271.
[201] *Id.* at 274.
[202] *See Fields*, 459 F.3d at 11.

and testimonial privileges, which may effectively block a plaintiff from presenting evidence of related legislative acts necessary to support the claim.[203]

Nondisclosure Privilege: A Continued Circuit Split

Although the precise scope of the protections afforded by the Clause have not been clearly articulated by the Supreme Court, there appears to be some agreement among the lower courts that the Clause provides immunity from direct liability for legislative acts; prohibits the use of legislative-act evidence in the course of litigation; and protects a Member from being compelled to respond to questioning regarding his legislative acts.[204] There is stark disagreement, however, as to whether the Clause encompasses a general documentary "non-disclosure privilege" that applies unrelated to whether such documents are introduced into evidence.[205] When accepted, this privilege appears to be included within the testimonial component of the Clause, and may apply in a variety of situations, including protecting Members from compelled compliance with an administrative[206] or civil discovery[207] subpoena for legislative-act documents, or from disclosures reflecting legislative acts that occur during a search executed as part of a criminal investigation.[208]

---

[203] *See Howard*, 720 F.3d at 949-50.

[204] *See, e.g., Renzi*, 651 F.3d at 1035 n. 27 ("To reiterate, the Court has identified three distinct privileges in the Clause: a testimonial privilege, an evidentiary privilege, and a privilege against liability."); Howard, 720 F.3d at 946 ("As a general matter, the Speech or Debate Clause affords three distinct protections: (a) an immunity from 'a civil or criminal judgment ...' (b) an evidentiary privilege ... and (c) a testimonial and non-disclosure privilege ...") (citations omitted).

[205] *Compare Rayburn*, 497 F.3d at 655 (holding that the testimonial component of the Clause includes a documentary nondisclosure privilege), with *Renzi*, 651 F.3d at 1034 (holding that the testimonial component of the Clause does not create the documentary nondisclosure privilege outlined in *Rayburn*).

[206] *See* Comm. on Ways & Means, 161 F. Supp. 3d at 238-45.

[207] MINPECO, S.A. v. Conticommodity Services, Inc., 844 F.2d 856, 857-59 (D.C. Cir. 1988).

[208] *Rayburn*, 497 F.3d at 660.

The D.C. Circuit has established the documentary nondisclosure privilege.[209] In a series of opinions, the circuit court determined that the Clause bars any compelled disclosure—not just the evidentiary use—of written materials that fall "within the sphere of legitimate legislative activity."[210] According to the D.C. Circuit, this privilege is broad and "absolute," and applies with equal "vigor" as the other aspects of the Clause.[211]

The U.S. Court of Appeals for the Ninth Circuit (Ninth Circuit) and the Third Circuit have rejected this documentary nondisclosure privilege, considering it an undue expansion of the Clause.[212] Instead, these courts have held, at least in criminal cases, that the Clause prohibits only the evidentiary *use* of privileged documents, not their mere disclosure to the government for review as part of an investigation.[213] The disagreement has not been addressed by the Supreme Court.[214]

The D.C. Circuit position is perhaps best exemplified by two cases: *Brown & Williamson Tobacco Corporation v. Williams* and *United States v. Rayburn House Office Building*.[215]

Brown & Williamson arose when a former employee of a law firm disclosed to a congressional committee stolen documents that were obtained while the firm was representing Brown & Williamson.[216] The law firm brought an action against the former employee in state court, and during that proceeding, the court issued subpoenas to two Members of the committee requiring the return of the stolen documents.[217] The case was removed to federal court, where the Members sought to quash the subpoenas on Speech or Debate grounds.[218]

---

[209] *See id.* at 660-62; *Brown & Williamson*, 62 F.3d at 420; *MINPECO*, 844 F.2d at 858.
[210] *Rayburn*, 497 F.3d at 660.
[211] *Brown & Williamson*, 62 F.3d at 420-21.
[212] *Renzi*, 651 F.3d at 1032-39; *Fattah*, 802 F.3d at 524-29; In re Grand Jury Investigation, 587 F.2d 589, 595-97 (3rd Cir. 1978).
[213] *Fattah*, 802 F.3d at 529.
[214] *Rayburn*, 651 F.3d at 1033 (noting that "to date the Court has not spoken on whether the privilege conferred by the Clause includes a non-disclosure privilege"); *Comm. on Ways & Means*, 161 F. Supp. 3d at 238.
[215] *Brown & Williamson*, 62 F.3d at 411-421; *Rayburn*, 497 F.3d at 659-63.
[216] *Brown & Williamson*, 62 F.3d at 411-12.
[217] *Id.*
[218] *Id.* at 412.

The court agreed with the Members, blocking the subpoenas and extending the Clause to include a general nondisclosure privilege.[219] In doing so, the court rejected three conclusions that had been reached by the Third Circuit in an earlier case. First, the court rebuffed the idea that a Member must be named as a party to the suit in order for litigation to "distract them from their legislative work."[220] "Discovery procedures" in any civil case, the court reasoned, "can prove just as intrusive" as being a party to a case.[221] The court similarly disagreed with the assertion that the testimonial component of the Clause applies only when Members or their aides are "personally questioned," suggesting instead that "documentary evidence can certainly be as revealing as oral communications."[222] Finally, the court dismissed the assertion that when applied to documents, the Clause's protection "is one of nonevidentiary use, not of nondisclosure." Instead, noting the antidistraction purpose of the Clause, the court held that "the nature of the use to which documents will be put ... is immaterial if the touchstone is interference with legislative activities."[223] The court concluded that "a party is no more entitled to compel congressional testimony—or production of documents—than it is to sue a congressman."[224]

The D.C. Circuit later extended the nondisclosure privilege to scenarios in which the government executes a search warrant as part of a criminal investigation of a Member.[225] In *United States v. Rayburn House Office Building*, a Member sought the return of documents seized by the Federal Bureau of Investigation (FBI) during a search of the Member's office, arguing the search—which was pursuant to a warrant for nonlegislative, unprotected documents—was executed in a way that violated

---

[219] *Id.* at 420 ("We do not accept the proposition that the testimonial immunity of the Speech or Debate Clause only applies when Members or their aides are personally questioned. Documentary evidence can certainly be as revealing as oral communications ...").

[220] *Id.* at 418 (citing *MINPECO*, 844 F.2d 856.).

[221] *Id.*

[222] *Brown & Williamson*, 62 F.3d at 420.

[223] *Id.* at 421.

[224] *Id.*

[225] *Rayburn*, 497 F.3d at 656.

the Clause.[226] In order to distinguish between protected and unprotected documents, the warrant permitted FBI agents to review "all of the papers in the Congressman's office."[227]

The D.C. Circuit held that the search violated the Clause because the Executive's procedures "denied the Congressman any opportunity to identify and assert the privilege with respect to legislative materials *before* their compelled disclosure to Executive agents."[228] The court noted that despite the limited scope of the warrant, the FBI's review of the Member's papers to determine which were responsive "must have resulted in the disclosure of legislative materials to agents of the executive."[229] That compelled disclosure was inconsistent with the protections of the Clause.[230] In reaching this conclusion, the court reaffirmed the nondisclosure privilege articulated in *Brown & Williamson*, and then extended it to the criminal context, concluding that "there is no reason to believe that the bar does not apply in the criminal as well as the civil context."[231] The court also reaffirmed its view of the absolute nature of the nondisclosure privilege, noting that the "non-disclosure privilege of written materials ... is [] absolute, and thus admits of no balancing."[232]

The court carefully distinguished between the lawfulness of searching a congressional office pursuant to a search warrant—which the court held was clearly permissible—and the lawfulness of the way the search was

---

226 *Id.* at 655.

227 *Id.* at 661. This instance was the first time a sitting Member's office was searched by the executive branch. *Id.* at 659.

228 *Id.* at 662.

229 *Id.* at 661. The court also held that the FBI's copying of hard drives was permissible, since procedures allowed for the Member to assert privilege prior to FBI review of the drive. *Id.* at 663.

230 In reaching its conclusion, the court invoked the distraction and disruption rationale, noting that:

> [T]his compelled disclosure clearly tends to disrupt the legislative process: exchanges between a Member of Congress and the Member's staff or among Members of Congress on legislative matters may legitimately involve frank or embarrassing statements; the possibility of compelled disclosure may therefore chill the exchange of views with respect to legislative activity. This chill runs counter to the Clause's purpose of protecting against disruption of the legislative process.

Id. at 661.

231 *Id.* at 660.

232 *Rayburn*, 497 F.3d at 662.

executed.[233] The court declined, however, to expressly delineate acceptable procedures that could avoid future violations, noting only that there appears to be "no reason why the Congressman's privilege under the Speech or Debate Clause cannot be asserted at the outset of a search in a manner that also protects the interests of the Executive in law enforcement."[234]

The D.C. Circuit's legal reasoning in *Rayburn* has been rejected by both the Ninth and Third Circuits.[235] In *United States v. Renzi*, the Ninth Circuit held that the Clause does not prohibit the compelled disclosure of legislative documents to the government in the course of executing a warrant in a criminal investigation, at least when the underlying criminal action is not itself barred by the immunity prong of the Clause.[236] *Renzi* involved a Speech or Debate Clause challenge brought by a former Member to portions of a 48-count indictment that included charges that he agreed to provide certain legislative favors in exchange for personal benefits.[237] Specifically, the Member relied on the nondisclosure privilege articulated in *Rayburn* to argue, in part, that the government's unlawful review of privileged documents allowed it to obtain evidence that was used against him.[238] The Ninth Circuit rebuffed Renzi's argument, as well as the reasoning in *Rayburn*, instead finding that the Clause does not encompass a documentary nondisclosure privilege.[239]

After noting that the Supreme Court has not recognized the existence of a general nondisclosure privilege, the *Renzi* court laid out the three principal reasons that led it to disagree with the D.C. Circuit's reasoning. First, the court objected to the D.C. Circuit's reliance on the notion that "distraction" from a Member's legislative duty, on its own, can serve "as a

---

[233] *Id.* at 659.

[234] *Id.* at 662. The court observed that the question of how these searches should proceed "is best determined by the legislative and executive branches in the first instance." *Id.* at 663.

[235] *Renzi*, 651 F.3d at 1032-39; *Fattah*, 802 F.3d at 524-29.

[236] *Renzi*, 651 F.3d at 1032-39.

[237] *Id.* at 1017-18.

[238] *Id.* at 1019. The court also rejected Renzi's assertion that the charges were based on "legislative acts." *Id.* at 1021- 27.

[239] *Id.* at 1032.

touchstone for application of the Clause's testimonial privilege."[240] Instead, the court reasoned that because "legislative distraction is not the primary ill the Clause seeks to cure," that rationale must be "anchored" to a barred action—for example, an investigation into a protected act—before it can preclude inquiry.[241] In cases where the underlying action is not precluded, the court stated that "other legitimate interests exist" and must be taken into account, most notably "the ability of the executive to adequately investigate and prosecute corrupt legislators for non-protected activity."[242]

Second, the circuit court indicated that previous decisions by the Supreme Court have suggested that the executive branch *may* review legislative materials as part of an investigation.[243] For example, in *United States v. Helstoski*, the Supreme Court reasoned that the executive branch could redact "legislative" aspects of certain documents so that the "remainder of the evidence would be admissible."[244] From this language, the circuit court noted that:

> Because the Executive would be hard pressed to redact a document it was constitutionally precluded from obtaining or reviewing, we see no tenable explanation for this caveat except that the Clause does not blindly preclude disclosure and review by the Executive of documentary "legislative act" evidence.[245]

Third, the court determined that any interpretation of the Clause that permitted the courts, but not the executive branch, to review protected legislative documents would be inconsistent with the separation-of-powers rationale that undergirds the Clause.[246] The Clause, the court noted, is a "creature born of separation of powers" and thus must apply "in equal scope and with equal strength to both the Executive and the Judiciary."[247]

---

240 *Id.* at 1034.
241 *Renzi*, 651 F.3d at 1037 ("Concern for distraction alone cannot bar disclosure and review when it takes place as part of an investigation into otherwise unprotected activity.").
242 *Id.* at 1036.
243 *Id.* at 1037.
244 *Helstoski*, 442 U.S. at 488 n.7.
245 *Renzi*, 651 F.3d at 1037.
246 *Id.* at 1037-38.
247 *Id.* at 1038.

The court specifically criticized the D.C. Circuit's opinion in *Rayburn* on the grounds that it prohibited "'any executive branch exposure to records of legislative acts' ... while noting that the Judiciary could review evidence claimed to be privileged."[248] "Such a distinction," the court stated, "cannot exist."[249]

The precise holding of *Renzi* appears to be that the Clause does not prohibit the government from reviewing protected legislative documents as part of the execution of a warrant connected to an investigation into nonlegislative acts.[250] However, the opinion suggests that there may be times when the testimonial component of the Clause would create a nondisclosure privilege in response to a *subpoena* for documents. Citing to the concurrence in *Rayburn*, the Ninth Circuit indicated that execution of a warrant has no testimonial aspects since the Member is not required to "respond" in any way.[251] However, the court reasoned that "it is entirely true that sometimes the very disclosure of documentary evidence in response to a subpoena duces tecum may have some testimonial import."[252] This language would appear to suggest that the Ninth Circuit has not foreclosed the idea of the existence of some form of documentary nondisclosure privilege—for instance, one more intimately connected to the testimonial privilege component—that may apply in situations where a subpoena is issued for legislative documents. The central focus for the court appears to have been whether the disclosure is "testimonial," and therefore more directly implicating the "question[ing]" prohibited by the Clause.[253]

The Third Circuit similarly rejected the existence of a documentary nondisclosure privilege during criminal investigations in *In re Fattah*.[254] There, a Member challenged a warrant, served on Google, authorizing the

---

[248] *Id.* (citing *Rayburn*, 497 F.3d at 660).
[249] *Id.*
[250] *Id.* at 1038-39.
[251] *Renzi*, 651 F.3d at 1037 n. 28.
[252] *Id.* at 1037 n. 28.
[253] *Id.*
[254] *Fattah*, 802 F.3d at 524-29. *See also*, In re Grand Jury Investigation, 587 F.2d 589, 595-97 (3rd Cir. 1978) (holding that "when applied to records or third-party testimony" the privilege afforded by the Clause "is one of nonevidentiary use, not of nondisclosure").

government to search his email on the grounds that such a search was barred by the Clause.[255] Specifically, the Member asserted that the privilege created by the Clause was "one of non-disclosure."[256] The court rejected this argument, holding that "it cannot be ... that the privilege prohibits disclosure of evidentiary records to the Government during the course of an investigation."[257] The court rested its decision primarily on the effect such a broad privilege would have on criminal prosecutions, noting that a nondisclosure privilege during criminal investigations would "shelter" Members from criminal responsibility and "eradicate the integrity of the legislative process" by "unduly amplify[ing] the protections" of the Clause.[258] The court ultimately refused to extend the testimonial component of the Clause to documentary disclosures, concluding that:

> ... while the Speech or Debate Clause prohibits hostile questioning regarding legislative acts in the form of testimony to a jury, it does not prohibit disclosure of Speech or Debate Clause privileged documents to the Government. Instead, as we have held before, it merely prohibits the evidentiary submission and use of those documents.[259]

How, and whether, the Supreme Court resolves this ongoing disagreement over the existence of a documentary nondisclosure privilege could have a significant impact on the protections afforded to Members by the Clause. For example, if the Court were to adopt the position of the Third and Ninth Circuits, that ruling would directly limit a Member's ability to invoke the Clause as a shield against the disclosure of documents to the executive branch during a criminal investigation. More generally, however, the disagreement between the D.C. Circuit and the Third and

---

[255] *Fattah*, 802 F.3d at 521-22.
[256] *Id.* at 524.
[257] *Id.* at 528.
[258] *Id.* at 529 ("Depriving the Executive of the power to investigate and prosecute and the Judiciary of the power to punish bribery of Members of Congress is unlikely to enhance legislative independence.") (quoting *Renzi*, 651 F.3d at 1036).
[259] *Id.*

Ninth Circuits is one relating to the fundamental purpose of the Clause.[260] The opinions in *Renzi* and *Fattah* appear to have adopted a legal reasoning that minimizes the role of the "distraction" rationale in defining the scope of the Clause. Were the Supreme Court to embrace that reasoning, it could potentially lead to a narrowing of the Clause's protections, especially in scenarios in which information is sought from a Member in a proceeding to which he is not a party.

THE ACQUISITION AND USE OF INFORMATION BY CONGRESS

A final line of cases relates to Speech or Debate Clause protections for the acquisition and use of information by Congress.[261] These cases typically arise from lawsuits in which a party asks a court to invalidate or block a congressional subpoena, or to direct Congress or its Members in how they may use information that is within their possession. Generally, a court will not interfere with lawful efforts by Congress to exercise its subpoena power, nor will a court act to limit the ability of Members to use or distribute information within the legislative sphere.[262] In some sense,

---

[260] In some sense, the debate concerns how, under the Clause, the purpose of preventing "distraction" should be weighed against the purpose of preserving "independence." *See Renzi*, 651 F.3d at 1034 ("*Rayburn* rests on the notion that 'distraction' of Members and their staffs from their legislative tasks is a principal concern of the Clause, and that distraction *alone* can therefore serve as a touchstone for application of the Clause's testimonial privilege ... We disagree with both *Rayburn*'s premise and its effect and thus decline to adopt its rationale.").

[261] *See, e.g.*, *Eastland*, 421 U.S. at 501-11; *Brown & Williamson,* 62 F.3d at 416-17; Hearst v. Black, 87 F.2d 68, 71 (D.C. Cir. 1936).

[262] *See Eastland*, 421 U.S. at 501; *Brown & Williamson*, 62 F.3d at 416 ("The privilege also permits Congress to conduct investigations and obtain information without interference from the courts, at least when these activities are performed in a procedurally regular fashion."); Dombrowski v. Burbank, 358 F.2d 821, 823-24 (1966) ("Since the documents are now held by the Subcommittee ... We cannot prohibit, nor are we asked to prohibit, [their] use of the documents in the course of their official business for the Subcommittee . ...").

these cases tend to emphasize the structural and institutional aspects of the Clause's role in the separation of powers.[263]

In *Eastland v. United States Serviceman's Fund*, the Supreme Court concluded that the Clause acts as a significant barrier to judicial interference in Congress's exercise of its subpoena power.[264] In this case, a private nonprofit organization filed suit against the Chairman of a Senate subcommittee asking the Court to enjoin a congressional subpoena issued to a bank for the nonprofit's account information.[265] The subpoena was issued as part of an investigation into alleged "subversive" activities harmful to the U.S. military conducted by the organization.[266] The Court held that because the "power to investigate and to do so through compulsory process plainly" constitutes an "indispensable ingredient of lawmaking," the Clause made the subpoena "immune from judicial interference."[267] *Eastland* is generally cited for the proposition that the Clause prohibits courts from entertaining preenforcement challenges to congressional subpoenas.[268] As a result, the lawfulness of a subpoena usually may not be challenged until Congress seeks to enforce the subpoena through either a civil action or contempt of Congress.[269]

While it is generally true that courts will not interfere in valid congressional attempts to obtain information, especially through the exercise of the subpoena power, the concurrence in *Eastland* and a subsequent appellate court decision suggests that the restraint exercised by

---

[263] See, *Dombrowski*, 358 F.2d at 824 (noting the importance of "considerations resting upon a proper allocation of powers and responsibilities among the co-ordinate branches of the federal system....").

[264] *Eastland*, 421 U.S. at 501.

[265] *Id.* at 494-96.

[266] *Id.* at 493.

[267] *Id.* at 501.

[268] In re Grand Jury, 821 F.2d 946, 957 (3d Cir. 1987) ("The Supreme Court has held analogously that the Speech or Debate Clause shields Congressmen from suit to block a Congressional subpoena because making the legislators defendants 'creates a distraction and forces Members [of Congress] to divert their time, energy, and attention from their legislative tasks to defend the litigation.'") (citing *Eastland*, 421 U.S. at 503.).

[269] United States v. Ryan, 402 U.S. 530, 532 (1971) (noting that in the judicial context that "one who seeks to resist the production of desired information [has a] choice between compliance with a trial court's order to produce prior to any review of that order, and resistance to that order with the concomitant possibility of an adjudication of contempt if his claims are rejected on appeal"); *Eastland*, 421 U.S. at. 515-16 (Marshall, J., concurring).

the courts in deference to the separation of powers is not absolute.[270] Justice Marshall's concurrence in *Eastland* clarified that the Clause "does not entirely immunize a congressional subpoena from challenge."[271] Rather, according to Justice Marshall, the Clause requires only that a Member "may not be called upon to defend a subpoena against constitutional objection."[272] Thus, Justice Marshall implied that if a challenge to the legitimacy of a subpoena is directed not at Congress or its Members, it may be permitted to proceed.[273]

Such a claim arose, however, in the case of *United States v. AT&T*.[274] In that case, a congressional subcommittee subpoena was issued to AT&T for all letters sent to the company by the Department of Justice (DOJ) that had identified certain phone lines the DOJ wished to monitor.[275] DOJ filed suit, seeking to enjoin AT&T from complying with the subpoena, citing national security concerns.[276] The subcommittee Chairman intervened in the case, asserting that judicial interference in the subcommittee's investigation was barred by the Clause.[277] After the court's attempts to initiate a settlement between the parties failed,[278] the D.C. Circuit ultimately rejected the Chairman's argument, noting generally that the Clause "was not intended to immunize congressional investigatory actions from judicial review."[279] Instead, the court concluded, the Clause "is personal to members of Congress" such that when Members or their aides are not "harassed by personal suit against them, the Clause cannot be invoked to immunize the congressional subpoena from judicial scrutiny."[280] The court went on to

---

[270] *Eastland*, 421 U.S. at 513-18; United States v. Am. Tel. & Telegraph Co., 567 F.2d 121, 129-30 (D.C. Cir. 1977).

[271] *Eastland*, 421 U.S. at. 513 (Marshall, J., concurring).

[272] *Id.* at 516.

[273] *Id.* at 517. Justice Marshall did not speculate as to what such a case may look like or "who might be the proper parties defendant." *Id.*

[274] United States v. AT&T, 567 F.2d 121, 123-25 (D.C. Cir. 1977).

[275] *Id.* at 123-24.

[276] *Id.*

[277] *Id.* at 124.

[278] In a prior iteration of the case, the D.C. Circuit had requested that the two branches seek a settlement, reasoning that "[b]efore moving on to a decision of such nerve-center constitutional questions, we pause to allow for further efforts at a settlement." United States v. AT&T, 551 F.2d 384, 394 (1976).

[279] *AT&T*, 567 F.2d at 129.

[280] *Id.* at 130.

establish an exception to the general prohibition on pre-enforcement interference with congressional subpoenas. When a party is "not in a position to assert its claim of constitutional right by refusing to comply with a subpoena," because the subpoena was issued to a neutral third party, the Clause "does not bar the challenge so long as members of the Subcommittee are not, themselves, made defendants in a suit to enjoin implementation of the subpoena."[281]

Once information is in the possession of Congress, courts generally will not curtail the ability of Members to use or distribute that information within the legislative sphere. For example, in *Doe v. McMillan*, a case dealing with the inclusion of specific students' names in a committee report on the D.C. public schools, the Supreme Court noted that "[a]lthough we might disagree with the Committee as to whether it was necessary, or even remotely useful, to include the names of individual children in the ... Committee Report, we have no authority to oversee the judgment of the Committee in this respect ..."[282]

The D.C. Circuit has also issued a series of opinions protecting Congress's authority to freely and independently assess and use information within its possession, no matter how it was obtained. In *Hearst v. Black*, the court concluded that it was not within its authority to tell a Senate committee that it was barred from "keeping" or "making any use of" certain unlawfully obtained documents.[283] Similarly, in *McSurely v. McClellan*, a case involving the receipt of documents by a committee that were obtained pursuant to an unlawful search by a congressional investigator, the court noted that "the law is clear that even though material comes to a legislative committee by means that are unlawful or otherwise subject to judicial inquiry the subsequent use of the documents by the committee staff in the course of official business is privileged legislative activity."[284] Finally, in *Brown & Williamson*, the court suggested that the Clause supplied Congress

[281] *Id.* at 129. This principle builds off the *Perlman* doctrine, which generally holds that a preenforcement challenge to a subpoena may be appropriate when the subpoena is issued to a neutral third party, rather than the party that owns the constitutional privilege. Perlman v. United States, 247 U.S. 7, 12 (1918).

[282] Doe v. McMillan, 412 U.S. 306, 313 (1973).

[283] Hearst v. Black, 87 F.2d 68, 71 (D.C. Cir. 1936).

[284] McSurely v. McClellan, 553 F.2d 1277, 1296-97 (D.C. Cir. 1976).

with the "privilege to use materials in its possession without judicial interference."[285]

These principles were applied recently in the case of *Senate Permanent Subcommittee on Investigations v. Ferrer*,[286] in which a Senate subcommittee initiated a civil action to enforce a subpoena issued to the Chief Executive Officer (CEO) of an online advertising website for documents relating to sex trafficking.[287] As part of that proceeding, the CEO asked the D.C. Circuit to order that the subcommittee destroy or return certain documents he had produced in response to the subpoena.[288] The court refused to comply with that request, citing to the aforementioned cases, and reasoning that "[t]o circumscribe the committee's use of material in its physical possession would ... 'destroy[]' the independence of the Legislature and 'invade[]' the constitutional separation of powers."[289] The court ultimately held that "the separation of powers, including the Speech or Debate Clause, bars this court from ordering a congressional committee to return, destroy, or refrain from publishing the subpoenaed documents."[290]

CONCLUSION

The Speech or Debate Clause is perhaps the greatest constitutional bulwark against inappropriate executive or judicial intrusions into both the functioning of Congress as an institution and the representative role of individual Members. The Clause seeks to ensure an independent legislature by providing Members with immunity from liability for legislative acts in both criminal and civil cases. That immunity appears to be complemented by both an evidentiary and a testimonial privilege that protects against the

---

[285] *Brown & Williamson*, 62 F.3d at 416. *See also*, *Dombrowski*, 358 F.2d at 823-24.

[286] Senate Permanent Subcomm. on Investigations v. Ferrer 856 F.3d 1080, 1085-87 (D.C. Cir, 2017).

[287] *Id.* at 1084.

[288] *Id.*

[289] *Id.* at 1086.

[290] *Id.*

compelled disclosure of information reflecting those acts. However, the scope of those privileges, especially with regard to the disclosure of documents for nonevidentiary purposes, is subject to debate among the federal courts. The issue would appear to be ripe for Supreme Court review.

In: Constitution
Editor: Jackelyn Haggerty

ISBN: 978-1-53614-198-6

Chapter 3

CONSTITUTIONAL AUTHORITY STATEMENTS AND THE POWERS OF CONGRESS: AN OVERVIEW*

Andrew Nolan

SUMMARY

On January 5, 2011, the House of Representatives adopted an amendment to House Rule XII to require that Members of the House state the constitutional basis for Congress's power to enact the proposed legislation when introducing a bill or joint resolution. This Constitutional Authority Statement (CAS) rule, found at House Rule XII, clause 7(c), was subsequently adopted in the 113th, 114th, and 115th Congresses.

Understanding the CAS rule first requires an understanding of both the powers provided to the Congress under the Constitution and Congress's role in interpreting the founding document. Article I's Vesting Clause creates a Congress of specified or "enumerated" powers, and every law Congress enacts must be based on one or more of its powers enumerated in the Constitution. The Constitution creates two central types

* This is an edited, reformatted and augmented version of Congressional Research Service report 7-5700, R44729, www.crs.gov, dated January 6, 2017.

of limitations on Congress's powers: (1) internal limits and (2) external limits. Internal limits are the restrictions inherent in the constitutional grants of power themselves, such as the limits on the scope of Congress's powers under the Commerce Clause. External limits, on the other hand, are the constraints contained in affirmative prohibitions found elsewhere in the text or structure of the document, such as the First Amendment's prohibition on Congress abridging the freedom of speech. While the Court's 1803 decision in *Marbury v. Madison* firmly cemented the judicial branch's role in interpreting the Constitution by recognizing the power of the Court to strike down legislation as unconstitutional, the early history of the nation is replete with examples of all three government branches playing a substantial role in constitutional interpretation. By the mid-20th century, however, the Supreme Court began articulating a theory of judicial supremacy that became widely accepted, wherein the federal judiciary is the final and exclusive arbiter of the Constitution's meaning. Nonetheless, in recent decades, a number of legal scholars and government officials have criticized this theory, instead promoting the view that the political branches of government possess the independent and coordinate authority to interpret the Constitution. In support of this view, some point to (1) the Constitution itself requiring all Members of Congress to be bound by an oath to support the Constitution; (2) the presumption of constitutionality that courts afford legislation enacted by Congress; and (3) the wide range of questions the Constitution requires Congress to resolve.

A CAS is fundamentally a congressional interpretation of the Constitution, in that House Rule XII requires each Member introducing a piece of legislation to attach a statement which cites the power(s) that allows Congress to enact the legislation. The submitted CAS appears in the *Congressional Record* and is published on Congress.gov. The House Rules Committee has indicated that Members have significant discretion in determining whether particular CASs comply with the rule. The CAS rule is enforced only insofar as "the House clerk ... acts to verify that each bill has a justification" and "not [in judging] the adequacy of the justification itself." The most common means of complying with the rule is to cite to a specific clause in Article I, Section 8, such as the Taxing and Spending Clause. The CAS rule has itself been subject to much debate, with proponents arguing that the rule promotes constitutional dialogue in the House, while critics contend that the rule provides minimal benefits and is administratively costly.

This chapter provides an overview of Congress's powers under the Constitution and Congress's role in interpreting the nation's founding document. The chapter then examines House Rule XII, clause 7(c), discussing the results of a recent study conducted by CRS of CASs that were submitted during the last six months of the 114th Congress. The chapter concludes by discussing trends with regard to the House's recent

CAS practices and by providing considerations for congressional personnel drafting CASs. The chapter contains two tables: one that identifies the most commonly cited provisions in recent CASs, and a second that lists suggested constitutional bases for various types of legislation.

INTRODUCTION

On January 5, 2011, the House of Representatives adopted an amendment to House Rule XII to require that Members of the House state the constitutional basis for Congress's power to enact the proposed legislation when introducing a bill or joint resolution.[1] The Constitutional Authority Statement (CAS) rule, found at House Rule XII, clause 7(c),[2] was subsequently adopted in the 113th, 114th, and 115th Congresses.[3] As the CAS rule begins its seventh year, the requirement continues to be a topic of congressional debate and inquiry, as Members of the House contemplate how to comply with the rule prior to every submission of a bill or joint resolution.[4]

This chapter aims to aid in understanding the CAS requirement. It begins by providing a broad overview of (1) Congress's powers under the Constitution and (2) Congress's role in interpreting this document. The chapter then specifically addresses House Rule XII, clause 7(c), discussing its key requirements and limits, the legal effect of a CAS, and the debate over the rule's value. The chapter concludes by discussing trends with regard to the House's recent CAS practices and by providing considerations for congressional personnel drafting CASs. The chapter

---

[1] *See* H.R. Res. 5, 112th Cong. (1st Sess. 2011) (adopting the rules for the 112th Congress, which included the Constitutional Authority Statement (CAS) requirement).

[2] *See* House Rule XII cl. 7(c)(1).

[3] *See* H.R. Res. 5, 113th Cong. (1st Sess. 2013) (adopting the rules for the 113th Congress, which were based on the "constituted rules of the House at the end of the" 112th Congress and did not alter the CAS requirement); H.R. Res. 5, 114th Cong. (1st Sess. 2015) (adopting the rules for the 114th Congress, which were based on the "constituted rules of the House at the end of the" 113th Congress and did not alter the CAS requirement); H.R. Res. 5, 115th Cong. (1st Sess. 2017) (adopting the rules for the 115th Congress, which were based on the "constituted rules of the House at the end of the" 114th Congress and did not alter the CAS requirement).

[4] *See infra* "House Rule XII, Clause 7(c), and Constitutional Authority Statements."

contains two tables: *Table 1* identifies the constitutional provisions most commonly cited in CASs during the last six months of the 114th Congress, and *Table 2* lists suggested constitutional authorities for various types of legislation.

SCOPE OF CONGRESS'S POWERS UNDER THE CONSTITUTION

Understanding the purpose and logic of the CAS rule first requires an understanding of both the powers provided to the Congress under the Constitution and Congress's role in interpreting the Constitution. The Framers of the Constitution feared tyranny as the result of the "accumulation of all powers" of government "in the same hands"[5] and, thus, "sought to guard against it by dispersing federal power to three interdependent branches of Government."[6] Reflecting this fear, the federal Constitution divides the government's power among the legislative, executive, and judicial branches, with the Congress exercising the legislative power, the President exercising the executive power, and the federal courts exercising the judicial power.[7] "It is a breach of the National fundamental law" if Congress "gives up its legislative power" to one of the other branches or if Congress "attempts to invest itself or its members with either executive power or judicial power."[8]

While only Congress may exercise the legislative power,[9] this power, like those belonging to the other branches of the federal government, is

---

[5] *See* THE FEDERALIST NO. 47, at 269 (James Madison) (Clinton Rossiter ed., 1999).

[6] *See* Thomas v. Union Carbide Agric. Prods. Co., 473 U.S. 568, 594 (1985) (Brennan, J., concurring).

[7] J. W. Hampton, Jr., & Co. v. United States, 276 U.S. 394, 406 (1928).

[8] *Id.*

[9] While Congress may not delegate its legislative powers to another branch, *see Field v. Clark*, 143 U.S. 649, 692 (1892), the Supreme Court has recognized that Congress can "obtain[] the assistance of its coordinate Branches" to help refine its general directives set forth in legislation. *See* Mistretta v. United States, 488 U.S. 361, 372 (1989) (noting that "our jurisprudence has been driven by a practical understanding that in our increasingly complex society, replete with ever changing and more technical problems, Congress simply cannot do its job absent an ability to delegate power under broad general directives."). To avoid an

cabined by the terms of the Constitution. Article I, Section 1, of the Constitution vests "all legislative Powers herein granted ... in a Congress of the United States," with the phrase "herein granted" indicating that the Congress's authority to legislate is "confined to those powers expressly identified in the document."[10] As a result, the Supreme Court has interpreted Article I's Vesting Clause as creating a Congress of specified or "enumerated powers."[11] As the Court noted in *United States v. Morrison,* "[e]very law enacted by Congress must be based on one or more of its powers enumerated in the Constitution."[12]

Congress's Powers

Congress's specified powers are primarily, but not exclusively, found in Section 8 of Article I of the Constitution. This section contains 18 clauses, 17 of which enumerate relatively specific powers granted to the Congress.[13] Among the powers enumerated are Congress's powers to

---

unlawful delegation of legislative authority, the Supreme Court has stated that "when Congress confers decisionmaking authority upon agencies Congress must 'lay down by legislative act an intelligible principle to which the person or body authorized to [act] is directed to conform.'" *See* Whitman v. Am. Trucking Ass'ns, 531 U.S. 457, 472 (2001) (quoting *J. W. Hampton, Jr.,* 276 U.S. at 409). In the history of the Supreme Court, the Court has "found the requisite 'intelligible principle' lacking in only two statutes, one of which provided literally no guidance for the exercise of discretion, and the other of which conferred authority to regulate the entire economy on the basis of no more precise a standard than stimulating the economy by assuring 'fair competition.'" *Id.* at 474 (citing A. L. A. Schechter Poultry Corp. v. United States, 295 U.S. 495 (1935); Panama Refining Co. v. Ryan, 293 U.S. 388 (1935)); *see generally* Cass R. Sunstein, *Nondelegation Canons,* 67 U. CHI. L. REV. 315, 315 (2000) ("It is often said that the nondelegation doctrine is dead.").

[10] *See* Zivotofsky v. Kerry, 135 S. Ct. 2076, 2098 (2015) (Thomas, J., concurring in part and dissenting in part); Printz v. United States, 521 U.S. 898, 919 (1997) ("[T]he Constitution[] confer[ed] upon Congress of not all governmental powers, but only discrete, enumerated ones."); Marbury v. Madison, 5 U.S. (Cranch) 137, 176 (1803) ("The powers of the legislature are defined, and limited.... ").

[11] Kansas v. Colorado, 206 U.S. 46, 81 (1907).

[12] 529 U.S. 598, 607 (2000).

[13] *See* U.S. CONST. art. I, §8.

- impose taxes,[14] and spend the money collected to pay debts and provide for the "common defence" and "general welfare,"[15]
- regulate commerce,[16]
- establish laws respecting naturalization and bankruptcy,[17]
- regulate currency,[18]
- establish post offices and roads,[19]
- promote the "Progress of Science and useful Arts" by giving authors and inventors "exclusive rights" to their writings and discoveries (i.e., copyright and patent protections),[20] and
- establish a judicial system.[21]

In addition, six of the clauses in Article I, Section 8, defining the substantive legislative jurisdiction of Congress, deal exclusively with wartime and military matters and include Congress's power to declare war and provide for an Army and Navy.[22]

Outside of Article I, Section 8, the Constitution contains several other provisions providing Congress with a specified power. For example, Article IV of the Constitution empowers Congress to enact laws regulating the validity of state "public Acts, Records, and judicial Proceedings"[23] and rules respecting the territory and property belonging to the United States.[24] And Article V authorizes Congress to propose amendments to the Constitution.[25] Outside of the original constitutional text, many of the

[14] *Id.* art. I, §8, cl. 1. The taxing power of Article I is limited by the requirements that money collected be spent to "pay the Debts and provide for the common Defence and general Welfare of the United States"; and taxes must be "uniform throughout the United States." The Sixteenth Amendment to the Constitution further empowers Congress to lay and collect taxes on incomes. *See id.* amend. XVI.

[15] *See id* . art. I, §8, cl. 1.

[16] *Id.* art. I, §8, cl. 3.

[17] *Id.* art. I, §8, cl. 4.

[18] *Id.* art. I, §8, cls. 5-6.

[19] *Id.* art. I, §8, cl. 7.

[20] *Id.* art. I, §8, cl. 8.

[21] *Id.* art. I, §8, cl. 9.

[22] *Id.* art. I, §8, cls. 11-16 (defining Congress's power to declare war and to raise, support, and regulate the military and militia).

[23] *Id.* art. IV, §1.

[24] *Id.* art. IV, §3, cl. 2.

[25] *Id.* art. V.

nforcement Clause as necessarily requiring a "congruence
lity" between the injury to be prevented or remedied by
egislation and the means that Congress adopted to that
this standard in *City of Boerne v. Flores*, the Court held
exceeded the scope of its enforcement power under the
nendment by enacting the Religious Freedom Restoration
nsofar as that law unduly invaded the sovereign rights of the
ted to protect the constitutional right to the free exercise of
A, in relevant part, invalidated any state law that imposed a
burden" on a religious practice without sufficient justification
ailoring.[48] Describing RFRA's operative standard as imposing
est" that amounted to a "considerable intrusion into the States'
rerogatives and general authority to regulate for the health and
heir citizens," the Court concluded that there was "a lack of
lity or congruence between the means adopted and the
nd to be achieved" by RFRA.[49]

l, beyond the internal limits on Congress's powers, the
n also imposes "external" constraints on congressional action,
tive prohibitions found elsewhere in the text or structure of the
.[50] Article I, Section 9, lists specific constraints on the power of
al government. Section 9 prohibits Congress from suspending the
abeas corpus in peacetime;[51] passing bills of attainder or ex post

nstrate that the firearm "moved in or that otherwise affects interstate or foreign
nerce." 18 U.S.C. §922(q)(2). This amended version of the statute has been upheld in
ace of constitutional challenges. *See, e.g.*, United States v. Dorsey, 418 F.3d 1038,
5 (9th Cir.2005); United States v. Danks, 221 F.3d 1037, 1039 (8th Cir.1999).

47 Boerne v. Flores, 521 U.S. 507, 520 (1997).

48 533.

49 hile the Supreme Court struck down RFRA's application to the states in *City of Boerne*,
RA has been held to still apply to the actions of the federal government. *See* United
ates v. Israel, 317 F.3d 768, 770 (7th Cir. 2003).

50 United States v. Comstock, 560 U.S. 126, 135 (2010) (noting that a "a federal statute, in
ddition to being authorized by Art. I, §8, must also 'not [be] prohibited' by the
onstitution.") (citing McCulloch v. Maryland, 17 U.S. (Wheat.) 316, 421 (1819)); *see also*
Saenz v. Roe, 526 U.S. 489, 508 (1999) ("[L]egislative powers are, however, limited not
only by the scope of the Framers' affirmative delegation, but also by the principle "that they
may not be exercised in a way that violates other specific provisions of the Constitution.").

51 *See* U.S. CONST. art. I, §9, cl. 2.

amendments to the Constitution explicitly restrict the power of Congress.[26] Several of the Constitution's amendments, however, provide Congress with the power to enact certain legislation. For instance, the Thirteenth, Fourteenth, and Fifteenth Amendments, adopted following the Civil War, empower Congress to "enforce" the amendments' provisions prohibiting slavery,[27] preventing the deprivations of certain civil rights,[28] and outlawing the denial or abridgement of the right to vote on account of "race, color, or previous condition of servitude."[29]

The final clause of Article I, Section 8, the Necessary and Proper Clause,[30] supplements Congress's enumerated powers, providing the legislative branch the power to adopt measures that assist in the achievement of ends contemplated by other provisions in the Constitution.[31] Specifically, that clause provides Congress with the power to make "all Laws which shall be necessary and proper for carrying into Execution the foregoing Powers and all other Powers vested by this Constitution in the Government of the United States, or in any Department or Officer thereof."[32] The Supreme Court has interpreted the scope of Congress's power under the Necessary and Proper Clause as "broad,"[33] in that the clause leaves to "Congress a large discretion as to the means that may be employed in executing a given power."[34] In so holding, the Court

26 *See, e.g., id.* amend. I ("Congress shall make no law respecting an establishment of religion, or prohibiting the free exercise thereof; or abridging the freedom of speech, or of the press; or the right of the people peaceably to assemble, and to petition the government for a redress of grievances.").

27 *Id.* amend. XIII.

28 *Id.* amend. XIV.

29 *Id.* amend. XV.

30 The Necessary and Proper Clause is also referred to as the "Elastic Clause" or the "Sweeping Clause." *See* Devotion Garner & Cheryl Nyberg, *Popular Names of Constitutional Provisions,* Univ. Of Wash. Gallagher Law Library (September 30, 2013), http://lib.law.washington.edu/ref/consticlauses.html.

31 For example, the Court has recognized that Congress, through the Necessary and Proper Clause, has the power to enact legislation to implement U.S. treaty obligations, as such legislation may be necessary to give effect to the federal government's power to make treaties, which is found in Article II, Section 2, clause 2. *See* Missouri v. Holland, 252 U.S. 416 (1920); Neely v. Hinkel, 180 U.S. 109 (1901).

32 *See* U.S. CONST. art. I, §8, cl. 18.

33 United States v. Kebodeaux, 133 S. Ct. 2496, 2503 (2013); United States v. Comstock, 560 U.S. 126, 133 (2010).

34 *Lottery Case*, 188 U.S. 321, 355 (1903).

has described the clause as providing the "broad power to enact laws that are 'convenient, or useful' or 'conducive' to" a more specific authority's "beneficial exercise."[35] Consistent with this view, the Court has upheld legislation criminalizing perjury and witness tampering as an extension of Congress's power to constitute federal tribunals.[36] Similarly, the Court upheld legislation prohibiting the bribery of officials who receive federal funds, as an extension of Congress's power to "appropriate federal moneys to promote the general welfare."[37] More broadly, the Court has taken the view that other powers, such as the power to conduct oversight, are implied from the general vesting of legislative powers in Congress.[38]

Importantly, however, the Necessary and Proper Clause is *not* an independent source of power for Congress that, standing in isolation, permits it to exercise the legislative power. As the Supreme Court has noted, the clause is "not itself a grant of power, but a *caveat* that the Congress possesses all the means necessary to carry out the specifically granted 'foregoing' powers of § 8 'and all other Powers vested by this Constitution....'"[39] Instead, in legislating, Congress "must rely upon its independent (though quite robust) Article I, § 8, powers" or in other powers implicitly or explicitly vested elsewhere in the Constitution to Congress.[40] Importantly as well, the Necessary and Proper Clause authorizes Congress to not only take action to assist in the execution of its own powers under the Constitution, but also to provide support for the execution of "all other Powers vested by this Constitution in the Government of the United States."[41] Pursuant to this authority, Congress

[35] *See Comstock,* 560 U.S. at 134 (quoting McCulloch v. Maryland, 17 U.S. (Wheat.) 316, 405 (1819)).
[36] Jinks v. Richland Cty., 538 U.S. 456, 462 (2003).
[37] Sabri v. United States, 541 U.S. 600, 605 (2004).
[38] *See, e.g.*, Nixon v. Adm'r of Gen. Servs., 433 U.S. 435 (1977); Eastland v. United States Servicemen's Fund, 421 U.S. 491 (1975); Barenblatt v. United States, 360 U.S. 109 (1959); Watkins v. United States, 354 U.S. 178 (1957); McGrain v. Daugherty, 273 U.S. 135 (1927).
[39] Kinsella v. United States *ex rel.* Singleton, 361 U.S. 234, 247 (1960) (emphasis in original).
[40] Bond v. United States, 134 S. Ct. 2077, 2099 (2014) (Scalia, J., concurring).
[41] *See* U.S. CONST. art. I, §8, cl. 18.

may permissibly enact legislation to assur
given to other branches of the federal gover

Limits on Congress's Powers

The Constitution imposes two central ty
powers of Congress. First, the concept of enume
is often referred to as an "internal limit" on Co
Congress's powers are restricted by and to the
grant.[43] For instance, in *United States v. Lope*
interpreted the Commerce Clause as empowering
"three broad categories of activities": (1) "ch
commerce," like roads and canals; (2) "persons or
commerce," and (3) activities that substantiall
commerce.[44] Having determined those limits to the cla
that Congress's power over commerce does not p
legislation prohibiting the possession of guns near a
connection to commercial activity) because such leg
regulate an economic activity that substantially
commerce.[45] Likewise, the Court has interpreted

[42] *See, e.g.*, Jinks v. Richland Cty., 538 U.S. 456, 462 (2003) (recogniz
provision in federal statute as being necessary and proper for carrying
Congress's power under Article I to constitute tribunals inferior to the
to assure that federal courts could "fairly and efficiently exercise 'the ju
United States'" under Article III); Neely v. Hinkel, 180 U.S. 109, 121 (1
congressional authority to enact legislation that is necessary and proper
stipulations of a treaty made by the President with the advice and consen
Stewart v. Kahn, 78 U.S. 493, 506 (1871) ("The President is the comma
the army and navy, and of the militia of the several States, when called int
the United States, and it is made his duty to take care that the laws are faith
Congress is authorized to make all laws necessary and proper to carry i
granted powers."); Wayman v. Southard, 23 U.S. 1, 22 (1835) (recognizing
authority to enact measures necessary and proper for carrying into execution
judgments).
[43] *See generally* Laurence H. Tribe, *American Constitutional Law* 794-95 (3
(distinguishing internal and external limitations on the federal legislative power).
[44] 514 U.S. 549, 558 (1995).
[45] *Id.* at 567-68. Congress subsequently amended the statute to expressly provide that,
the possession of a firearm in a school zone to be a federal offense, the govern

facto laws;[52] imposing taxes or duties on exports "from any state";[53] and granting titles of nobility.[54] Section 9 also provides that Congress can suspend the writ of habeas corpus only in "cases of rebellion or invasion" when "public safety may require" such a suspension.[55] Similarly, money can be drawn from the Treasury only upon an appropriation made by law.[56]

More broadly, Congress's powers are constrained by three principles undergirding the Constitution: federalism, separation of powers, and individual rights. Federalism constraints are grounded in states' status as separate and distinct sovereign entities[57] and seek to preserve states' retained prerogatives under the U.S. constitutional system by enforcing certain limits on the federal government's jurisdiction.[58] For instance, the Supreme Court has identified federalism-based constraints stemming from the Tenth Amendment—the provision of the Bill of Rights that reads, "The powers not delegated to the United States by the Constitution, nor prohibited by it to the States, are reserved to the States respectively, or to the people."[59] More specifically, the Court has interpreted the Tenth Amendment to prevent the federal government from "commandeering" or requiring state executive officers or state legislators to carry out federal directives.[60] Similarly, the Court has held that Congress cannot indirectly commandeer state governments by imposing limits on monetary grants that go so far as to functionally coerce states, leaving them with no choice but to comply with a federal directive.[61]

---

[52] *Id.* art. I, §9, cl. 3.

[53] *Id.* art. I, §9, cl. 5.

[54] *Id.* art. I, §9, cl. 8.

[55] *Id.* art. I, §9, cl. 3.

[56] *Id.* art. I, §9, cl. 7.

[57] Shelby Cty. v. Holder, 133 S. Ct. 2612, 2623 (2013) ("Outside the strictures of the Supremacy Clause, States retain broad autonomy in structuring their governments and pursuing legislative objectives.").

[58] *See* Gary Lawson & Patricia B. Granger, *The "Proper" Scope of Federal Power: A Jurisdictional Interpretation of the Sweeping Clause,* 43 DUKE L.J. 267, 297 (1993).

[59] *See* U.S. CONST. amend. X.

[60] Printz v. United States, 521 U.S. 898, 935 (1997).

[61] South Dakota v. Dole, 483 U.S. 203, 211 (1987). In *South Dakota v. Dole*, the Supreme Court upheld legislation requiring states to raise their legal drinking age or lose 5% of federal highway funds, viewing the condition as amounting to "relatively mild encouragement to the States to enact higher minimum drinking ages.... " *See id.* In contrast, in *National Federal of Independent Businesses (NFIB) v. Sebelius,* the Court

Second, separation of powers constraints are concerned with the proper allocation of authority among the three branches within the federal government.[62] The Constitution assigns each branch of government distinct, but interrelated, roles, and one branch may not aggrandize its power by attempting to exercise powers assigned to another branch.[63] For example, the Appointments Clause of the Constitution gives the President the authority to appoint principal officers of the United States with the Senate's advice and consent.[64] Thus, when Congress purported to reserve to itself the right to appoint certain members of the Federal Election Commission in 1971, the Supreme Court struck down that law as being in violation of the Appointments Clause.[65]

Finally, constraints based on individual rights serve to prohibit congressional interference with the rights that individuals retain under the Constitution[66] and, in particular, under the first 10 amendments to the Constitution, the Bill of Rights.[67] The First Amendment, for example, prohibits Congress from enacting a law that abridges the freedom of

---

invalidated provisions of the Patient Protection and Affordable Care Act of 2010 that required states to expand their Medicaid programs or risk losing their current Medicaid funding, describing the Medicaid expansion as "accomplish[ing] a shift in kind, not merely degree." *See* 132 S. Ct. 2566, 2605 (2012) (opinion of Roberts, C.J.); *see also id.* at 2667-68 ("Seven Members of the Court agree that the Medicaid Expansion, as enacted by Congress, is unconstitutional.") (Scalia, Kennedy, Thomas & Alito, JJ., dissenting). For the controlling plurality opinion in *NFIB*, the threatened loss of funds in *Dole* preserved the states' voluntary choices, while the threat of losing "over 10 percent of a State's overall budget ... is economic dragooning that leaves the States with no real option but to acquiesce in the Medicaid expansion." *Id.* at 2605 (opinion of Roberts, C.J.).

62 *See* Clinton v. Jones, 520 U.S. 681, 699 (1997).

63 *See* Buckley v. Valeo, 424 U.S. 1, 122 (1976) (per curiam) ("The Framers regarded the checks and balances that they had built into the tripartite Federal Government as a self-executing safeguard against the encroachment or aggrandizement of one branch at the expense of the other."). The Court has allowed Congress to confer decisionmaking authority upon executive agencies so long as the legislature lays "lay[s] down ... an intelligible principle to which the person or body authorized to [act] is directed to conform." J. W. Hampton, Jr., & Co. v. United States, 276 U.S. 394, 409 (1928). For further discussion on the intelligible principle test, see *supra* note 9.

64 *See* U.S. CONST. art. II, §2, cl. 2.

65 *See Buckley*, 424 U.S. at 140.

66 *See, e.g.,* U.S. CONST. art. III, §2, cl. 3 (providing for the right to a trial by jury in all criminal cases).

67 *See* Lawson & Granger, *supra* note 58, at 297; *see* U.S. CONST. amend. IX ("The enumeration in the Constitution, of certain rights, shall not be construed or disparage others retained by the people.").

amendments to the Constitution explicitly restrict the power of Congress.[26] Several of the Constitution's amendments, however, provide Congress with the power to enact certain legislation. For instance, the Thirteenth, Fourteenth, and Fifteenth Amendments, adopted following the Civil War, empower Congress to "enforce" the amendments' provisions prohibiting slavery,[27] preventing the deprivations of certain civil rights,[28] and outlawing the denial or abridgement of the right to vote on account of "race, color, or previous condition of servitude."[29]

The final clause of Article I, Section 8, the Necessary and Proper Clause,[30] supplements Congress's enumerated powers, providing the legislative branch the power to adopt measures that assist in the achievement of ends contemplated by other provisions in the Constitution.[31] Specifically, that clause provides Congress with the power to make "all Laws which shall be necessary and proper for carrying into Execution the foregoing Powers and all other Powers vested by this Constitution in the Government of the United States, or in any Department or Officer thereof."[32] The Supreme Court has interpreted the scope of Congress's power under the Necessary and Proper Clause as "broad,"[33] in that the clause leaves to "Congress a large discretion as to the means that may be employed in executing a given power."[34] In so holding, the Court

---

[26] *See, e.g., id.* amend. I ("Congress shall make no law respecting an establishment of religion, or prohibiting the free exercise thereof; or abridging the freedom of speech, or of the press; or the right of the people peaceably to assemble, and to petition the government for a redress of grievances.").

[27] *Id.* amend. XIII.

[28] *Id.* amend. XIV.

[29] *Id.* amend. XV.

[30] The Necessary and Proper Clause is also referred to as the "Elastic Clause" or the "Sweeping Clause." *See* Devotion Garner & Cheryl Nyberg, *Popular Names of Constitutional Provisions,* Univ. Of Wash. Gallagher Law Library (September 30, 2013), http://lib.law.washington.edu/ref/consticlauses.html.

[31] For example, the Court has recognized that Congress, through the Necessary and Proper Clause, has the power to enact legislation to implement U.S. treaty obligations, as such legislation may be necessary to give effect to the federal government's power to make treaties, which is found in Article II, Section 2, clause 2. *See* Missouri v. Holland, 252 U.S. 416 (1920); Neely v. Hinkel, 180 U.S. 109 (1901).

[32] *See* U.S. CONST. art. I, §8, cl. 18.

[33] United States v. Kebodeaux, 133 S. Ct. 2496, 2503 (2013); United States v. Comstock, 560 U.S. 126, 133 (2010).

[34] *Lottery Case*, 188 U.S. 321, 355 (1903).

has described the clause as providing the "broad power to enact laws that are 'convenient, or useful' or 'conducive' to" a more specific authority's "beneficial exercise."[35] Consistent with this view, the Court has upheld legislation criminalizing perjury and witness tampering as an extension of Congress's power to constitute federal tribunals.[36] Similarly, the Court upheld legislation prohibiting the bribery of officials who receive federal funds, as an extension of Congress's power to "appropriate federal moneys to promote the general welfare."[37] More broadly, the Court has taken the view that other powers, such as the power to conduct oversight, are implied from the general vesting of legislative powers in Congress.[38]

Importantly, however, the Necessary and Proper Clause is *not* an independent source of power for Congress that, standing in isolation, permits it to exercise the legislative power. As the Supreme Court has noted, the clause is "not itself a grant of power, but a *caveat* that the Congress possesses all the means necessary to carry out the specifically granted 'foregoing' powers of § 8 'and all other Powers vested by this Constitution....'"[39] Instead, in legislating, Congress "must rely upon its independent (though quite robust) Article I, § 8, powers" or in other powers implicitly or explicitly vested elsewhere in the Constitution to Congress.[40] Importantly as well, the Necessary and Proper Clause authorizes Congress to not only take action to assist in the execution of its own powers under the Constitution, but also to provide support for the execution of "all other Powers vested by this Constitution in the Government of the United States."[41] Pursuant to this authority, Congress

---

[35] *See Comstock,* 560 U.S. at 134 (quoting McCulloch v. Maryland, 17 U.S. (Wheat.) 316, 405 (1819)).

[36] Jinks v. Richland Cty., 538 U.S. 456, 462 (2003).

[37] Sabri v. United States, 541 U.S. 600, 605 (2004).

[38] *See, e.g.*, Nixon v. Adm'r of Gen. Servs., 433 U.S. 435 (1977); Eastland v. United States Servicemen's Fund, 421 U.S. 491 (1975); Barenblatt v. United States, 360 U.S. 109 (1959); Watkins v. United States, 354 U.S. 178 (1957); McGrain v. Daugherty, 273 U.S. 135 (1927).

[39] Kinsella v. United States *ex rel.* Singleton, 361 U.S. 234, 247 (1960) (emphasis in original).

[40] Bond v. United States, 134 S. Ct. 2077, 2099 (2014) (Scalia, J., concurring).

[41] *See* U.S. CONST. art. I, §8, cl. 18.

may permissibly enact legislation to assure the proper exercise of powers given to other branches of the federal government.[42]

Limits on Congress's Powers

The Constitution imposes two central types of limitations on the powers of Congress. First, the concept of enumerated powers creates what is often referred to as an "internal limit" on Congress's powers—that is, Congress's powers are restricted by and to the terms of their express grant.[43] For instance, in *United States v. Lopez*, the Supreme Court interpreted the Commerce Clause as empowering Congress to regulate "three broad categories of activities": (1) "channels of interstate commerce," like roads and canals; (2) "persons or things in interstate commerce," and (3) activities that substantially affect interstate commerce.[44] Having determined those limits to the clause, the Court held that Congress's power over commerce does not permit it to enact legislation prohibiting the possession of guns near a school (absent a connection to commercial activity) because such legislation does not regulate an economic activity that substantially affects interstate commerce.[45] Likewise, the Court has interpreted the Fourteenth

---

[42] *See, e.g.,* Jinks v. Richland Cty., 538 U.S. 456, 462 (2003) (recognizing judicial tolling provision in federal statute as being necessary and proper for carrying into execution both Congress's power under Article I to constitute tribunals inferior to the Supreme Court and to assure that federal courts could "fairly and efficiently exercise 'the judicial Power of the United States'" under Article III); Neely v. Hinkel, 180 U.S. 109, 121 (1901) (recognizing congressional authority to enact legislation that is necessary and proper to carry out the stipulations of a treaty made by the President with the advice and consent of the Senate); Stewart v. Kahn, 78 U.S. 493, 506 (1871) ("The President is the commander-in-chief of the army and navy, and of the militia of the several States, when called into the service of the United States, and it is made his duty to take care that the laws are faithfully executed. Congress is authorized to make all laws necessary and proper to carry into effect the granted powers."); Wayman v. Southard, 23 U.S. 1, 22 (1835) (recognizing congressional authority to enact measures necessary and proper for carrying into execution federal court judgments).

[43] *See generally* Laurence H. Tribe, *American Constitutional Law* 794-95 (3d ed. 2000) (distinguishing internal and external limitations on the federal legislative power).

[44] 514 U.S. 549, 558 (1995).

[45] *Id.* at 567-68. Congress subsequently amended the statute to expressly provide that, in order for the possession of a firearm in a school zone to be a federal offense, the government must

Amendment's Enforcement Clause as necessarily requiring a "congruence and proportionality" between the injury to be prevented or remedied by congressional legislation and the means that Congress adopted to that end.[46] Applying this standard in *City of Boerne v. Flores*, the Court held that Congress exceeded the scope of its enforcement power under the Fourteenth Amendment by enacting the Religious Freedom Restoration Act (RFRA) insofar as that law unduly invaded the sovereign rights of the states.[47] Adopted to protect the constitutional right to the free exercise of religion, RFRA, in relevant part, invalidated any state law that imposed a "substantial burden" on a religious practice without sufficient justification and narrow tailoring.[48] Describing RFRA's operative standard as imposing a "stringent test" that amounted to a "considerable intrusion into the States' traditional prerogatives and general authority to regulate for the health and welfare of their citizens," the Court concluded that there was "a lack of proportionality or congruence between the means adopted and the legitimate end to be achieved" by RFRA.[49]

Second, beyond the internal limits on Congress's powers, the Constitution also imposes "external" constraints on congressional action, or affirmative prohibitions found elsewhere in the text or structure of the document.[50] Article I, Section 9, lists specific constraints on the power of the federal government. Section 9 prohibits Congress from suspending the writ of habeas corpus in peacetime;[51] passing bills of attainder or ex post

---

demonstrate that the firearm "moved in or that otherwise affects interstate or foreign commerce." 18 U.S.C. §922(q)(2). This amended version of the statute has been upheld in the face of constitutional challenges. *See, e.g.,* United States v. Dorsey, 418 F.3d 1038, 1046 (9th Cir.2005); United States v. Danks, 221 F.3d 1037, 1039 (8th Cir.1999).

[46] City of Boerne v. Flores, 521 U.S. 507, 520 (1997).

[47] *Id.*

[48] *Id.* at 533.

[49] *Id.* While the Supreme Court struck down RFRA's application to the states in *City of Boerne,* RFRA has been held to still apply to the actions of the federal government. *See* United States v. Israel, 317 F.3d 768, 770 (7th Cir. 2003).

[50] *See* United States v. Comstock, 560 U.S. 126, 135 (2010) (noting that a "a federal statute, in addition to being authorized by Art. I, §8, must also 'not [be] prohibited' by the Constitution.") (citing McCulloch v. Maryland, 17 U.S. (Wheat.) 316, 421 (1819)); *see also* Saenz v. Roe, 526 U.S. 489, 508 (1999) ("[L]egislative powers are, however, limited not only by the scope of the Framers' affirmative delegation, but also by the principle "that they may not be exercised in a way that violates other specific provisions of the Constitution.").

[51] *See* U.S. CONST. art. I, §9, cl. 2.

speech.[68] The Supreme Court has interpreted the First Amendment to mean that speech restrictions promulgated as a result of the *content* of the speech are presumptively unconstitutional.[69] In keeping with this presumption, in *United States v. Alvarez*, the Court struck down a law that made it a crime to falsely claim that one had received military medals or decorations on the grounds that the law risked "significant First Amendment harm" by broadly empowering prosecutions of speech based on its content, without any notable limitations.[70]

ROLE OF CONGRESS IN INTERPRETING THE CONSTITUTION

Given the powers of Congress and the limits on those powers under the Constitution, the question remains as to which branch of the federal government may interpret the scope of Congress's powers. The question is one that has been debated from the very beginnings of the country. In its 1803 decision in *Marbury v. Madison,* the Supreme Court held that the logic of having a written Constitution that enumerates the legal limits imposed on the federal government, coupled with the tenure protections provided to the federal judiciary under the Constitution,[71] confirmed the Supreme Court's role in interpreting the Constitution and invalidating acts of other branches of government that contravene this document.[72] Pursuant

---

[68] *See* U.S. CONST. amend. I.

[69] *See* Ashcroft v. Am. Civil Liberties Union, 542 U.S. 656, 660 (2004).

[70] *See* 132 S. Ct. 2537, 2555 (2012).

[71] The key sources of the judiciary's insulation from the political process are the Good Behavior Clause and the Compensation Clause of Article III. *See, e.g.,* U.S. CONST. art. III, §1. The Good Behavior Clause, by creating a "permanent tenure of judicial offices," ensures an "independent spirit in judges," *see* THE FEDERALIST NO. 78, at 437 (Alexander Hamilton) (Clinton Rossiter ed., 1999). Likewise, the Compensation Clause, by creating a "fixed provision for [the judiciary's] support," prevents the political branches from having power over a judge's subsistence and, with that, "power over his will." *See* THE FEDERALIST NO. 79, at 440 (Alexander Hamilton) (Clinton Rossiter ed., 1999).

[72] *See* 5 U.S. (1 Cranch) 137, 177-78 (1803); *see generally* Michael Stokes Paulsen, *The Irrepressible Myth of* Marbury, 101 MICH. L. REV. 2706, 2707 (2003) (criticizing the widely held belief that judicial review was established by *Marbury* and instead pointing out that *Marbury* merely applied well-established principles respecting the Court's powers).

to *Marbury*'s famous command, it is "the province and duty of the judicial department to say what the law is."[73]

While *Marbury* firmly established that the judicial branch has *a* role in interpreting the Constitution, including the power to strike down laws held to be incompatible with the founding document, it did not, however, expressly state that the judiciary has a *final* or even *exclusive* role in defining the basic powers and limits of the federal government. To the contrary, the early history of the United States is replete with examples of all three branches of the federal government playing a role in constitutional interpretation, with Congress and the Executive openly questioning the Supreme Court's pronouncements on constitutional law, such as the Court's rulings on the National Bank or slavery.[74] As these examples show, *Marbury* was not seen to interfere with the ability of either Congress or the President to interpret the Constitution. Rather, *Marbury* only asserted the judiciary's power to act as the ultimate expositor of the Constitution in the limited context of cases that were properly before the Court.[75] Instead, Thomas Jefferson's view that "each of the three departments has equally the right to decide for itself what is its duty under the Constitution, without any regard to what the others may have decided for themselves under a similar question,"[76] appears to have prevailed in Congress during the early days of the United States. This is evidenced by the fact that Members of Congress spent "a considerable amount of time" "debating the constitutional limitations on" legislation during the first 100 years of the nation.[77]

---

[73] *See* 5 U.S. (1 Cranch) at 177.

[74] *See generally* CRS Report R43706, *The Doctrine of Constitutional Avoidance: A Legal Overview*, by Andrew Nolan, at 4-5 (providing an overview of various debates between the three branches over the meaning of the Constitution).

[75] 75 *See, e.g.*, Edward Corwin, Marbury v. Madison *and the Doctrine of Judicial Review*, 12 MICH. L. REV. 538, 571 (1914).

[76] Letter from Thomas Jefferson to Judge Spencer Roane Poplar Forest (September 6, 1819), *available at* http://www.let.rug.nl/usa/presidents/thomas-jefferson/letters-of-thomas-jefferson/jefl257.php.

[77] *See* Russ Feingold, *The Obligation of Members of Congress to Consider Constitutionality While Deliberating and Voting: The Deficiencies of House Rule XII and A Proposed Rule for the Senate,* 67 VAND. L. REV. 837, 846-49 (2014); *see generally* DAVID P. CURRIE, THE CONSTITUTION IN CONGRESS 120 nn.25-27 (1997) (cataloging various constitutional debates during early Congresses).

In the mid-20th century, however, the Supreme Court began articulating a theory of judicial supremacy, wherein the Court no longer shared its role in interpreting the Constitution with the other branches of the federal government, but rather characterized its role as being the preeminent arbiter of the Constitution's meaning. For example, in *Cooper v. Aaron,* the Court read *Marbury* as "declaring the basic principle that the federal judiciary is supreme in the exposition of the law of the Constitution, and [this] principle has ever since been respected by this Court and the Country as a permanent and indispensable feature of our constitutional system."[78] In other words, the *Cooper* Court concluded that the "interpretation[s] of the [Constitution] enunciated by this Court ... [are] the supreme law of the land,"[79] with constitutional interpretations by other actors, including Congress, necessarily lacking the same force.[80] Supporters of the judicial supremacy view assert that it promotes stability and uniformity in constitutional interpretation,[81] as well as preserves constitutional norms from majoritarian pressures.[82] The Court's decision in *Cooper*, coupled with broader institutional factors that may further constrain Congress's ability to engage in constitutional interpretation,[83] has provided support for the notion of

---

[78] 58 U.S. 1, 16-17 (1958).

[79] *Id.* at 18.

[80] The Court has, at times, grounded this principle in the concern that if Congress were the "final judge of its own power under the Constitution," such a system would run contrary to notions of a limited and checked government. Baltimore & O. R. Co. v. United States, 298 U.S. 349, 364 (1936).

[81] *See* Larry Alexander & Frederick Schauer, *On Extrajudicial Constitutional Interpretation,* 110 HARV. L. REV. 1359, 1369-81 (1997) (defending judicial supremacy because finality in constitutional interpretation provides stability and coordination in a constitutional democracy).

[82] *See* Erwin Chemerinsky, *In Defense of Judicial Review: A Reply to Professor Kramer*, 92 Calif. L. Rev. 1013, 1018- 24 (2004) (arguing for judicial supremacy because of concerns that a majoritarian Congress might interpret the Constitution in such a way as to not adequately protect minority rights).

[83] *See* Feingold, *supra* note 77, at 851 (arguing that Members of Congress lack "the time and technical sophistication" to understand the constitutional complexities of each bill, as well as the "political incentive to inquire into the constitutionality of each piece of legislation."); *see also* Hon. Abner Mikva, *How Well Does Congress Support and Defend the Constitution?*, 61 N.C. L. Rev. 587, 587 (1983) (concluding that Congress has neither the institutional nor the political capacity to engage in effective constitutional interpretation); *but see* Louis Fisher, *Constitutional Interpretation by Members of Congress*, 63 N.C. L. Rev. 707, 708 (1985) (arguing that "Congress can perform an essential, broad, and ongoing role in shaping the meaning of the Constitution.").

judicial supremacy in constitutional interpretation within the coordinate branches of government.[84] As a result, while Congress certainly continues to debate about the Constitution during the legislative process,[85] in the modern era, the Court's views on the Constitution appear to have taken on an elevated role vis-á-vis those views of the other branches of government.[86]

The theory of judicial supremacy is far from a consensus view,[87] however, and several aspects of the American constitutional system may counsel for a more robust role for Congress in constitutional interpretation. In recent decades, a number of legal scholars and government officials have criticized the judicial supremacy view,[88] instead advancing the view that the Constitution should more regularly be the subject of interpretation

---

[84] *See generally* Paul Brest, *Congress as Constitutional Decisionmaker and Its Power to Counter Judicial Doctrine*, 21 GA. L. REV. 57 (1986) ("By the second half of the twentieth century, both the House and the Senate had abandoned the tradition of deliberating over ordinary constitutional issues."); *see also* Feingold, *supra* note 77, at 849-850 (noting the decline of constitutional interpretation by Members of Congress following *Cooper v. Aaron* and the "rise of judicial supremacy").

[85] *See* Bruce G. Peabody, *Congressional Constitutional Interpretation and the Courts: A Preliminary Inquiry into Legislative Attitudes, 1959-2001,* 29 LAW & SOC. INQUIRY 127, 148 (2004) (noting that "today's [Members of Congress] ... seek advice on constitutional questions within Congress itself, turning to colleagues, committees, and respected institutions like the [Congressional Research Service].")

[86] This view has, at times, been articulated by Members of Congress. *See generally* Feingold, *supra* note 77, at 839-40 (collecting statements of a number of Senators in the wake of the Court's ruling in *Shelby County v. Holder*); *see also* Hanah Metchis Volokh, *Constitutional Authority Statements in Congress,* 65 FLA. L. REV. 173, 185 (2013) (noting that some Members of Congress have "tak[en] the judicial supremacy position," "claiming that the Constitution is the domain of the courts.").

[87] *See* Volokh, *supra* note 86, at 179 ("Most scholars believe that the Supreme Court is not the sole authorized interpreter of the Constitution.").

[88] Gary Lawson, *What Lurks Beneath: NSA Surveillance and Executive Power*, 88 B. U. L. Rev. 375, 381 n.30 (2008) ("The standard tendency in the legal academy is to treat Supreme Court decisions as privileged pronouncements on constitutional meaning. It is a very, very bad tendency. There is nothing in the Constitution on which to ground any such idea, nor does the Supreme Court's actual track record as a constitutional interpreter inspire much confidence.... [A]s a matter of objective constitutional meaning, there is no good reason to think that Supreme Court opinions are better evidence of that meaning than are the pronouncements of the Department of Justice, the Congressional Research Service, or Gary Lawson - and there are good reasons to think them worse."); *see also* Mark V. Tushnet, *The Constitution Outside the Courts: A Preliminary Inquiry*, 26 Val. U. L. Rev. 437, 437-38 (1992) (arguing that "Constitutional law is obsessed with the Supreme Court," and there is a "much richer terrain to explore" with regard to non-Court actors and their interpretations of the Constitution).

by those outside of the judicial branch.[89] This view posits that Congress and others outside of the government possess independent and coordinate authority to interpret the Constitution.[90] Supporters of this view point to the fact that the Constitution requires all Members of Congress to "be bound by Oath or Affirmation ... to support [the] Constitution...,"[91] a requirement that presumes Senators and Representatives must understand and interpret the Constitution in their work in Congress.[92] Similarly, courts' practice of affording a presumption of constitutionality to laws passed by Congress[93] necessarily assumes that Members of Congress engage in constitutional interpretation during the legislative process.[94] In addition, if Congress opts not to engage in interpreting the Constitution, a vacuum could arise in constitutional dialogue[95] because various judicially crafted doctrines generally serve to keep the courts from making pronouncements on a wide

---

[89] *See* Larry Kramer, *The People Themselves* 8 (2004) ("Both in its origins and for most of our history, American constitutionalism assigned ordinary citizens a central and pivotal role in implementing their Constitution. Final interpretive authority rested with 'the people themselves,' and courts no less than elected representatives were subordinate to their judgments."); *see generally* Doni Gewirtzman, *Glory Days: Popular Constitutionalism, Nostalgia, and the True Nature of Constitutional Culture*, 93 Geo. L. J. 897, 899 (2005) (describing a "growing body of scholarship" discussing the concept of "popular constitutionalism," the idea that "the People and their elected representatives should—and often do—play a substantial role in the creation, interpretation, evolution, and enforcement of constitutional norms.").

[90] *See* Edwin Meese III, *The Law of the Constitution*, 61 Tul. L. Rev. 979, 985-86 (1987) ("The Supreme Court, then, is not the only interpreter of the Constitution. Each of the three coordinate branches of government created and empowered by the Constitution—the executive and legislative no less than the judicial—has a duty to interpret the Constitution in the performance of its official functions."); *see also* Hon. David H. Coar, *"It Is Emphatically the Province and Duty of the Judicial Department to Say" Who the President Is?*, 34 Loy. U. Chi. L. J. 121, 129-30 (2002) ("While it is beyond question that within its sphere, it is the duty of the Supreme Court to determine the constitutionality of laws passed by Congress, the Supreme Court is not the only branch of government entrusted with the power to interpret the Constitution.").

[91] *See* U.S. CONST. art. VI, §1, cl. 3.

[92] *Cf.* Boumediene v. Bush, 553 U.S. 723, 738 (2008) ("The usual presumption is that Members of Congress, in accord with their oath of office, considered the constitutional issue and determined the amended statute to be a lawful one.... "); *see generally* Volokh, *supra* note 86, at 183-84.

[93] *See* U.S. R. Ret. Bd. v. Fritz, 449 U.S. 166, 184 (1980) ("The enactments of Congress are entitled to a presumption of constitutionality...").

[94] *See* Volokh, *supra* note 86, at 182-83.

[95] *See id.* at 181-82.

range[96] of constitutional questions.[97] These arguments can be seen as relevant to the current CAS requirement imposed under the House rules insofar as they suggest that Congress should have some role in interpreting the Constitution.[98]

House Rule XII, Clause 7(c), and Constitutional Authority Statements

Originally adopted as an amendment to House Rule XII on January 5, 2011,[99] the CAS rule prohibits Members from introducing a bill or joint resolution without a "statement citing as specifically as practicable the power or powers granted to Congress in the Constitution to enact the bill or joint resolution."[100] The current CAS rule functionally replaced a requirement that existed during the 105th through 111th Congresses, mandating that committee reports for bills reported out of committee "include a statement citing the specific powers granted to the Congress in the Constitution to enact the law proposed by the bill or joint resolution."[101] A CAS is not part of the text of the legislation; instead, it "accompanie[s]" the legislation.[102] The CAS must be "submitted at the time the bill or joint resolution" is presented for introduction and referral,

[96] *See* Michael J. Gerhardt, *The Constitution Outside the Courts*, 51 DRAKE L. REV. 775, 777 (2003) ("It is hard to overstate the range or significance of constitutional decision making that occurs outside the Court.").

[97] *See* Elizabeth Garrett & Adrian Vermeule, *Institutional Design of a Thayerian Congress*, 50 Duke L. J. 1277, 1278 (2001) ("Consider the large domain of constitutional decisionmaking over which the Supreme Court has essentially ceded control to the political branches by articulating deferential standards of review, limits on standing and justiciability, and the political-question doctrine. Impeachments and many issues involving electoral processes generally lie within this domain, and other questions do as well.").

[98] *See infra* "Debate over the Rule."

[99] *See* H.R. Res. 5, 112th Cong. (1st Sess. 2011) (adopting the rules for the 112th Congress).

[100] *See* House Rule XII cl. 7(c)(1). The House Rules permit the chair of a committee of jurisdiction to submit a CAS with regard to any Senate bill or joint resolution before that committee. *See id.* XXII cl. 7(c)(2).

[101] *See* H.R. Res. 5, §13, 105th Cong (1st Sess. 1997).

[102] *See* House Rule XII cl. 7(c)(1).

that is, when the legislation is dropped in the "hopper."[103] The submitted CAS appears in the *Congressional Record* and is published electronically on Congress.gov.[104]

Compliance with the CAS Rule

While the rule, on its face, requires Members to provide as "specific[] as practicable" "a statement citing ... the power or powers to Congress in the Constitution to enact the bill or joint resolution," the CAS rule itself is silent on various issues.[105] For example, the rule does not prescribe any particular format or level of detail for CASs. Guidance provided by the House Committee on Rules (Rules Committee) soon after the rule was adopted provided the following five examples of citations to constitutional authority:

1. "The constitutional authority on which this bill rests is the power of Congress to make rules for the government and regulation of the land and naval forces, as enumerated in Article I, Section 8, Clause 14 of the United States Constitution."
2. "This bill is enacted pursuant to Section 2 of Amendment XV of the United States Constitution."
3. "This bill is enacted pursuant to the power granted to Congress under Article I, Section 8, Clause 3 of the United States Constitution."
4. "The Congress enacts this bill pursuant to Clause 1 of Section 8 of Article I of the United States Constitution and Amendment XVI of the United States Constitution."

---

103 *See Constitutional Authority Statement Forms,* U.S. House of Representatives, Office of Legislative Counsel, https://legcoun.house.gov/members/HOLC/Resources/const_auth_statement.html (last accessed January 5, 2017). House Legislative Counsel has prepared a form to facilitate submission of CASs. *See Constitutional Authority Statement,* U.S. House of Representatives, Office of Legislative Counsel, https://legcoun.house.gov/members/HOLC/Resources/casform.pdf (last accessed Jan. 5, 2017).

104 *See* House Rule XII cl. 7(c)(1).

105 *Id.*

5. "This bill makes specific changes to existing law in a manner that returns power to the States and to the people, in accordance with Amendment X of the United States Constitution."[106]

This guidance suggests that compliant CASs should generally discuss the affirmative constitutional authority that empowers Congress to enact particular legislation, but need *not* discuss any external constraints on Congress's powers to enact the legislation. For example, under this guidance, a CAS for a bill that proposed to ban all interstate shipments of religious pamphlets could be seen as compliant if it cited the Commerce Clause as the source of congressional power, even though the bill may run afoul of the Free Exercise and Free Speech Clauses of the First Amendment.[107] Nonetheless, the last example provided by the Rules Committee suggests that a citation to a provision of the Constitution that does not explicitly grant power to the Congress— such as the Tenth Amendment, which preserves the powers of the states[108]—may suffice to comply with the rule. More broadly, the Rules Committee guidance indicates that Members have significant discretion in determining whether particular CASs comply with the rule. The Rules Committee guidance notes that it is ultimately "the responsibility of the bill sponsor to determine what authorities [he or she] wish[es] to cite and to provide that information to the Legislative Counsel staff."[109]

In practice,[110] outside commentators have noted that Members have generally complied with House Rule XII, clause 7(c).[111] Such observations

---

[106] *See New Constitutional Authority Requirement for Introduced Legislation,* Comm. On Rules, House of Representatives (Jan. 5, 2011), *available at* https://web.archive.org/web/20110406150854/http://www.rules.house.gov/about/PolicyDetail.aspx?NewsID=72 (hereinafter Comm. On Rules- CAS Requirement).

[107] *See* Church of Lukumi Babalu Aye v. City of Hialeah, 508 U.S. 520, 533 (1993) (noting that laws targeting religious practices are "never permissible"); Org. for a Better Austin v. Keefe, 402 U.S. 415, 419 (1971) ("This Court has often recognized that the activity of peaceful pamphleteering is a form of communication protected by the First Amendment.").

[108] *See* U.S. CONST. amend. X ("The powers not delegated to the United States by the Constitution, nor prohibited by it to the States, are reserved to the States respectively, or to the people.").

[109] *See* Comm. on Rules- CAS Requirement, *supra* note 106.

[110] For additional discussion on the procedural requirements related to the CAS rule, see CRS Report R44001, *Introducing a House Bill or Resolution*, by Mark J. Oleszek.

may be the result of how the rule is enforced. The Rules Committee has noted, "The adequacy and accuracy of the citation of constitutional authority is a matter for debate in the committees and in the House."[112] This statement suggests that the CAS rule is enforced only insofar as "the House clerk ... acts to verify that each bill has a justification" and "not [in judging] the adequacy of the justification itself."[113]

Studies of CAS Practices

Practices with Regard to Specificity

Studies of past practices under House Rule XII, clause 7(c), support the view that Members have considerable leeway and discretion in crafting CASs. Professor Hanah Volokh of Emory University conducted a study of CAS practices early in the 112th Congress, aggregating more than 1,700 statements submitted during the first four months of 2011.[114] According to Professor Volokh, a "handful" of these CASs "engage[d]," in her opinion, "in a thorough and highly detailed explanation of the constitutional

---

[111] *See* Feingold, *supra* note 77, at 843 ("The early scholarship on these new CASs shows substantial compliance with the new rule ... "); *see also* Volokh, *supra* note 86, at 174 (noting that CASs are "flowing through Congress at the rate of several hundred per month."). In the CRS study conducted for this report, *see infra* note 119, of the 937 pieces of legislation examined, all had a corresponding CAS.

[112] *See* Comm. On Rules- CAS Requirement, *supra* note 106.

[113] *See* Comm. On Rules, House Of Representatives, Text And Section-By-Section Analysis Of The 112th Congress House Rules Package (2011), *available at* https://rules.house.gov/sites/republicans.rules.house.gov/files/other%20home%20files/HRes%205%20Sec-by-Sec.pdf. An early dispute in the Subcommittee on Health of the Energy and Commerce Committee over the sufficiency of a CAS was resolved by the Chair of the Subcommittee, acting on advice from the Parliamentarian and the House Rules Committee, to have a fairly broad interpretation of what is required to comply with the CAS rule. *See* Volokh, *supra* note 86, at 194-96 (detailing a debate that occurred at a hearing whose transcript and video are no longer publicly available). Specifically, the Chair ruled that a point of order "cannot be used to object that the content of a CAS was incorrect or insufficient." *Id.* at 196; *see generally* Abby Brownback & Louis Jacobson, *Lawmakers Abiding by New Constitutional Justification Rule,* St. Petersburg Times (March 18, 2011), http://www.politifact.com/trutho-meter/promises/gop-pledge-o-meter/promise/665/require-bills-to-include-a-clause-citingits-autho/. This ruling prompted one commentator to suggest that "The fact that the CAS document [is] filed with something written on it is enough to fulfill the requirement in the House Rules." *See* Volokh, *supra* note 86, at 196.

[114] *See* Volokh, *supra* note 86, at 178.

ramifications of the proposed legislation" by discussing the Federalist Papers or Supreme Court doctrine, among other things.[115] The remainder, however, were less specific in their identification of Congress's powers. For example, 8% of the statements reviewed by Professor Volokh generally cited Article I, Section 8–without providing any further specificity as to the particular clauses within that section providing constitutional support for the proposed legislation.[116] A study of the CASs for "every bill and joint resolution introduced" from January 5, 2011, to January 5, 2012, of that same Congress reported similar findings.[117]

According to the House Republican Study Committee, 15% of submitted CASs relied on Article I, Section 8 alone.[118]

In preparing this chapter, CRS conducted a similar study of CASs from the 114th Congress.[119] Specifically, CRS staff examined the 937 statements submitted between July 1, 2016, and January 1, 2017, consisting of 13 joint resolutions and 924 bills.[120] Most commonly, in 58% of cases, the CAS cited to a specific clause in Article I, Section 8, such as the Taxing and Spending Clause or the Commerce Clause.[121] Few submitted CASs consisted of more than a bare citation to an affirmative power granted to Congress in the Constitution. For example, four CASs explicitly discussed Supreme Court case law that purportedly support the bill or joint resolution. Forty-four of the statements also cited to provisions of the Constitution that constrain rather than empower Congress or one of the other federal branches, such as the restrictions in Article I, Section 9 or the Bill of Rights. Few CASs went beyond the scope of the rule to detail why

---

[115] *See* Volokh, *supra* note 86, at 178.

[116] *Id.* (noting that 142 of 1,709 statements "cite Article I, Section 8 without further specificity.").

[117] *See Constitution Authority Statements,* Republican Study Comm. (Jan. 5, 2012), *available at* https://web.archive.org/web/20121213105104/http://rsc.jordan.house.gov/uploadedfiles/rsc_one_pager_-_constitutional_authority_statements—01-05-12.pdf.

[118] *Id.* (noting that of the 3,865 CASs examined, 617 cited "only Article I, Section 8.").

[119] In part, CRS's survey arguably provides an insight into whether initial practices with regard to the CAS rule may have reflected an initial zealousness of Members, or whether "compliance might improve as Representatives and their staff become more familiar with constitutional analysis." *See* Volokh, *supra* note 86, at 196.

[120] Of the 937 CASs examined, 611 or 65% cited a specific provision within the Constitution, as opposed to a general section or Article of the Constitution. *See Table 1.*

[121] Of the 937 examined CASs, 542 or 58% cited to a specific clause in Article I, Section 8. *See Table 1.*

the constitutional provision cited empowers Congress to enact the proposed legislation.

Table 1. Top 10 Most Frequently Cited Constitutional Sources in Constitutional Authority Statements (CASs) in Recent Legislation Based on a Review of 937 Pieces of Legislation Introduced from July 1, 2016, to January 1, 2017

Section or Clause	**Number of Times Cited**
General reference to Article I, Section 8	284
Article I, Section 8, clause 18 (Necessary and Proper Clause)	226[a]
Article I, Section 8, clause 1 (Taxing and Spending Clause)	205
Article I, Section 8, clause 3 (Commerce Clause)	174
Article IV, Section 3, clause 2 (Property Clause)	40
Article I, Section 8, clause 4 (Naturalization Clause)	30
Article I, Section 9, clause 7 (Appropriations Clause)	23
Article I, Section 8, clause 14 (Military Regulation Clause)	19
General reference to Article I	17
Article I, Section 8, clause 7 (Postal Clause)	15

Source: Congressional Research Service, based on a search of Congress.gov for bills and joint resolutions introduced in the House from July 1, 2016, to January 1, 2017.

Note: A single bill may have multiple sources cited in the bill's CAS.

[a] In 133 cases, the Necessary and Proper Clause was the sole authority source cited.

In line with the studies on CASs in the 112th Congress, CRS found that numerous statements submitted during the sample period contained general, rather than specific, references to the Constitution. As *Table 1* below indicates, the most frequent citation in CASs accompanying recent legislation was a general reference to Article I, Section 8, of the Constitution.[122] This occurred in 30% of all CASs during the sample period, a marked increase from the House Republican Study Committee and Volokh studies of the 112th Congress.[123] Similarly, the ninth most frequently cited constitutional provision in submitted statements during the

[122] *See Table 1.*

[123] Of the 937 CASs examined, 249 had a general reference to Article I, Section 8.

sample period was even broader: a general reference to Article I of the Constitution.[124]

Practices with Regard to Particular Clauses

Beyond CAS practices with regard to specificity, the sample of recently submitted Rule XII statements is also noteworthy in that it highlights the specific clauses of the Constitution that Members have most frequently relied upon in submitted CASs.[125] In particular, numerous recently submitted CASs are notable in that the statements raise certain questions about how a particular clause has been interpreted, both as a matter of historical practice and by the courts, and how that same clause is being cited by the relevant CAS.[126] Among the most prominent examples of CASs that could be seen as adopting an interpretation of the Constitution that potentially diverges from historical understandings or judicial interpretations of a particular clause include statements that cite to the following clauses:

Necessary and Proper Clause

One of the most frequently cited clauses in recent CASs was the Necessary and Proper Clause, which allows Congress to "make all Laws which shall be necessary and proper for carrying into Execution" the powers enumerated in Article I and "all other Powers vested by [the] Constitution in the Government of the United States, or in any Department

---

[124] *See Table 1.*
[125] *See id.*
[126] The content of CASs with regard to particular clauses has, at times, spurred criticism from a wide range of commentators. *See, e.g.,* Horace Cooper & Nathaniel Stewart, Constitutional Authority Statements: in Defense of House Rule XII, http://www.constitutingamerica.org/docs/WhitePaper.pdf ("Members on both sides of the aisle have made a number of common, substantive mistakes in drafting their Constitutional Authority Statements."); Ilya Shapiro, *Whither Constitutional Authority Statements?,* CATO AT LIBERTY (October 18, 2011), https://www.cato.org/blog/whither-constitutional-authority-statements (describing the CASs surveyed by the Republican Study Group as "[p]retty thin gruel"); *Constitutional Authority Statements in the 112th Congress: How Did the Members Do?,* Constitutional Accountability CTR., (Jan. 15, 2013), http://theusconstitution.org/text-history/1771/constitutional-authority-statements-112th-congress-how-did-members-do (noting several perceived errors in submitted CASs).

or Officer thereof."[127] About 24% of all CASs in the CRS study contained a citation to that clause, with 14% of all CASs citing the Necessary and Proper Clause as the sole power to enact the underlying legislation.[128] Citations to the Necessary and Proper Clause in isolation could be seen as somewhat anomalous, as that clause has never been viewed by the Court or by the Framers of the Constitution as a general source of power for Congress to do whatever is "necessary and proper."[129] Instead, "[w]hile the Necessary and Proper Clause authorizes congressional action 'incidental to [an enumerated] power, and conducive to its beneficial exercise,'"[130] it does not provide Congress with "great substantive and independent power."[131]

General Welfare Clause

The General Welfare Clause refers to a specific phrase contained within the language in Article I, Section 8, clause 1 empowering Congress to enact certain taxes and spend the money collected from taxation. Specifically, the first clause of Section 8 of Article I affords Congress the power to "lay and collect Taxes, Duties, Imposts and Excises, to pay the Debts and provide for the Common Defence and *general Welfare of the United States....*"[132] In

---

[127] *See* U.S. CONST. art. I, §8, cl. 18.

[128] *See Table 1.*

[129] *See* Kansas v. Colorado, 206 U.S. 46, 88 (1907) ("The last paragraph of the section which authorizes Congress to make all laws which shall be necessary and proper for carrying into execution the foregoing powers, and all other powers vested by this Constitution in the Government of the United States, or in any department or office thereof, is not the delegation of a new and independent power, but simply provision for making effective the powers theretofore mentioned."); McCulloch v. Maryland, 17 U.S. (Wheat.) 316, 420-21 (1819) (noting that the Necessary and Proper Clause is not a "great substantive and independent power" like the "power of making war, or levying of taxes, or of regulating commerce"). *See also* The Federalist NO. 33, at 171 (Alexander Hamilton) (Clinton Rossiter ed., 1999) ("[T]he sweeping clause ... authorizes the national legislature to pass all necessary and proper laws. If there is anything exceptionable, it must be sought for in the specific powers upon which this general declaration is predicated. The declaration itself, though it may be chargeable with tautology or redundancy, is at least perfectly harmless.").

[130] *See* United States v. Kebodeaux, 133 S. Ct. 2496, 2507 (2013) (Roberts, C.J., concurring) (citing McCulloch v. Maryland, 17 U.S. (Wheat.) 316, 420-21 (1819)).

[131] *See McCulloch,* 17 U.S. at 418; *see also* Kinsella v. United States *ex rel.* Singleton, 361 U.S. 234, 247 (1960) ("The [Necessary and Proper Clause] is not itself a grant of power, but a *caveat* that the Congress possesses all the means necessary to carry out the specifically granted 'foregoing' powers of § 8 'and all other Powers vested by this Constitution.... '") (emphasis in original).

[132] *See* U.S. CONST. art. I, §8, cl. 1 (emphasis added).

CRS's study, the Taxing and Spending Clause was the third most frequently cited clause by CASs.[133] Not infrequently, a citation to this clause—commonly described in CASs as the "General Welfare Clause"—was used for legislation unrelated to the spending of money by the federal government. Importantly, the phrase "general Welfare" does not exist in isolation in the clause, which might otherwise empower Congress to enact laws that broadly promote the general welfare of the nation.[134] Instead, the phrase "general Welfare" in Article I, Section 8, clause 1, is tied to the preceding language in the clause regarding the raising of revenue, and thus requires Congress to spend the money it collects from taxation to promote the general welfare.[135] While this power is considerable,[136] it is necessarily tied to spending legislation.[137]

Military Regulation Clause

The constitutional provision affording Congress with the power to "make rules for the Government and Regulation of the land and naval forces"[138] is another frequently cited clause in recent CASs.[139] Several of the bills to which such CASs are attached, however, do not purport to regulate

---

[133] *See Table 1.*

[134] *See* United States v. Butler, 297 U.S. 1, 64 (1936) ("The view that the clause grants power to provide for the general welfare, independently of the taxing power, has never been authoritatively accepted."); *see also* 2 Joseph Story, *Commentaries on the Constitution of The United States* § 904 (Leonard W. Levy ed., 1970) (stating that if the "generality of the words to 'provide for the ... general welfare'" constituted a "distinct and substantial power" in the Constitution, "it is obvious" that the government of the United States would be transformed into one of "general and unlimited powers.... "); The Federalist NO. 41, at 230 (James Madison) (Clinton Rossiter ed., 1999) (rejecting the view that the Taxing and Spending Clause "amounts to an unlimited commission to exercise every power which may be alleged to be necessary for the common defense or general welfare.").

[135] *See* United States v. Butler, 297 U.S. 1, 64 (1936) (holding that "the only thing granted [by the Taxing and Spending Clause] is the power to tax for the purpose of providing funds for payment of the nation's debts and making provision for the general welfare.").

[136] *See* Agency for Int'l Dev. v. Alliance for Open Soc'y Int'l, Inc., 133 S. Ct. 2321, 2327-28 (2013) ("The Clause provides Congress broad discretion to tax and spend for the 'general welfare'.... "); *see also* Helvering v. Davis, 301 U.S. 619, 640-41 (1937) (holding that the "discretion" to decide how to "spend money in aid of the 'general welfare'" "belongs to Congress, unless the choice is clearly wrong, a display of arbitrary power, not an exercise of judgment.").

[137] *See Butler,* 297 U.S. at 64.

[138] *See* U.S. CONST. art. I, §8, cl. 14.

[139] *See Table 1* (ranking the Military Regulation Clause as the eighth most frequently cited clause).

the United States' armed forces, but instead prescribe broad regulations for the government as a whole. Such references to the Military Regulation Clause appear to stem from reading the first phrase of the clause—"make rules for the Government"—in isolation from the rest of the clause, as an independent power. However, such an understanding of the clause is inconsistent with traditional interpretations of the scope of that clause, which view it as solely related to Congress's power over the military.[140] This interpretation also runs contrary to traditional rules of legal interpretation that counsel for reading phrases in a legal text in their context and not in isolation from the rest of the text.[141] More broadly, interpreting the Military Regulation Clause to allow Congress to direct the actions of the federal government generally in whatever manner Congress wishes would arguably transform the clause from a narrow power, confined to matters

---

[140] Traditionally, the Military Regulation Clause is viewed as a "natural incident" to Article I's preceding powers to make war, raise armies, and provide for and maintain a navy. *See* 3 Joseph Story, *Commentaries on the Constitution of the United States* § 1192 (Leonard W. Levy ed., 1970). By placing the power to govern and regulate the military among Congress's powers, the Constitution can be seen to have rejected British precedents that allowed the King, on his own authority, to impose military rules unilaterally. *See id.* ("In Great Britain, the king, in his capacity of generalissimo of the whole kingdom, has the sole power of regulating fleets and armies.... The whole power is far more safe in the hands of congress, than of the executive; since otherwise the most summary and severe punishments might be inflicted at the mere will of the executive."). In practice, the Military Regulation Clause has been viewed by the Supreme Court to allow Congress to regulate matters like the discipline of service members. *See, e.g.,* United States v. Kebodeaux, 133 S. Ct. 2496, 2503 (2013) ("[U]nder the authority granted to it by the Military Regulation and Necessary and Proper Clauses, Congress could promulgate the Uniform Code of Military Justice."); Carter v. Roberts, 177 U.S. 496, 497-98 (1900) ("The eighth section of Art. I of the Constitution provides that the Congress shall have power 'to make rules for the government and regulation of the land and naval forces' and in the exercise of that power Congress has enacted rules for the regulation of the army known as the Articles of War.... Every officer, before he enters on the duties of his office, subscribes to these articles, and places himself within the power of courts martial to pass on any offence which he may have committed in contravention of them.").

[141] *See* Deal v. United States, 508 U.S. 129, 132 (1993) (noting a "fundamental principle of statutory construction (and, indeed, of language itself) that the meaning of a word cannot be determined in isolation, but must be drawn from the context in which it is used."). In this context, reading the phrase "make rules for the Government" as a separate and distinct power from the rest of the clause would render the last phrase in the clause, regarding "Regulation of the Land and Naval Forces," meaningless. *Cf.* United States v. 144,744 pounds of Blue King Crab, 410 F.3d 1131, 1134 (9th Cir. 2005) ("It is an accepted canon of statutory interpretation that we must interpret the statutory phrase as a whole, giving effect to each word and not interpreting the provision as to make other provisions meaningless or superfluous.").

related to the armed forces, to an open-ended police power, something otherwise rejected by the Framers of the Constitution.[142]

Appropriations Clause

A number of recent CASs cite provisions in Article I, Section 9, including several CASs that cite the Appropriations Clause as the authority for Congress to provide money for a particular project.[143] The Appropriations Clause states, in relevant part, that "No Money shall be drawn from the Treasury, but in Consequence of Appropriations made by Law."[144] Like other provisions found in Section 9 of Article I,[145] this clause generally has not been interpreted to grant Congress any affirmative power.[146] Instead, in keeping with other provisions in Section 9, the Appropriations Clause has been seen to function as a *restriction* on the

---

[142] *See* United States v. Morrison, 529 U.S. 598, 619 n.8 (2000) ("With its careful enumeration of federal powers and explicit statement that all powers not granted to the Federal Government are reserved, the Constitution cannot realistically be interpreted as granting the Federal Government an unlimited license to regulate.").

[143] *See Table 1* (ranking the Appropriations Clause as the seventh most frequently cited clause).

[144] *See* U.S. CONST. art. I, §9, cl. 8.

[145] *See* North American Co. v. SEC, 327 U.S. 686, 704-05 (1946) (noting that the powers of the federal government under Section 8 of Article I are limited by "express provisions" of other sections of the Constitution, such as "[Section] 9 of Article I and the Bill of Rights."); *see also* Warren v. Paul, 22 Ind. 276, 277 (1864) ("The powers delegated to the general government are specified in sec. 8 of art. 1. Section 9 of the same article contains restrictions and limitations on the powers granted generally in section 8, and section 10 of the same article contains the prohibitions upon the States.").

[146] *See* Cincinnati Soap Co. v. United States, 301 U.S. 308, 321 (1937) ("The provision of the Constitution ... that 'No Money shall be drawn from the Treasury, but in Consequence of Appropriations made by Law' was intended as a restriction upon the disbursing authority of the Executive department, and is without significance here. It means simply that no money can be paid out of the Treasury unless it has been appropriated by an act of Congress."); *see generally* Robert G. Natelson, *Federal Land Retention and the Constitution's Property Clause: The Original Understanding*, 76 U. COLO. L. REV. 327, 363 (2005) (noting that the Appropriation Clause does "not actually authorize appropriations" and instead appropriations are "authorized by other parts of the document."); *id.* ("Rather, the Appropriations Clause (a) assumed as a background fact that there would be federal funds and appropriations arising from the exercise of other powers and (b) established rules for them."); *Panel Discussion, The Appropriations Power and the Necessary and Proper Clause*, 68 WASH. U. L.Q. 623, 651 (1990) (remarks of then-Assistant Attorney General William Barr) ("The appropriations clause is not an independent 'power' of Congress. It is not a power clause.... The appropriations clause is simply a procedural provision – a requirement that Congress pass a law before it can take money out of the treasury.").

powers of the federal government.[147] Specifically, the Appropriations Clause ensures that when the federal government spends money, "the payment of money from the Treasury must be authorized by a statute."[148] It thus serves as an affirmative restriction on the power of the Executive and makes Congress's "power over the purse" exclusive in nature.[149] As discussed above, Congress's power to spend money derives from the Taxing and Spending Clause.[150]

Bill of Rights

While not among the most frequent citations in CASs, occasionally one of the first 10 amendments to the Constitution—the Bill of Rights—has been cited in support of Congress's power to enact legislation. Congress may certainly have an interest in protecting the rights listed in the Bill of Rights, but it should be noted that the first 10 amendments to the Constitution do not themselves empower Congress to take any action, and they instead consist of "negative rights" protecting individuals from certain government conduct.[151] The Bill of Rights often *prohibits* congressional

---

147 Reeside v. Walker, 52 U.S. (11 How.) 272, 291 (1851) ("It is a well-known constitutional provision, that no money can be taken or drawn from the Treasury except under an appropriation by Congress.... However much money may be in the Treasury at any one time, not a dollar of it can be used in the payment of anything not thus previously sanctioned. Any other course would give to the fiscal officers a most dangerous discretion.").

148 OPM v. Richmond, 496 U.S. 414, 424 (1990).

149 *See* 3 Joseph Story, *Commentaries on the Constitution of the United States* § 1342 (Leonard W. Levy ed., 1970) ("As all the taxes raised from the people, as well as the revenues arising from other sources, are to be applied to the discharge of the expenses, and debts, and other engagements of the government, it is highly proper, that congress should possess the power to decide, how and when any money should be applied for these purposes. If it were otherwise, the executive would possess an unbounded power over the public purse or the nation; and might apply all its monied resources at his pleasure. The power to control, and direct the appropriations, constitutes a most useful and salutary check upon profusion and extravagance, as well as upon corrupt influence and public peculation.").

150 *See* Helvering v. Davis, 301 U.S. 619, 640-41 (1937) (holding that the Taxing and Spending Clause provides Congress with the "discretion" to decide how to "spend money in aid of the 'general welfare'").

151 *See* Daniel v. Cook Cnty., 833 F.3d 728, 733 (7th Cir. 2016) ("The individual rights in our Bill of Rights have long been understood as negative rights, meaning that the Constitution protects individuals from some forms of government intrusions upon their liberty, without imposing affirmative duties on governments to care for their citizens."); *see generally* DeShaney v. Winnebago Cty. Dep't of Soc. Servs., 489 U.S. 189, 196 (1989).

action.[152] As a result, if a sponsor proposes legislation intended to support individual liberties protected by the Constitution, the CAS for such legislation could instead rely on an affirmative power of the Congress, such as the powers provided in Article I, Section 8 of the Constitution. Another alternative would be the enforcement power of the Fourteenth Amendment, which the Supreme Court has held allows "Congress [to] enact so-called prophylactic legislation" aimed at "prevent[ing] and deter[ing] unconstitutional conduct."[153] Nonetheless, it should be noted that the House Rules Committee has suggested that a citation to a provision of the Constitution that does not explicitly grant power to Congress may suffice to comply with the CAS rule.[154] For example, a Member seeking to rescind or narrow the scope of an existing law could arguably believe it appropriate to identify constitutional principles found in the Bill of Rights or elsewhere that the Member believes are advanced by the proposed legislation.[155]

Legal Implications of a CAS

CASs have limited legal import, in that the CAS of a bill enacted into law will likely not alter a court's view of the constitutionality of the legislation. At bottom, a CAS is a statement by one Member of Congress (i.e., the sponsor) when a piece of legislation is introduced. It is not formally part of a bill or joint resolution. Therefore, even if the underlying legislation is enacted into law, the CAS would have no formal legal effect because the CAS was not subject to the approval of both houses of Congress, or presented to the President, as is required by Article I, Section

---

[152] *See, e.g.,* U.S. CONST. amend. I ("*Congress shall make no law* respecting an establishment of religion, or prohibiting the free exercise thereof; or abridging the freedom of speech, or of the press; or the right of the people peaceably to assemble, and to petition the government for a redress of grievances.") (emphasis added).

[153] *See* Nev. Dep't of Human Res. v. Hibbs, 538 U.S. 721, 727-28 (2003).

[154] *See* Comm. On Rules- CAS Requirement, *supra* note 106 (providing, as an example of a CAS, "This bill makes specific changes to existing law in a manner that returns power to the States and to the people, in accordance with Amendment X of the United States Constitution.").

[155] *See id.*

7.[156] Instead, CASs are a type of legislative history material that describes the initial thoughts of a single Member as to Congress's power to enact the bill.[157] In this sense, one might view a CAS as akin to an isolated statement in the *Congressional Record* or a statement issued by the sponsor of a bill, which courts generally regard as "weak" forms of legislative history when considering Congress's intent in passing a law.[158]

In practice, in the few court cases that cite to a law's CAS, the underlying statement is mentioned merely in passing and had no apparent effect on the decision, as courts have independently evaluated the constitutionality of the legislation in question notwithstanding the existence of the CAS.[159] This practice is in keeping with broader principles of constitutional law as adopted by the courts. One such principle holds that Congress generally may not independently and without further scrutiny in the context of a case or controversy before a court define its own powers under the Constitution.[160] Another principle holds that an

---

[156] Zedner v. United States, 547 U.S. 489, 509-10 (2006) (Scalia, J., concurring) ("[T]he only language that constitutes 'a Law' within the meaning of the Bicameralism and Presentment Clause of Article I, § 7, and hence the only language adopted in a fashion that entitles it to our attention, is the text of the enacted statute."); *see also* Exxon Mobil Corp. v. Allapattah Servs., 545 U.S. 546, 568 (2005) ("As we have repeatedly held, the authoritative statement is the statutory text, not the legislative history or any other extrinsic material.").

[157] *See* Volokh, *supra* note 86, at 204 ("As currently structured, CASs are a form of legislative history, and a very weak form at that."); *see also* COMM. ON RULES- CAS REQUIREMENT, *supra* note 106 ("To the extent that a court looks at the legislative history of an Act, the Constitutional Authority Statement would be part of that history.").

[158] Landgraf v. USI Film Prods., 511 U.S. 244, 262 n.15 (1994) ("[A] court would be well advised to take with a large grain of salt floor debate and statements placed in the Congressional Record which purport to create an interpretation for the legislation that is before us.") (quoting 137 CONG. REC. S15325 (daily ed. October 29, 1991) (statement of Sen. Danforth)); *see generally* Zachary M. Ista, *No Vacancy: Why Congress Can Regulate Senate Vacancy-Filling Elections Without Amending (or Offending) the Constitution*, 61 Am. U. L. Rev. 327, 360 (2011) (describing the "hierarchy of the extrinsic sources of legislative history, ranging from the most persuasive to the least persuasive: conference committee reports; regular committee reports; earlier versions of a bill, including rejected amendments; statements made by the bill's supporters during its floor debate, with special consideration sometimes given to the bill's drafters and sponsors; and, finally, statements made by the bill's opponents during floor debate").

[159] *See, e.g.*, United States v. Bollinger, 798 F.3d 201, 207 (4th Cir. 2015) (independently evaluating the constitutionality of a law after noting that the CAS for the law cited the Commerce Clause); United States v. Clark, 435 F.3d 1100, 1104 (9th Cir. 2006) (same).

[160] *See* City of Boerne v. Flores, 521 U.S. 507, 529 (1997) ("If Congress could define its own powers ... no longer would the Constitution be 'superior paramount law, unchangeable by ordinary means.' It would be 'on a level with ordinary legislative acts, and, like other acts, ...

otherwise unconstitutional law will not be found to be permissible by a court merely because Congress believes the provision to be within its powers.[161]

Debate over the Rule

Given the seeming ease of compliance with House Rule XII, clause 7(c),[162] and the tendency of some CASs to cite to general[163] or arguably inapplicable constitution provisions,[164] questions might be raised about the desirability of the CAS rule.[165] Critics have argued for its repeal, contending that the rule is symbolic and has little impact on congressional debate or dialogue about Congress's authority under the Constitution.[166] In

---

alterable when the legislature shall please to alter it.'") (quoting *Marbury*, 5 U.S. (1 Cranch) at 177); *see also Marbury*, 5 U.S. (1 Cranch) at 177 (holding that in a case or controversy properly before a federal court that it is "the province and duty of the judicial department to say what the law is").

161 *See* City of Rome v. United States, 446 U.S. 156, 207 (1980) (Rehnquist, J., dissenting) ("While the presumption of constitutionality is due to any act of a coordinate branch of the Federal Government or of one of the States, it is this Court which is ultimately responsible for deciding challenges to the exercise of power by those entities.").

162 *See supra* "Compliance with the CAS Rule."

163 *See supra* "Practices with Regard to Specificity."

164 *See supra* "Practices with Regard to Particular Clauses."

165 The Rules Committee addressed the question of the CAS rule's value in its initial guidance on the rule. *See* Comm. On Rules- CAS Requirement, *supra* note 106 ("Q. So why have this Rule at all? A. Just as a cost estimate from the Congressional Budget Office informs the debate on a proposed bill, a statement outlining the power under the Constitution that Congress has to enact a proposed bill will inform and provide the basis for debate. It also demonstrates to the American people that we in Congress understand that we have an obligation under our founding document to stay within the role established therein for the legislative branch.").

166 *See* Feingold, *supra* note 77, at 842 ("[C]ritics have suggest that this new House rule is symbolic at best and meaningless at worst.... "); *see also* Volokh, *supra* note 86, at 176 ("CASs are so unobjectionable that the main argument against them is that they are useless."); Norman Ornstein, as quoted in Brownback & Jacobson, *supra* note 113 ("Frankly, this is just symbolic, so I have no real feelings one way or the other.... Of course, you could offer a bill that repeals the Internal Revenue Code, or Medicare, by claiming it is unconstitutional as your basis, and be utterly wrong. But what difference does it really make? You can also justify almost any bill you want by claiming a broad constitutional authority under the health and welfare clause or the commerce clause. So I see the disagreements here as being just as symbolic as the promise in the first place."); *see also* David W. Rohde, as quoted in Brownback & Jacobson, *supra* note 113 (describing the rule as "utterly trivial.").

addition, some have asserted that Congress lacks the institutional capacity to interpret the Constitution,[167] and the CAS rule demonstrates this insofar as there have been few meaningful debates in Congress over the scope of Congress's powers under the rule.[168] Others contend that the administrative costs of complying with the rule outweigh any benefits from the CAS requirement.[169]

On the other hand, proponents characterize House Rule XII, clause 7(c), as an extension of the broader debate[170] over Congress's role in interpreting the Constitution, providing a limited means by which Members of Congress may expressly engage in constitutional interpretation.[171] As one commentator notes, "[f]undamentally, a [CAS] is a congressional interpretation of the Constitution,"[172] and supporters of the rule see several benefits to having the House of Representatives engage in a limited form of constitutional interpretation through the submission of CASs. According to the rule's proponents, statements submitted under House Rule XII are a "simple and straightforward self-monitoring mechanism" to ensure that Congress does not "usurp" powers not granted to it in the Constitution.[173] In this sense, according to its proponents, the

---

[167] *See supra* note 83.

[168] *See* Stephen Dinan, *Congress Has a Constitution Problem—Many Don't Understand Document*, WASH. TIMES (Jan. 14, 2013), *available at* http://www.washingtontimes.com/news/2013/jan/14/defenders-of-constitution-dont-always-useit-for-l/("Many lawmakers ignored the rule, while others sliced and diced the clauses to justify what they were trying to do. One thumbed his nose at the exercise altogether, saying it's up to the courts, not Congress, to determine what is constitutional. Most striking of all is how little the statements mattered in the debates on the bills. They were mentioned just a handful of times on the floor, and didn't foster the constitutional conversation that Republican lawmakers said they wanted to spark.").

[169] *See* Pete Kasperowicz, *Democrat: Citing Constitution Will Cost Taxpayers $570K,* THE HILL (Jan. 10, 2011), *available at* http://thehill.com/blogs/floor-action/house/136995-democrat-citing-constitutional-authority-in-bills-willcost-you (quoting one opponent of the rule who argued that the "requirement that lawmakers cite the Constitution in each bill they introduce will cost $570,000 in additional printing costs."); *see also* Feingold, *supra* note 77, at 844 (arguing that requiring a CAS at the introduction of a bill that may not advance in the legislative process is "unnecessary and bureaucratic.").

[170] *See supra* "Role of Congress in Interpreting the Constitution."

[171] *See* Feingold, *supra* note 77, at 842-43 (arguing that the CAS rule has "generated some interesting discourse in the House on specific pieces of legislation.").

[172] *See* Volokh, *supra* note 86, at 178.

[173] *Id.* at 176.

CAS rule serves to remind Members of the limits on Congress's institutional power.[174]

Additionally, supporters of House Rule XII, clause 7(c), argue that the rule enhances constitutional dialogue outside of the judiciary and promotes constitutional literacy within Congress by formally requiring Members to engage in even limited constitutional interpretation when introducing legislation.[175] According to one commentator, the CAS rule could

> provide a foundation for a new sense within ... [Congress] ... that there is both reason and need for its members to develop deeper and broader understandings of the Constitution and constitutional interpretation—in the direction of Congress becoming ... not only a co-equal branch of the federal government, but a co-equal interpreter of the federal Constitution, if not more.[176]

Proponents of the rule have further contended that the rule could enhance the institutional credibility and reputation of Congress by making clear to constituents that Members "take seriously the constitutionality of their actions."[177] According to one former Member,

> Congress's reputational problems partially relate to a belief that Congress is not really debating or deliberating in good faith but is simply retreating to partisan battle lines. This concern has been exacerbated by Congress abdicating and leaving to the courts its historical responsibility to consider constitutionality on its own. In this respect, the House Rule ... is a foot in the door. Under the House Rule, all members of the House are

---

[174] *See* Cooper & Stewart, *supra* note 126, at 3 ("Rule XII reminds Congress—even if subtly—that the Constitution has meaning and should be respected ... it reinforces the principle that Congress has limited, enumerated powers derived from a specific, foundational source.").

[175] *See* Marc Spindelman, *House Rule XII: Congress and the Constitution,* 72 OHIO ST. L.J. 1317, 1340 (2011) ("Through engagement with the Constitution and constitutional deliberations of the sort that the new House Rule calls for, members of the House may come to share, whatever their political affiliation, a political desire for full fluency and literacy in constitutional deliberation and debate. Following and flowering from that desire could well come a desire to change ... the wider political culture, which has for so long left the Constitution so firmly and finally in the hands of the courts."); *see also* Cooper & Stewart, *supra* note 126, at 3 ("[T]he Rule allows Congress to engage the other federal branches in a conversation about the meaning of the laws and the Constitution itself.").

[176] *See* Spindelman, *supra* note 175, at 1339.

[177] *See* Feingold, *supra* note 77, at 872.

required, essentially for the first time, to take at least one aspect of their obligation to consider constitutionality more seriously.[178]

Nonetheless, even amongst proponents of the rule, informal suggestions have been made to improve the constitutional dialogue surrounding CASs. Among the primary changes proposed are the following:

Enhancing the Content of CASs

Prompted by criticisms about how "thin many of [the CASs] are,"[179] some have suggested that the House rules be altered to require more formal and robust debate over the constitutionality of proposed legislation. One proposal called for time to be set aside for formal debate on the House floor about the constitutionality of legislation upon the motion of a single Member.[180] Other proposals focus on changing the content of the CASs themselves by requiring more expansive statements that discuss the relationship between the cited provision of the Constitution and the bill itself.[181] In addition, others have advocated that the CAS rule formally require that the statement discuss "[w]ith some depth" any "precedent germane to the authority to enact the" legislation.[182] Finally, several commentators have proposed altering the rule so that Members must not only cite to the Constitution's *affirmative* grants of authority to Congress,

---

[178] *Id.*

[179] *See* Neil Siefring, *Three Commitments Conservatives Should Get from a New Speaker*, PJ MEDIA (October 2, 2015), https://pjmedia.com/blog/what-conservatives-should-ask-from-a-new-speaker/?print=true&singlepage=true.

[180] *Id.* ("To reform this process, a new speaker should commit to change the rules of the House to require that during general debate, the minority and the majority shall each be allowed one specific 'motion regarding constitutional authority.' This motion would allow a House member to ask the bill's sponsor, or the sponsor's designee, to respond on the floor to questions about the constitutional authority statement attached to the bill. The motion would allow for up to ten minutes of back-and-forth discussion about the statement."). Currently, Members may send a written request to the chair of the Rules Committee for debate on the constitutionality of the proposed measure. If at least 25 Members sign the request, the chair will schedule up to 20 minutes of floor debate, evenly divided between a member specified in the letter and the majority bill manager. *See* Oleszek, *supra* note 110, at 4-5.

[181] *See* COOPER & STEWART, *supra* note 126, at 21 ("Second, to increase transparency and accessibility, the Rule should require that each Statement be accompanied by a short description of the bill's purpose.").

[182] *See* Feingold, *supra* note 77, at 870.

but also discuss any potential *limitations* the Constitution may impose on Congress's power to legislate.[183]

Better Enforcing the CAS Rule

Given the large number of CASs that lack specificity or cite seemingly inapplicable clauses of the Constitution, supporters of the rule have argued that Members must be held accountable for ensuring that submitted CASs comply with both the letter and spirit of the requirement.[184] One early version of the current CAS rule proposed in the 111th Congress would have deemed general citations to the "common defense clause, the general welfare clause, or the necessary and proper clause" insufficient to satisfy House Rule XII, clause 7(c).[185] In addition, this proposal would have allowed a Member to initiate a point of order challenging the adequacy of a CAS, thereby subjecting the measure to a short debate that would resolve whether the submitted statement complied with House Rule XII.[186] Others have urged that the Clerk of the House or a designee be empowered to "evaluate the content" of a submitted statement formally and "add a note indicating that the Statement submitted does not properly satisfy the Rule's specificity requirement."[187] Under this proposal, any bill with such a notation could be "subject to a special privileged motion by a Member to recommit the bill for failure to follow the Rule."[188]

Changing Other Procedures Regarding CASs

Currently, the CAS focuses on a single moment: the initial introduction of a bill or joint resolution. Viewing this limitation on the use

---

[183] *See id.* at 845 ("By merely requiring a statement describing *the source* of Congress's constitutional authority but not *a limit* to that authority, the House Rule addresses at best only half of the constitutional equation."); *see also* Volokh, *supra* note 86, at 216 ("The current CAS rule focuses Congress's attention only on its grants of authority, not on other clauses of the Constitution that set limits on the exercise of its powers. For a full debate of constitutionality, Congress must consider both.").

[184] *See* Volokh, *supra* note 86, at 199 ("Some critics might say that citing these very general, open-ended clauses defeats the purpose of the rule.").

[185] *See* H.Res. 1754, 111th Cong. (2010).

[186] *Id.*

[187] *See* COOPER & STEWART, *supra* note 126, at 20.

[188] *Id.* at 21.

of a CAS as a shortcoming that prevents more robust constitutional debate, several proponents of the CAS rule have argued that the rule should apply during all stages of the legislative process, including during committce deliberations, so that the constitutionality of a bill or resolution is subject to broader consideration.[189] Relatedly, because the CAS rule only applies at the beginning of the legislative process, the only Member who currently assesses Congress's authority to enact the legislation in question is the Member who introduced the legislation.[190] In order to ensure that Members, who ordinarily must decide how to vote on *another* Member's bill, consider the constitutional implications of the legislation in question, some have suggested that the House rule "explicitly acknowledge" the independent "obligation" of Members to be "mindful of any constitutional objections" regarding the bill that is the subject of a vote.[191] In what may be the broadest means to allow more Members to weigh in on the constitutional implications of a bill, at least one commentator has suggested (but ultimately rejects) changing the House rule so that the CAS is part of the text of a bill, as opposed to a statement attached to the bill.[192] Such an approach could, at least in theory, formalize and elevate the role of the CAS because when a bill that contains a CAS in its text is put to a vote, multiple Members could potentially voice their agreement or disagreement with the bill's language assessing Congress's power to enact the underlying legislation.[193]

---

[189] *Id.* ("But Rule XII should ensure that at each step in the legislative labyrinth, from submission to the floor, the bill and its Authority Statement are attached thereto and immediately available to Members for their consideration and debate."); *see also* Feingold, *supra* note 77, at 864-65 (noting that one "area[] that need[s] expansion and improvement" with regard to the CAS rule is that the rule "requires a CAS only at the time the bill is introduced" and has "no rules regarding proposed amendments that may be attached to any legislation."); Volokh, *supra* note 86, at 215 ("CASs should be required *both* at introduction *and* in the committee report.") (emphasis in original).

[190] *See* Feingold, *supra* note 77, at 865.

[191] *Id.*; *see also* Volokh, *supra* note 86, at 218 ("Changes could be made to the rule that would turn CASs into statements of the entire House of Representatives or the entire Congress.").

[192] *See* Volokh, *supra* note 86, at 220. Notably, Professor Volokh concludes that the "costs of putting CASs in statutory text," such as the risks of the statement being watered down, "are substantial, and probably outweigh the benefits." *Id.* at 226.

[193] *See id.* at 220 (describing the proposal to place CASs in a bill's text as "the strongest way for Congress to make its constitutional views binding.... "). Nonetheless, even if placing a CAS in the legislative text would elevate congressional dialogue about the Constitution by

Each of the proposed modifications to the CAS rule could raise new concerns, however. For example, if House Rule XII were modified to require more robust discussions of the constitutionality of a given piece of legislation throughout the legislative process, such a modification could amplify the criticisms that the CAS rule requires considerable resources to ensure compliance.[194] Moreover, if the rule were modified to require that CASs include additional content, without any changes to its current enforcement regime, the additional requirements could, in the view of at least one commentator, be ignored.[195]

POTENTIAL RESOURCES AND CONSIDERATIONS FOR DRAFTING CASS

This section of the chapter identifies issues that Members and congressional staffers may find useful to consider when assessing whether and how a constitutional provision may provide a source of authority for legislation. First, the section notes available resources that may aid in interpreting the Constitution. Second, the section suggests potential constitutional bases for various types of legislation.

---

requiring each Member to participate in a vote on the constitutional basis for the act, it is unclear what effect the statement would have with regard to constitutional interpretation by other branches, particularly the courts. *See supra* note 161 and accompanying text. Moreover, the argument for placing the CAS in the text of a bill is based on the assumption that a Member's vote on a bill is necessarily an endorsement or rejection of the entire bill, which may not reflect the realities of modern legislation. *See* Cindy G. Buys & William Isasi, *An "Authoritative" Statement of Administrative Action: A Useful Political Invention or a Violation of the Separation of Powers Doctrine?* 7 N.Y.U. J. LEGIS. & PUB. POL'Y 73, 100 n.135 (2004) ("While we may hold legislators responsible for the statutes they vote on, given the number and complexity of bills before Congress, it is a fiction to assume they are familiar with every provision of every bill.").

[194] *See supra* notes 162-169 and accompanying text.

[195] *See* Feingold, *supra* note 77, at 871 (noting, but ultimately rejecting, the argument that "members of the Congress may still not take seriously their obligations to consider constitutionality."). Ultimately, Senator Feingold suggests that "members [would] take [their] obligations seriously" even if there were no enforcement mechanism for a more robust CAS rule. *Id.* at 872 ("Nevertheless, anecdotal evidence suggests that, at least in the case of similar rules governing the behavior of senators, many members take such obligations seriously.").

Resources on the Constitution That May Be Relevant for CASs

There are numerous resources that Members and staff could use to learn more about the affirmative powers afforded Congress by the Constitution and the limitations on those powers. The Constitution and its current amendments contain a little more than 7,500 words,[196] and Congress regularly authorizes the printing and distribution of pocket versions of the Constitution for Members and staff.[197] Moreover, a host of primary historical documents from the founding era are available electronically for those interested, including the following:

- *Farrand's Records:* Documentary records from the Constitutional Convention, including the notes gathered by various attendees, complied by historian Max Farrand.[198]
- *The Federalist Papers*: A series of newspaper articles written by Alexander Hamilton, John Jay, and James Madison urging the ratification of the Constitution.[199]
- *Founder's Constitution*: A joint venture of the University of Chicago Press and the Liberty Fund, providing various primary sources for each clause of the Constitution.[200]
- *Constitutional Sources Project (ConSource): ConSource* provides free access to a "digital library of historical sources related to the creation, ratification, and amendment of the United States Constitution."[201]

---

[196] *See* Stephen Gardbaum, *The Myth and the Reality of American Constitutional Exceptionalism*, 107 MICH. L. REV. 391, 399 (2008) ("Overall, the U.S. Constitution is exceptional among written constitutions both in its age and its brevity. It is the oldest currently in effect and ... is among the shortest at 7591 words including amendments.... ").

[197] *See, e.g.,* H.Con.Res. 54, 114th Cong. (2015).

[198] *See Farrand's Records,* Library Of Congress (last accessed January 5, 2017), https://memory.loc.gov/ammem/amlaw/lwfr.html.

[199] *See The Federalist Papers,* CONGRESS.GOV (last accessed January 5, 2017), https://www.congress.gov/resources/display/content/The+Federalist+Papers.

[200] *See* The Founders' Constitution (Philip B. Kurland & Ralph Lerner, eds., 1987), *available at* http://presspubs.uchicago.edu/founders.

[201] *See Welcome to ConSource,* CONSOURCE (last accessed January 5, 2017), http://www.consource.org/.

In addition to these primary sources, Members and staff may wish to consult a number of secondary sources that are publicly available explaining the various clauses of the Constitution, including the following:

- *Constitution Annotated (CONAN*): The Library of Congress, through the Congressional Research Service, regularly publishes and updates *The Constitution of the United States of America: Analysis and Interpretation* (popularly known as the Constitution Annotated or CONAN). CONAN contains an in-depth, accessible, and objective record of how each provision in the Constitution has been interpreted by the Supreme Court and other entities.[202]
- *Commentaries on the Constitution of the United States*: *Commentaries on the Constitution of the United States* is a three-volume treatise written by Associate Justice Joseph Story in 1833. It is widely cited as an authoritative understanding of the Constitution.[203]
- *Interactive Constitution*: For an overview of the Constitution, the congressionally chartered National Constitution Center has created the *Interactive Constitution* wherein "scholars of different perspectives discuss what they agree upon, and what they disagree about" with regard to broad concepts in constitutional law.[204]
- *The Heritage Foundation's Guide to the Constitution:* The Heritage Foundation's *Guide to the Constitution* provides a clause-by-clause analysis of the Constitution with a series of explanatory essays from a number of legal scholars.[205]

---

[202] *See* Cong. Research Serv., Library Of Cong., The Constitution Of The United States Of America: Analysis And Interpretation, S. Doc. No. 112-9, 112th Cong., 2d Sess. 1611-16 (2016), *available at* https://www.congress.gov/ constitution-annotated/.

[203] *See* Joseph Story, *Commentaries on the Constitution of the United States* (Leonard W. Levy ed., 1970). Several versions of Story's *Commentaries* are available online, including at http://www.constitution.org/js/js_005.htm.

[204] *See Interactive Constitution,* Nat'l Constitution Ctr., (last accessed January 5, 2017), *available at* http://constitutioncenter.org/interactive-constitution/index_no_flash.php.

[205] *See The Heritage Guide to the Constitution,* HERITAGE FOUND., 2012, *available at* http://www.heritage.org/ constitution.

- The American Constitution Society's *Keeping Faith With the Constitution*: The American Constitution Society's *Keeping Faith With the Constitution* examines the text and history of the Constitution with a view toward how the Constitution's "words and principles" have been interpreted throughout U.S. history.[206]

In addition, beginning in 2017, the American Law Division of CRS will offer a seminar for Members and staff on the "Powers of Congress," which will serve as an introductory course on Congress's powers under the Constitution and strategies for crafting CASs.[207]

ADDITIONAL CONSIDERATIONS IN CRAFTING CASS

To aid drafters of CASs, *Table 2* provides a list of suggested citations that could potentially be submitted in a CAS pursuant to House Rule XII, clause 7(c), for various types of commonly introduced legislation.

Beyond these suggestions for citations to specific provisions of the Constitution,[208] given the broader trends with regard to CAS practices discussed above,[209] it may also be helpful to consider the following questions before submitting a CAS:

- *Does the CAS cite to a specific clause of the Constitution?* While several recent CASs have adopted the practice of citing to an entire Article of the Constitution or a section of the Constitution, such as Article I, Section 8,[210] the prevailing customary practice has been

[206] *See* Goodwin Liu, Pamela S. Karlan, & Christopher H. Schroeder, Keeping Faith with the Constitution (2009), *available at* https://www.acslaw.org/pdf/ACS_KeepFaith_FNL.pdf.

[207] To request information about this seminar, please contact Jeanne Dennis (7-5812, jdennis@crs.loc.gov.

[208] *See supra* notes 120-121 for a discussion of the primary means by which Members comply with the CAS rule.

[209] *See supra* "House Rule XII, Clause 7(c), and Constitutional Authority Statements."

[210] *See Table 1.*

to cite to a specific clause of the Constitution.[211] To the extent a Member wishes to cite to a specific clause in a CAS, *Table 2* may be a helpful resource to consult.

- *Does the CAS cite only to the Necessary and Proper Clause?* While a considerable number of CASs cite exclusively to the Necessary and Proper Clause,[212] such a citation may raise questions with regard to whether the clause is intended to do more than supplement Congress's other enumerated powers under the Constitution.[213] To the extent a Member may wish to cite to Congress's other, more specific enumerated powers for support for a given piece of legislation, *Table 2* may be a helpful resource to consult.
- *Does the CAS cite to a clause that affirmatively empowers Congress to take an action?* Citations in CASs to clauses in Article I, Section 9 of the Constitution, which contains a list of limitations on the powers of the federal government, or the Bill of Rights, which consists of a number of rights retained vis-á-vis the federal government, may suggest a broader interpretation of such clauses. To the extent a Member prefers to cite to a clause that is more generally recognized to grant an affirmative power to Congress, Article I, Section 8 contains the vast majority of commonly cited clauses that provide Congress the power to legislate with respect to various subjects.
- *Does the CAS cite to a clause that relates to and authorizes the underlying legislation?* Perhaps most importantly, a Member may wish cite to a provision of the Constitution whose power, based on either historical understandings or judicial interpretations of a particular clause, has some relationship with the subject matter of the legislation. As discussed earlier in this chapter, citations to constitutional provisions like the General Welfare Clause and the

---

[211] *See supra* notes 120-121 for a discussion of the primary means by which Members comply with the CAS rule.

[212] *See Table 1.*

[213] McCulloch v. Maryland, 17 U.S. (Wheat.) 316, 418 (1819); Kinsella v. United States *ex rel.* Singleton, 361 U.S. 234, 247 (1960).

Military Regulation Clause may be more limited than the language of the Constitution might suggest at first blush.[214] To the extent a Member may want to confirm that a particular CAS citation relates to and authorizes the underlying legislation, attorneys in CRS's American Law Division (x7-6006) can provide advice with regard to specific CAS citations.

Table 2. Suggested CAS Citations for Commonly Introduced Legislation

<table>
<tr><th>Subject Matter of Legislation</th><th>Suggested Citation</th></tr>
<tr><td>Appropriations (i.e., legislation that sets aside a sum of money for a specific purpose)</td><td>Article I, Section 8, clause 1 provides Congress with the power to "lay and collect Taxes, Duties, Imposts and Excises" in order to "provide for the ... general Welfare of the United States."
* Note: Article I, Section 9, clause 7 prohibits money from being drawn from the Treasury absent an appropriation made by law.</td></tr>
<tr><td>Appropriations Related to the Military</td><td rowspan="2">Article I, Section 8, clause 1 provides Congress with the power to "lay and collect Taxes, Duties, Imposts and Excises" in order to "provide for the common Defence ... of the United States."
Article I, Section 8, clause 12 provides Congress with the power to raise and support armies.
Article I, Section 8, clause 13 provides Congress with the power to "provide and maintain" a navy.
Article I, Section 8, clause 1 provides Congress with the power to "lay and collect Taxes, Duties, Imposts and Excises" in order to "provide for the ...general Welfare of the United States."
Article I, Section 8, clause 18 allows Congress to make all laws "which shall be necessary and proper for carrying into execution" any of Congress's enumerated powers, including Congress's powers over appropriations.</td></tr>
<tr><td>Appropriations that Place Conditions on an Expenditure (e.g., a grant to the states)</td></tr>
</table>

[214] *See supra* "Practices with Regard to Particular Clauses."

Table 2. (Continued)

Subject Matter of Legislation	Suggested Citation
	* Note: According to the Supreme Court, "[i]ncident to Congress's [spending] power, Congress may attach conditions on the receipt of federal funds.... " *See* South Dakota v. Dole, 483 U.S. 203, 207 (1987).
Awards—Military Awards (e.g., Congressional Medal of Honor)	*Article I, Section 8, clause 14* provides Congress with the power to make rules for the government and regulation of the land and naval forces.
Awards—Non-Military Awards (e.g., Congressional Gold Medal)	*Article I, Section 8, clause 6* empowers Congress to coin money. The U.S. Treasury through the United States Mint has historically exercised its power over coinage to strike national medals.
Civil Rights Legislation	* Note: A variety of constitutional provisions have been utilized with regard to civil rights legislation, depending on the nature of the legislation, including the following: *Article I, Section 8, clause 3* provides Congress with the power to "regulate commerce with foreign nations, and among the several states, and with the Indian tribes." The Supreme Court has held that the "power of Congress to promote interstate commerce also includes the power to regulate ... local activities in both the States of origin and destination, which might have a substantial and harmful effect upon that commerce," including local discriminatory activities that have a "disruptive effect ... on commercial intercourse." *See* Heart of Atlanta Motel v. United States, 379 U.S. 241, 257-58 (1964). *Thirteenth Amendment, Section 2* provides Congress the power "to enforce" the substantive guarantees of the Amendment, which centrally prohibits slavery and involuntary servitude, by enacting "appropriate legislation." The Supreme Court has recognized that the Thirteenth Amendment provides Congress with the authority to pass laws for abolishing all

Subject Matter of Legislation	**Suggested Citation**
	"badges or incidents" of slavery or servitude. *See* Jones v. Alfred H. Mayer Co., 392 U.S. 409, 437-44 (1968). *Fourteenth Amendment, Section 5* provides Congress the power "to enforce" the substantive guarantees of the amendment, including the Due Process and Equal Protection Clauses, by enacting "appropriate legislation." The Supreme Court has recognized that, under Section 5, Congress may both proscribe unconstitutional conduct, as well as enact legislation that remedies and deters violations of rights guaranteed under the Fourteenth Amendment. *See* Nev. Dep't of Human Res. v. Hibbs, 538 U.S. 721, 728 (2003). *Fifteenth Amendment, Section 2* provides Congress the power to enforce the substantive guarantees of the amendment, namely, that the right to vote shall not be denied or abridged on account of race or color, by enacting "appropriate legislation." The Supreme Court has recognized that "Congress has full remedial powers [under the Fifteenth Amendment] to effectuate the constitutional prohibition against racial discrimination in voting." *See* South Carolina v. Katzenbach, 383 U.S. 301, 326 (1966).
Constitutional Amendment Courts—Regulation of the Jurisdiction of Federal Courts	*Article V* authorizes Congress, whenever two-thirds of both houses "deem it necessary," to propose amendments to the Constitution. *Article I, Section 8, clause 9* provides Congress with the power to constitute "Tribunals inferior to the Supreme Court." * Note: *Article III, Section 2* allows Congress to make "Exceptions" to the Supreme Court's appellate jurisdiction.
Courts—Procedures, Practices, and Rules of Federal Courts	*Article III, Section 1* vests the judicial power of the United States in the Supreme Court and any inferior courts Congress establishes.

Table 2. (Continued)

Subject Matter of Legislation	Suggested Citation
	Article I, Section 8, clause 18 allows Congress to make all laws "which shall be necessary and proper for carrying into execution" any "other" powers vested by the Constitution in the Government of the United States. * Note: According to the Supreme Court, the Necessary and Proper Clause gives Congress the "power to make laws for carrying into execution all the judgments which the judicial department has power to pronounce" (Wayman v. Southard, 10 Wheat. 1, 22 (1825)), and, thereby, Congress has "undoubted power to regulate the practice and procedure of federal courts." *See* Sibbach v. Wilson & Co., 312 U.S. 1, 9 (1941).
Economic Regulations (e.g., regulations regarding a particular business; regulations pertaining to labor standards)	*Article I, Section 8, clause 3* provides Congress with the power to "regulate commerce with foreign nations, and among the several states, and with the Indian tribes." * Note: According to the Supreme Court, the Commerce Clause authorizes Congress to regulate the use of the channels of interstate commerce; the instrumentalities of interstate commerce, or persons or things in interstate commerce; and those activities having a substantial relation to or affecting interstate commerce. *See* United States v. Lopez, 514 U.S. 549, 558-59 (1995).
Election Regulations	*Article I, Section 4, clause 1* allows states to prescribe the "Time, Places and Manner of holding Elections for Senators and Representatives," but allows Congress "at any time" to "make or alter such regulations."

Subject Matter of Legislation	**Suggested Citation**
Federal Land Regulation (e.g., selling federal lands; creating rules for national parks)	*Article IV, Section 3, clause 2* provides Congress with the power to "dispose of and make all needful Rules and Regulations respecting the Territory and other Property belonging to the United States." * Note: The Supreme Court has described this power to be "without limitations," holding that "Congress may constitutionally limit the disposition of the public domain to a manner consistent with its views of public policy." *See* United States v. San Francisco, 310 U.S. 16, 29 (1940).
Immigration—Naturalization (i.e., granting of citizenship to a foreign-born person)	*Article I, Section 8, clause 4* provides Congress with the power to establish a "uniform Rule of Naturalization." * Note: The Supreme Court has recognized that the power to establish a uniform rule of naturalization can, in part, be more broadly viewed to provide Congress power "over the subject of immigration and the status of aliens." *See* Arizona v. United States, 132 S. Ct. 2492, 2498 (2012).
Immigration—Outside of Naturalization (e.g., granting of temporary visas to nonimmigrants, regulating the entry and deportation of aliens)	* Note: According to the Supreme Court, the formulation of immigration policy is "entrusted exclusively to Congress." *See* Galvan v. Press, 347 U.S. 522, 531 (1954); *see also* Fiallo v. Bell, 430 U.S. 787, 792 (1977) ("This Court has repeatedly emphasized that 'over no conceivable subject is the legislative power of Congress more complete than it is over' the admission of aliens."). Notwithstanding such language, the Constitution does not directly address the sources of federal power to regulate which non-U.S. nationals (aliens) may enter and remain in the United States or to establish the conditions of their continued presence within the country. Several of the enumerated powers in the Constitution, however, have been construed as authorizing such regulations, including the following:

Table 2. (Continued)

Subject Matter of Legislation	Suggested Citation
	Article I, Section 8, clause 3 provides Congress with the power to "regulate commerce with foreign nations, and among the several states, and with the Indian tribes." The Supreme Court has held that Congress's power to regulate foreign commerce includes the power to regulate the entry of persons into the country. *See* Henderson v. Mayor of New York, 92 U.S. 259, 270-71(1876). *Article I, Section 8, clauses 11-16,* which collectively provide Congress with various authorities related to foreign affairs, have been cited as providing support for congressional regulation of immigration. *See* Toll v. Moreno, 458 U.S. 1, 10 (1982). Other cases from the Supreme Court have looked beyond the powers in Article I, Section 8 for support for Congress's power over immigration. *See The Chinese Exclusion Case,* 130 U.S. 581, 604 (1889) (listing the powers to "declare war, make treaties, suppress insurrection, repel invasion, regulate foreign commerce, secure republican governments to the States, and admit subjects of other nations to citizenship" as authorizing Congress to enact legislation excluding Chinese laborers); Fong Yue Ting v. United States, 149 U.S. 698, 705-09 (1893) (relying on the same sources to affirm Congress's power to deport noncitizens).
Internal Rules of the House	*Article I, Section 5, clause 2* provides that each house of Congress "may determine the Rules of its Proceedings."
Intellectual Property—Patents and Copyright	*Article I, Section 8, clause 8* provides Congress with the power to promote the "Progress of Science and useful Arts, by securing for limited Times to Authors and Inventors the exclusive Right to their respective Writings and Discoveries."

Subject Matter of Legislation	**Suggested Citation**
Military Rules and Regulations (e.g., amending the Uniform Code of Military Justice)	*Article I, Section 8, clause 14* provides Congress with the power to make rules for the government and regulation of the land and naval forces.
Post Offices (e.g., naming post offices; creating honorary stamps)	*Article I, Section 8, clause 7* provides Congress with the power to establish post offices and post roads.
Taxes, Duties, Imposts, and Excises	*Article I, Section 8, clause 1* provides Congress with the power to "lay and collect Taxes, Duties, Imposts and Excises."
Taxes (Income)	*Sixteenth Amendment* provides Congress the power to "lay and collect taxes on incomes."

Source: Congressional Research Service.

CONCLUSION

A House Rule XII, clause 7(c), statement regarding the constitutionality of legislation is required only when a Member of the House *introduces* legislation. The CAS, by its nature, is just the starting point for constitutional dialogue respecting a bill or joint resolution. Nothing in the rule prohibits further discussions about the constitutional issues that a piece of legislation may implicate. While the customary practice with regard to CASs, to date, has been to provide a short citation to the provision in the Constitution that affirmatively grants Congress the authority to enact the underlying legislation,[215] it is not unprecedented for Members to cite sources beyond the text of the Constitution, such as Supreme Court case law, primary source materials on the Constitution, or a constitutional law treatise.[216] Other CASs have gone beyond citing to the affirmative powers that the Constitution provides Congress and have

---

[215] *See supra* note 120.

[216] *See* Cooper & Stewart, *supra* note 126, at 9-10 (providing examples of more detailed CASs); *see also* Volokh, *supra* note 86, at 198 (noting that a "handful of CASs engage in a thorough and highly detailed explanation of the constitutional ramifications of the proposed legislation," such as including "several paragraphs of discussion about the Federalist Papers and Supreme Court doctrine as well as three particular clauses of the Constitution."); *supra* at 13 (noting that four CASs of the 937 examined by CRS explicitly discussed Supreme Court case law supporting the bill or joint resolution.).

discussed potential restraints the Constitution imposes that may prohibit the enactment of the underlying legislation.[217]

Outside of a CAS, Members can request a formal floor debate respecting the constitutionality of pending legislation,[218] and constitutional debate and dialogue can occur in a host of other contexts, including voting to enact legislation, committee hearings, committee reports, and more "informal practices, norms, and traditions."[219] Also, Members of Congress have a variety of resources available to help inform their participation in constitutional debate, including "expert witnesses at hearings, their legally trained staff, [and] constitutional experts at the [CRS]."[220] In particular, CRS's American Law Division regularly provides legal advice to Members and their staff on constitutional questions regarding pending legislation, whether by providing suggestions for a CAS or by formally rendering an opinion on the constitutionality of pending legislation.[221] In this vein, Members and their staff have the capability to meaningfully participate in ongoing debates over the interpretation of the Constitution, beginning with the CAS.

---

217 *See* Cooper & Stewart, *supra* note 126, at 11 (noting an example of a CAS that discussed why the underlying legislation was "consistent with" various constitutional provisions).

218 *See supra* note 180.

219 *See* Michael J. Gerhardt, *Non-Judicial Precedent,* 61 Vand. L. Rev. 713, 738-39 (2008) (chronicling the various contexts in which Congress interprets the Constitution).

220 *See* Volokh, *supra* note 86, at 189; *see generally* Fisher, *supra* note 83, at 729-30 (discussing Congress's various "sources of legal assistance" to aid in constitutional interpretation).

221 *See* Fisher, *supra* note 83, at 730 ("Committee staff can analyze constitutional questions and call on the American Law Division of the Library of Congress... ").

In: Constitution
Editor: Jackelyn Haggerty

ISBN: 978-1-53614-198-6

Chapter 4

THE ARTICLE V CONVENTION TO PROPOSE CONSTITUTIONAL AMENDMENTS: CONTEMPORARY ISSUES FOR CONGRESS*

Thomas H. Neale

SUMMARY

Article V of the U.S. Constitution provides two ways to amend the nation's fundamental charter. Congress, by a two-thirds vote of both houses, may propose amendments to the states for ratification, a procedure that has been used for all 27 current amendments. Alternatively, on the application of the legislatures of two-thirds of the states, 34 at present, Article V directs that Congress "shall call a Convention for proposing Amendments..." This alternative, known as an "Article V Convention," has yet to be implemented. This chapter examines the Article V Convention alternative, focusing on related contemporary issues for Congress. From the 1960s through the early 1980s, supporters of Article V conventions mounted vigorous unsuccessful campaigns to call conventions to consider then-contentious

* This is an edited, reformatted and augmented version of Congressional Research Service report 7-5700, R42589, www.crs.gov, dated March 29, 2016.

issues of national policy, including a ban on school busing to achieve racial balance, restrictions on abortions, apportionment of state legislatures, and, most prominently, a requirement that the federal budget be balanced, except in wartime or other extraordinary circumstances. Although they came close to the constitutional requirement, none of these campaigns attained applications from 34 states.

With the failure of these efforts, interest in the Article V Convention alternative declined for more than 20 years, but over the past decade, there has been a gradual resurgence of attention to and support for a convention. Advocacy groups across a broad range of the political spectrum have embraced the convention mechanism as an alternative to perceived policy deadlock at the federal level. Using the Internet and social media to build campaigns and coalitions that once took much longer to assemble, they are pushing for a convention or conventions to consider various amendments, including the well-known balanced budget requirement, restrictions on the authority of the federal government, repeal of the corporate political contributions elements of the Supreme Court's *Citizens United* decision, and others.

This chapter identifies a range of policy questions Congress might face if an Article V Convention seemed imminent. Some of these include the following: what constitutes a legitimate state application? Does Congress have discretion as to whether it *must* call a convention? What legislative vehicle would be appropriate to call a convention? Could a convention consider any issue, or would it be limited to the specific issue cited in state applications? Could a "runaway" convention propose amendments outside its mandate? Could Congress choose *not* to propose a convention-approved amendment to the states? What role, if any, does the President have? What role would Congress have in the mechanics of a convention, including rules of procedure and voting, number and apportionment of delegates, funding and duration, service by Members of Congress, and other related questions? Congress could consult a range of information resources under these circumstances, including the record of the founders' intentions and actions in establishing the Article V Convention alternative, scholarly works cited in this chapter, historical examples and precedents, and the body of relevant hearings, reports, and bills produced by Congress, particularly when it examined this question between the 1970s and the 1990s.

INTRODUCTION

Article V of the U.S. Constitution provides two methods by which the nation's founding charter may be amended. The first, proposal of amendments by Congress, requires the adoption of an amendment or amendments by a two-thirds vote in both houses of Congress. The second, generally referred to as the "Article V Convention," authorizes the states to apply for a convention to propose an amendment or amendments. If the legislatures of two-thirds of the states—34 at present—apply for a convention, Congress is directed by the Constitution to convene one. All proposed amendments require the approval of three-fourths of the states—38 at present—in order to become part of the Constitution.

While the Article V Convention option was the subject of advocacy campaigns from the 1960s through the 1980s, it was largely dormant for two decades thereafter. The past 10 years, however, have seen a gradual resurgence of interest in and support for the Article V Convention alternative. Advocacy groups across a wide range of the political spectrum are pushing for conventions to consider various amendments to remedy what they regard as legislative and policy deadlock at the federal level.

Dramatic progress in communications technology during this period has arguably facilitated this development. In the past, the need to mobilize support, coupled with time limitations on most state legislative sessions, guaranteed that an organized movement would require a considerable period to develop public awareness and support and to move the application process forward. The comparatively swift emergence of a range of new convention advocacy organizations suggests that the time-consuming organization and development once considered prerequisite to an effective Article V Convention advocacy movement has been greatly compressed, and that much of the infrastructure previously considered necessary for such a campaign might be avoided altogether.

This chapter opens with a brief overview of the provisions of Article V of the U.S. Constitution, which established the alternative procedures for proposing amendments to the states. It then addresses, from the standpoint of policy, the role of Congress in calling a convention, the form and function of Article V conventions, the amendments they might propose, the ratification process, and such ancillary issues as the role of the President.

Background: Article V of the U.S. Constitution

As noted directly above, Article V of the U.S. Constitution provides two procedures to amend the nation's fundamental charter. The first, "Proposal by Congress," authorizes proposal of amendments by Congress:

> The Congress, whenever two thirds of both Houses shall deem it necessary, shall propose Amendments to this Constitution ... which ... shall be valid to all Intents and Purposes, as Part of this Constitution, when ratified by the Legislatures of three fourths of the several States, or by Conventions in three fourths thereof, as the one or the other Mode of Ratification may be proposed by the Congress....[1]

The second, the "Article V Convention" alternative, requires Congress, "on the Application of the Legislatures of two thirds of the several States"—34 at present—to call "a Convention for Proposing Amendments...."

Amendments ratified by the states under either procedure are indistinguishable and have equal force; they are both "valid to all Intents and Purposes, as Part of this Constitution...."[2] Both modes of amendment share key constitutional requirements.

- Amendments proposed either by Congress or an Article V Convention must be ratified by the legislatures or conventions in three-fourths of the states—38 at present.
- Congress has authority to choose the method of ratification in the states. The options are ratification by ad hoc conventions called by the states for the specific purpose of considering the ratification, or ratification by the legislatures of the states. Here again, the three-fourths requirement applies in both instances.[3]

---

[1] U.S. Constitution, Article V.

[2] Ibid.

[3] To date, Congress has specified ratification by convention only for the 21st Amendment, which repealed the 18th "Prohibition" Amendment.

In addition, over the past century, three elements not included in the Constitution have been customarily incorporated in the ratification process when Congress proposes amendments. As precedents, they would likely be followed, but would not necessarily be required for an amendment or amendments proposed by an Article V Convention.[4]

- First, amendments are not incorporated into the existing text of the constitution as adopted in 1788, but are included as supplementary articles.[5]
- Second, Congress may set a time limit on the ratification process. Beginning with the 18th Amendment, proposed in 1917, and continuing with the 20th through 26th Amendments, Congress set a seven-year time limit on ratification. Proposed amendments covered by this provision must be approved by the requisite number of states in order to become part of the Constitution.
- Finally, the Constitution does not require approval of proposed amendments by the President. Nor are amendments duly proposed by Congress or an Article V Convention subject to the President's veto or pocket veto.[6]

---

[4] A fourth element applies specifically to amendments proposed by Congress. The Constitution requires only that amendments be proposed by the vote of "two thirds of both Houses....", but Congress expanded this requirement by internal rulemaking, so that a congressional vote to propose an amendment must be approved by *two-thirds of the Members present and voting, a quorum being present*, in both chambers. Although it was established by internal action, this requirement was ruled to be constitutional by the Supreme Court in its 1920 decision in *National Prohibition Cases,* 253 U.S. 350, 386 (1920).

[5] As a Member of the House of Representatives, James Madison sponsored the amendments now known as the Bill of Rights, suggesting that they should be incorporated in the body of the Constitution. Congress decided instead to place them at the end of the Constitution as additional articles when ratified. This precedent has been followed for all subsequent amendments.

[6] This issue was determined as part of the Supreme Court's 1798 decision in *Hollingsworth v. Virginia*, 3 Dall. (3 U.S.) 378 (1798). In 1978, President Jimmy Carter signed a joint resolution (H.J. Res. 638, 95th Congress) extending the deadline for ratification of the proposed Equal Rights Amendment as an indication of his support for the measure. For additional information, see CRS Report R42979, *The Proposed Equal Rights Amendment: Contemporary Ratification Issues*, by Thomas H. Neale, p. 10.

Thirty-three amendments have been proposed to the states by Congress to date, beginning with 12 amendments proposed in 1789, 10 of which were ratified as the Bill of Rights. Twenty-seven of the 33 were approved by the states; 26 of them are currently in effect, while one, the 18th Amendment that prohibited the “manufacture, sale, or transportation of intoxicating liquors,” was ultimately repealed by the 21st Amendment.

By comparison, the Article V Convention option has yet to be successfully invoked, although not for lack of activity in the states. Proponents of various amendments took concerted efforts to secure the necessary number of applications several times in the 20th century. The most successful example to date was the early-20th century campaign for an amendment to provide popular election of U.S. Senators. Although only 25 of 48 states applied for a convention, this effort is frequently credited with “prodding” the Senate to join the House of Representatives in proposing what became the 17th Amendment in 1912.[7] Two Article V Convention campaigns of the 1960s-1980s came even closer to the constitutional requirement, but were ultimately unable to attain applications from the legislatures of two-thirds of the states.

The Article V Convention in the 21st Century: Renewed Interest

During the last third of the 20th century, two campaigns came close to achieving the constitutional threshold of 34 state applications for an Article V Convention. The first sought a convention to consider an amendment authorizing states to use criteria other than strict equality of population in apportioning districts in one chamber of their legislatures. The second advocated a convention to consider an amendment to require a balanced federal budget under most circumstances. Both campaigns ultimately failed to attain their goal. Various reasons are cited for their failure, including

---

[7] For further information on the prodding effect and the 17th Amendment, see CRS Report R42592, *The Article V Convention for Proposing Constitutional Amendments: Historical Perspectives for Congress*, by Thomas H. Neale, pp. 9-10.

second thoughts in state legislatures; for the apportionment amendment, the death of Senator Everett Dirksen, its principal advocate; changing public attitudes concerning the issues; and, in the case of the balanced federal budget amendment campaign, congressional legislation to address concerns over the persistent budget deficits.[8] Many advocates assert, however, that convention applications remain valid indefinitely and that those submitted at any time in the past still count toward the constitutional threshold. Three decades have passed since the high-water mark of the balanced budget amendment convention campaign in the 1980s; consequently, few current Members of either chamber have had the occasion to consider the prospect of an Article V Convention. This situation may, however, be changing, as new communications technology and changing patterns in issue advocacy may offer convention proponents ways to counteract traditional deterrents to the convention alternative.

Traditional Deterrents to an Article V Convention

In the past, several factors tended to impede the progress of campaigns for an Article V Convention.

The Constitution's stringent requirement that a super-majority of two-thirds of the state legislatures must apply for an Article V Convention has always served as the principal deterrent to calling a convention that did not enjoy broad support. This was intended by the founders; as Supreme Court Justice and constitutional scholar Joseph Story noted, "[t]he great principle to be sought is to make the changes practicable, but not too easy; to secure due deliberation, and caution; and to follow experience, rather than to open a way for experiments, suggested by mere speculation or theory."[9]

Moreover, it was not easy, even after the advent of mass electronic communications in the 20th century, to mount a campaign able to secure convention applications from a large number of states. As late as the 1960s

---

[8] For further information on these campaigns for an Article V Convention, see ibid., pp. 10-14.

[9] Joseph Story, *Commentaries on the Constitution of the United States* (Boston: Hilliard, Gray & Co., 1833), § 1821, in *The Founders Constitution*, Web edition, at http://press-pubs.uchicago.edu/founders/documents/a5s12.html.

through the 1980s, it took time for a grass-roots movement to emerge, communicate with like-minded individuals and groups, coalesce around an agreed-upon program, establish a national structure of groups sharing the same interest to promote a particular cause, and gradually to develop the ancillary skills necessary for nationwide advocacy, most importantly in the state legislatures.

The measured pace of the legislative process in the states also traditionally served as a check to a convention. While most state legislatures convene annually, their sessions are frequently limited by law. Thirty-two states place some form of time constraint on their sessions, frequently limiting them to as little as 60 to 90 session days.[10] Convention advocates arguably faced a daunting task in securing timely action on a convention proposal, given the generally hectic pace and urgent demands faced by most state legislators during their sessions. In the case of the balanced budget amendment campaign, seven years of organized activity were needed to gain applications from 32 state legislatures.

Factors Contributing to the Revival of the Article V Convention

As noted previously, from the 1960s through the early 1980s, supporters of the Article V Convention alternative mounted campaigns to consider diverse issues. Although these gained broad support, none attained the constitutional threshold of 34 state applications. The failure of these efforts was followed by nearly three decades of relative inactivity. In the 21st century, however, the convention alternative began to experience a revival among groups that span the political spectrum. Advocacy organizations as disparate as the Tea Party and Occupy Wall Street view the convention as an alternative to perceived policy deadlock at the federal level.[11]

---

[10] *The Book of States*, 2015 edition, volume 47 (Lexington, KY: Council of State Governments, 2015), pp. 66-67.

[11] These groups and their convention agendas are examined in a companion CRS Report, R00000, *The Article V Convention to Propose Constitutional Amendments: Current Developments*, by Thomas H. Neale.

A major contributing factor in facilitating these advocacy "start-ups" has been progress in communications technology in recent years. The emergence and subsequent ubiquity of the Internet, e-mail, and social media provided a new and compelling model for issue-driven mass policy advocacy campaigns. The emergence of social media-driven groups such as MoveOn.org, the Tea Party movement, and Occupy Wall Street provide the most obvious examples.[12] Their swift rise, when combined with widespread publicity, proved that a contemporary campaign, using today's communication strategies and devices, could move the issue of an Article V Convention to a substantial level of public awareness on a shorter cycle than was previously possible.

Also noted earlier in this chapter, renewed interest in the Article V Convention alternative has arguably been driven by public perceptions of policy deadlock on the national level and discontent with the nation's direction. One political analyst recently argued that the nation is in a period of unusual political volatility, reflected in part by "eleven straight years in wrong track pessimism in national polling. This is the longest period of pessimism ever measured."[13] In late 2014, moreover, the Pew Research Center found that 81% of respondents expected political divisions to grow deeper and to continue. Eighty-six percent of respondents believed the nation would experience continuing partisan gridlock, but only 20%

---

[12] MoveOn.org emerged in 1998 as an ad hoc online coalition supporting President Bill Clinton; it later grew to a membership of 5 million. The Tea Party movement originated in late 2008 through online discussions among conservative-oriented social networking websites and frequent conference calls. On February 9, 2009, a television cable network business commentator made an on-air call for rallies to oppose government spending. His emotionally charged remarks were picked up by various websites and went viral. In two months, the newly-named Tea Party movement was able to rally over 600,000 supporters in demonstrations around the nation. Occupy Wall Street originated with Canadian activists on July 13, 2011; by September 17, it had begun its protests in New York City, and within a month, it claimed to have mounted demonstrations in 70 major cities around the country.

[13] Glen Bolger, "Republican Incumbents Beware: There's Something Happening Here, What It Is Ain't Exactly Clear," GCA Public Opinion Strategies, September 16, 2015, at http://pos.org/2015/09/REPUBLICAN-INCUMBENTSBEWARE-THERES-SOMETHING-HAPPENING-HERE-WHAT-IT-IS-AINT-EXACTLY-CLEAR/.

believed that there would be progress on the most important national problems in the near future.[14]

Critics might argue that, notwithstanding these conditions, the convention movement, in its present incarnation, has yet to attract widespread support among the general public or to influence action on this issue by more than a few state legislatures.

Issues for Congress in the Context of Renewed Interest in the Article V Convention

Article V delegates important and exclusive responsibilities related to the amendment process to Congress. First among these is the right, on the vote of two-thirds of the Members of the House and Senate, to propose amendments to the states for their consideration. Article V also vests in Congress the obligation to summon a convention to consider amendments on application of the legislatures of two-thirds of the states, and then refer any amendments proposed by the convention to the states for the ratification process.

Among the many competing demands for its time and energy, what compelling interest might draw the attention of Congress to the Article V Convention alternative? As noted previously in this chapter, advances in communications technology and public concern over perceived policy deadlock have arguably contributed to the rise of groups advocating an Article V Convention on a wide range of issues. Whether this activity can be translated into widespread state legislative action calling for a convention remains an open question: to date, none of the newly emerged Article V Convention advocacy groups has been able to persuade more than a limited number of state legislatures to adopt their proposals. The potential arguably exists, given the existing situation that a policy "prairie fire" could ignite, bringing the convention issue to the forefront with unprecedented speed and presenting Congress with a range of substantial

[14] Pew Research Center, "Few See Quick Cure for Nation's Political Divisions," December 11, 2014, at http://www.people-press.org/2014/12/11/few-see-quick-cure-for-nations-political-divisions/.

and urgent policy considerations. The next section of this chapter will identify and provide an analysis for Congress of the most important policy questions Congress might be called on to address.

The Role of Congress in the Article V Convention

The state legislatures are indispensable actors in the Article V Convention process—nothing can happen unless 34 or more apply for one. Congress is equally indispensable to the process by which a convention is summoned, convened, and defined. The Constitution, with characteristic economy of phrase, simply directs that "Congress ... on the application of the Legislatures of two thirds of the several States, shall call a Convention for the proposing of Amendments...." Beyond this language, however, observers have identified subsidiary issues for consideration by Congress, of which five may be among the most important:

- What is the overall role of Congress in the convention process? Would it call a convention and then stand aside, or would it be the "guardian" of a convention?
- More specifically, what is Congress's obligation under Article V to call a convention if it receives sufficient state applications?
- What sort of convention does Article V authorize?
- If an Article V Convention proposes an amendment or amendments, does Congress have any discretion as to whether they must be submitted to the states for consideration?
- What is the constitutional status of an Article V Convention?

Congress: "Clerk" or "Guardian" of the Convention Process?

Article V's barebones provisions provide little guidance as to the general role of Congress in the convention process. Supporters of a minimalist interpretation would assign a purely ministerial or clerical role to Congress: it should call the convention; establish minimal requirements as to form, procedures, and agenda; and then refer whatever amendment or amendments are proposed to the states in timely fashion. In other words, call a convention, make the arrangements, and then stand aside. There is justification for this "hands off" course of action from the founders themselves: the records of the Philadelphia Convention show that the Article V alternative was deliberately placed in the Constitution as a check to an intransigent or unresponsive Congress. Alexander Hamilton explained the Article V Convention process in unmistakable terms, "[t]he words of this article are peremptory. The Congress 'shall call a convention.' Nothing in this particular is left to the discretion of that body."[15] This point of view is generally held, with variations, by proponents of the Article V Convention. For instance, a 2010 Goldwater Institute study summarized this position as follows:

> The ministerial nature of congressional duties and the requirement that it call a convention at the behest of two-thirds of the state legislatures supports the conclusion that ... Congress acts primarily as the legislatures' agent. From the nature of that role, it follows that Congress may not impose rules of its own on the states or on the convention.... In the state application-and-convention procedures, the states are in the position of the property owner, Congress in the position of the manager, and the convention for proposing amendments in the place of the contractor.[16]

In contrast to this assertion, some scholars hold that Congress should be the "guardian" of an Article V Convention, exercising broad authority over the process. Their assertions will be identified and analyzed with respect to more specific questions as they are raised in this chapter. The House Judiciary Committee considered both points of view in its 1993

---

[15] Alexander Hamilton, in *The Federalist*, Number 85, "Conclusion," (Cambridge, MA: the Belknap Press of Harvard University Press, 1961), p. 546.

[16] Robert G. Natelson, *Amending the Constitution by Convention: A Complete View of the Founders' Plan*, Goldwater Institute, Policy Report No. 241, September 16, 2010, pp. 20-22. The Goldwater Institute identifies itself as a public policy research organization focusing on research oriented to individual rights, the free market economy, and limited constitutional government.

print, *Is There a Constitutional Convention in America's Future?* The committee suggested that Congress would have a role beyond that of calling the convention and then standing aside; the chapter suggested, however, that the extent of that function would be open to considerable discussion:

> Congress, according to most commentators, has only two roles in the Convention process: To Call the Convention and to choose a method of ratification. However, all are agreed that a range of ancillary functions are necessary and proper to carry out the primary roles. The disagreement begins in deciding the limits of the ancillary functions.[17]

An American Bar Association study of the Article V alternative sought to achieve a balance, suggesting a limited, but important role for Congress: "to be sure, Congress has discretion in interpreting Article V and in adopting implementing legislation. It cannot be gainsaid that Congress has the primary power of administering Article V. We do not believe, however, that Congress is, or ought to be, the final dispositive power in every situation."[18]

Calling a Convention: The Requirement

Moving beyond the fundamental issue of its role in the Article V Convention process, the Constitution instructs Congress in plain language to call an Article V Convention once the legislatures of two-thirds of the states have submitted applications: Congress "... *shall* [emphasis added] call a Convention for proposing Amendments" While a legal analysis is beyond the scope of this chapter, most legal scholars conclude that Congress must call a convention. The founders' intentions in this respect

---

[17] U.S. Congress, House, Committee on the Judiciary, *Is There a Constitutional Convention in America's Future?* 103rd Congress, 1st session, Serial No. 1(Washington: GPO, 1993), pp. 28-29.

[18] American Bar Association, Special Constitutional Convention Study Subcommittee, *Amendment of the Constitution by the Convention Method under Article V* (Chicago (?): American Bar Association, 1974), p. 21.

seem unmistakable: as noted previously, no less an authority than Alexander Hamilton wrote that, once the threshold is met,

> ... the Congress will be obliged ... to call a convention for proposing amendments. The words of this article are peremptory. The Congress 'shall call a convention.' *Nothing in this particular is left to the discretion of that body* [emphasis added]. And of consequence, all the declamation of disinclination to a change vanishes in air.[19]

Constitutional scholar Russell Caplan confirmed the founders' unanimity on the issue; he noted that, "[t]he founding generation spoke with one voice on this duty," and went on to quote the writings of John Marshall, James Iredell, John Dickinson, and James Madison, in which they all asserted the obligation of Congress to call a convention once the two-thirds threshold was attained.[20]

Given the founders' intentions, on what grounds could Congress decline to call a convention? Several factors concerning state applications might be used to represent them as defective and therefore invalid. For instance, many constitutional scholars hold that applications proposing a specifically-worded amendment are invalid. As one observer noted, "these resolutions seek to make the 'Convention' part of the *ratifying* [emphasis in the original] process, rather than part of the deliberative process for 'proposing' constitutional amendments.... They are applications for a convention powered solely to approve or disapprove the submission to the states of particular amendments 'proposed' elsewhere."[21] Another reason for hesitation in calling an Article V Convention centers on the issue of its scope—general versus limited. A further potential impediment is the question of contemporaneity: Are applications perpetually valid, or do they expire after a certain length of time?[22] Convention proponents generally

---

[19] Hamilton, *The Federalist*, p. 546.

[20] Russell L. Caplan, Constitutional Brinksmanship, Amending the Constitution by National Convention (New York: Oxford University Press, 1988), pp. 115-117.

[21] Arthur Earl Bonfield, "Proposing Constitutional Amendments by Convention: Some Problems," Notre Dame Law Review, volume 39, issue 6, 1963-1964, pp. 662-663.

[22] The question of application contemporaneity is examined more closely in CRS Report R42592, The Article V Convention for Proposing Constitutional Amendments: Historical Perspectives for Congress, pp.18-19.

claim that state applications never expire,[23] while the 2010 Goldwater Institute's study asserted that Congress lacks the authority to decide this question:

> ... Congress may not impose rules of its own on the states or on the convention. For example, it may not limit the period within which states must apply. Time limits are for principals, not agents to impose: if a state legislature believes its application to be stale, that legislature may rescind it.[24]

In a 1957 report to the House Judiciary Committee, committee counsel Cyril Brickfield suggested that Congress might not be obliged to summon an Article V Convention, even if the requisite number of state applications were submitted: "[i]t is doubtful, however, that there is any process or machinery by which the [C]ongress could be *compelled* [emphasis added] to perform this duty."[25] Congress, he noted, had the mandate to perform, but "its failure to do so apparently gives rise to no enforcible (sic) cause of action."[26]

Still another potential option would be preemption of the call for a convention. Supporters of this tactic maintain that Congress can legally respond to state applications by proposing its own relevant amendment. During the 1980s campaign for a convention to consider a balanced budget amendment, the National Taxpayers' Union exemplified this opinion, asserting that the convention movement was designed to force Congress to propose an amendment, that the call for a convention was "just a way of getting attention—something akin to batting a mule with a board."[27] The House Judiciary Committee offered support to this argument in its 1993

---

[23] See, for instance, "What Does Contemporaneous Mean As It Relates to Counting Applications," Friends of the Article V Convention (FOAVC) website, at http://www.article-5.org/file.php/1/Articles/FAQ.htm#Q4.06.

[24] Natelson, Amending the Constitution by Convention: A Complete View of the Founders' Plan, p. 212.

[25] U.S. Congress, House of Representatives, Committee on the Judiciary, *Problems Relating to a Federal Constitutional Convention*, by Cyril F. Brickfield, 85th Congress, 1st sess., Committee Print (Washington: GPO, 1957), p. 27.

[26] Ibid.

[27] Baltimore Evening Sun, March 11, 1983; quoted in *Is There a Constitutional Convention in America's Future?*, p. 13.

print, *Is There a Constitutional Convention in America's Future?* The committee noted that during the 1980s a number of states had forwarded conditional applications that specifically stated their petitions would be canceled in the event Congress proposed a balanced budget amendment that incorporated the general principles embodied in their proposals.[28]

In the final analysis, it may be difficult to conceive that Congress would fail to heed the deliberate call of the nation's citizens, acting through the agency of their state legislatures and meeting the clearly-stated requirements of Article V. As Cyril Brickfield noted, however, "[p]ublic opinion and, ultimately, the ballot box are the only realistic means by which the Congress can be persuaded to act."[29] In its 1993 print, the House Judiciary Committee speculated that congressional failure to call a convention in the aforementioned circumstances might trigger court challenges that could lead to a constitutional crisis.[30] Another legal scholar expressed doubts that the courts would intervene: "... even conceding the reach of the judicial power as exercised these days, I find it difficult to believe that the Supreme Court would issue an order compelling Congress to carry out a duty which can hardly be called a simple ministerial duty, or would, in the alternative, take it upon itself to prescribe the procedures for a convention. I much prefer to rely on the integrity of Congress in carrying out a constitutional duty."[31]

Constitutional Status of an Article V Convention

Another question turns on the status of an Article V Convention: where does it fit in the constitutional framework? Some commentators assert that it would be a near-sovereign body. Others claim that it is an instrument of state constitutional authority, hence the title "a Convention of States"

---

[28] Ibid. For additional information on conditional applications, see CRS Report R42592, *The Article V Convention for Proposing Constitutional Amendments: Historical Perspectives for Congress*, pp. 17-18.

[29] Brickfield, Problems Relating to a Federal Constitutional Convention, p. 28.

[30] Is There a Constitutional Convention in America's Future?, p. 14.

[31] Paul G. Kaupfer, "The Alternative Amendment Process: Some Observations," Michigan Law Review, vol. 66, issue 5, March 1967-1968 (sic), pp. 905-906.

frequently used by advocacy groups. Still others suggest that it fits comfortably within the constitutional matrix, fully incorporated within the framework of checks, balances, and separation of powers.

One commentator, law professor Michael Stokes Paulsen, invoked "original intent" and the founders' understanding of such a gathering to claim a unique status for the Article V Convention. He asserted that that the founders would have considered a "convention" to be a body that enjoyed broad powers, similar to the Constitutional Convention itself:

> "Convention" had a familiar ... public meaning in 1787. It referred to a deliberative political body representing the people, as it were, "out of doors." Representatives or delegates to such a convention might well operate to some extent pursuant to "instructions" of the people thus represented, but a convention was not a pass-through or a cipher, but rather an agency—a deliberative political body.[32]

His interpretation comported with that of Cyril Brickfield, who identified a doctrine of "conventional sovereignty" in his 1957 study for the House Judiciary Committee:

> According to this theory, a convention is, in effect, a premier assembly of the people, a representative body charged by the people with the duty of framing the basic law of the land, for which purpose there devolves upon it all the power which the people themselves possess. In short, that for the particular business of amending and revising our Constitution, the convention is possessed of sovereign powers and therefore is supreme to all other Government branches or agencies.[33]

Brickfield also presented contrary arguments, however, reporting that conventional sovereignty was not a universally accepted doctrine, primarily on the grounds that an Article V Convention can only be summoned subject to conditions set out in the Constitution:

---

[32] Michael Stokes Paulsen, "How to Count to Thirty-Four: The Constitutional Case for a Constitutional Convention," *Harvard Journal of Law and Public Policy*, volume 34, issue 3, 2011, p. 842.

[33] Brickfield, *Problems Relating to a Federal Constitutional Convention*, p. 16.

> ... [T]hose who assert the right of the Congress to bind a convention contend that the convention is, in no proper sense, a sovereign. It is, they argue, but an agency employed by the people to institute or revise fundamental law. While there may be a special dignity attaching to a convention by reason of its framing fundamental law, no such dignity or power should attach which would invest it with a primacy over other branches of government having equally responsible functions.[34]

Some contemporary advocates assert that Article V was intended by the founders to place the convention firmly in the hands of the states, with only a minimal role assigned to Congress, noting that "the Founders retained the Articles of Confederation model. In other words, during that procedure, the state legislatures are the principals, and Congress and the convention for proposing amendments are their agents."[35] Former Solicitor General Walter Dellinger, however, expressed concern about the role of the state legislatures in the Article V Convention process. Writing at the height of the 1980s debate over the campaign for a convention to consider an amendment requiring a balanced federal budget, he asserted that the framers deliberately sought to provide a means of amending the Constitution that would be insulated from excessive influence, not only from Congress, but from the state legislatures as well. He asserted that a convention, once summoned, possessed sufficient constitutional authority to undertake its own deliberations and make its own decisions, referential to, but not dominated by the state legislatures that summoned it or the Congress that would propose any amendments it produced. Dellinger reasoned that, while a convention "should be influenced in its agenda by the grievances that led the states to apply for its convocation, the authority to determine the agenda and draft the amendments to be proposed should rest with the convention, rather than with Congress or the state legislatures."[36]

---

[34] Ibid.

[35] Natelson, Amending the Constitution by Convention: A Complete View of the Founders' Plan, p. 26.

[36] See Walter E. Dellinger, "The Recurring Question of the 'Limited" Constitutional Convention," Yale Law Journal, volume 88, issue 8, July 1979, pp. 1623-1640, especially p. 1635.

What Sort of Convention Does Article V Authorize?

One of the issues that has provoked the most controversy is the nature of the convention contemplated by the Constitution. What did the founders envision when they drafted the convention alternative?

Alternative Convention Models

Three alternative models for the Article V Convention are generally recognized:

- The general convention, which would be free to consider any and all additions to the Constitution, as well as alterations to existing constitutional provisions.
- The limited convention, which would be restricted by its "call," or authorizing legislation, to consideration of a single issue or group of issues, as specified by the states in their applications.
- The "runaway" convention, frequently identified by convention opponents as one of the dangers inherent in the process, is essentially a limited convention that departs from its prescribed mandate and proceeds to consider proposals in a range of issues that were not included in the original "call."

Each of these variants has been the subject of scholarly attention and gained both proponents and detractors over the years.

The General Convention

The first state applications for an Article V Convention, submitted in 1789, as government under the Constitution was just beginning, requested a general convention. Since that time, the general convention option has arguably generated less opposition than either of the other convention models presented in this chapter. Advocates of a general convention note that the language of Article V is broadly inclusive: "... on the Application of the Legislatures of two thirds of the several States, [Congress] shall call Convention for proposing *Amendments* [emphasis added]...." Few sources suggest that a general convention would be contrary to the intent of Article V: "no one appears to take the position—quite untenable as a matter of Article V text, history or practice—that a constitutional convention *must* be limited to a single subject. Article V at the very least *permits* a general convention [emphases in the original]."[37] Similarly, the American Bar Association's 1974 accepted the validity of a general convention as a given:

> ... we consider it essential that implementing legislation not preclude the states from applying for a general convention. Legislation which did so would be of questionable validity since neither the language nor history of Article V reveals an intention to prohibit another general convention.[38]

Not all observers support the wisdom of a general convention, however. Writing in *Constitutional Brinksmanship*, Russell Caplan presented a contrary view. He warned against unlimited conventions, more from a practical standpoint than from constitutional principle. Noting state conventions of the 1960s and 1970s that were called to propose constitutional revisions, he asserted that these assemblies frequently transcended their mandates unless strictly limited by their convening documents:

> The trend toward aggrandizement of power at a convention is supported by modern experience in the states. When delegates are presented with the choice of writing a new constitution or submitting a number of amendments to the existing document, they have exhibited a desire to become part of history by framing a new constitution.[39]

Some scholars have adopted the position that *any* Article V Convention would be general, notwithstanding language to the contrary in

---

[37] Michael Stokes Paulson, "A General Theory of Article V: The Constitutional Lessons of the 27th Amendment," *Yale Law Journal*, vol.103, no. 3, December 1993, pp. 737-738.

[38] American Bar Association, *Amendment of the Constitution by the Convention Method under Article V*, p. 18.

[39] Caplan, *Constitutional Brinksmanship*, p. 147.

the convention call. They assert that the language of Article V places no limitation on either the number *or* the scope of amendments that that would be within a convention's purview. Constitutional scholar Charles Black offered emphatic support of this viewpoint in the 1970s: "I believe that, in Article V, the words 'a Convention for proposing such amendments' mean 'a convention for proposing such amendments as that convention decides to propose.'"[40]

Defenders of the general convention could counter opponents by asserting that the founders included ample checks on the work of a general or unlimited convention. They could point to the requirement that any proposed amendment or amendments would face the same requirements as those proposed by Congress. They might also note that Congress retains the considerable authority to choose whether such amendments will be considered by the state legislatures or ad-hoc conventions called for the specific purpose of ratification. In the final analysis, as one observer noted, "... a convention can only *propose* [emphasis in the original] amendments, not ratify them."[41]

The Limited Convention

The concept of a limited convention has commanded considerable support in the debate over the Article V alternative. A range of constitutional scholars maintains that, contrary to Charles Black's assertion, quoted earlier, a convention *may* be limited to a specific issue or issues contained in state applications; in fact, some observers maintain that it *must* be so limited. A fundamental assumption from their viewpoint is that the framers did *not* contemplate a general or large-scale revision of the Constitution when they drafted Article V. The late Senator Sam Ervin, who supported the Article V alternative and championed advance congressional planning for a convention, expounded this point of view:

---

[40] Charles Black, "Amending the Constitution: A Letter to a Congressman," *Yale Law Journal*, volume 82, number 2, December 1972, p. 199, at http://digitalcommons.law.yale.edu/cgi/viewcontent.cgi?article=3579&context=fss_papers.

[41] Michael A. Almond, "Amendment by Convention: Our Next Constitutional Crisis?" *North Carolina Law Review*, volume 53, issue 3, February 1975, p. 507.

> ... there is strong evidence that what the members of the [original constitutional] convention were concerned with ... was the power to make specific amendments.... [The] provision in article V for two exceptions to the amendment power[42] underlines the notion that the convention anticipated a specific amendment or amendments rather than general revision.[43]

Another commentator, championing state authority in the convention issue, asserted that the founders' intention in establishing the alternative amendment process was to check the ability of Congress to impede proposal of an amendment that enjoyed widespread support. He claimed that a convention limited to an issue specified by the states in their applications would be constitutional, but that a convention could be limited by the states, but not by Congress:

> Congress may not impose its will on the convention.... The purpose of the Convention Clause is to allow the States to circumvent a recalcitrant Congress. The Convention Clause, therefore, must allow the States [but not Congress] to limit a convention in order to accomplish this purpose.[44]

The primacy of the states in this viewpoint thus suggests that a convention could be open and general, or limited, depending on the applications of the legislatures.

For its part, Congress has historically embraced the limited convention. When considering this question in the past, it has claimed the authority to call the convention, but also asserted a constitutional duty to respect the state application process, and to limit the subject of amendments to the

---

[42] Senator Ervin was referring to Article V's prohibition of amendments that would: restrict the slave trade before 1808; impose a capitation tax outside the census formula previously agreed to (i.e., slaves counted as three-fifths of a person for purposes of taxation and apportionment of House seats; see Article I, Section 2, clause 3); or deprive states of equal suffrage in the Senate.

[43] Sam J. Ervin, Jr., "Proposed Legislation to Implement the Convention Method of Amending the Constitution," *Michigan Law Review*, volume 66, issue 5, March 1967-1968 (sic), p. 882.

[44] Caplan, *Constitutional Brinksmanship*, p. 147.

subject areas cited therein. For instance, in 1984, the Senate Judiciary Committee claimed Congress's power both to set and to enforce limits on the subject or subjects considered by an Article V Convention to those included in the state petitions. The committee's report on the Constitutional Convention Implementation Act of 1984 (S. 119, 98th Congress), stated:

> Under this legislation, it is the States themselves, operating through the Congress, which are ultimately responsible for imposing subject-matter limitations upon the Article V Convention.... the States are authorized to apply for a convention "for the purpose of proposing one or more specific amendments." Indeed, that is the only kind of convention within the scope of the present legislation, although there is no intention to preclude a call for a "general" or "unlimited" convention.[45]

Twenty-six years later, a 2010 study by the Goldwater Institute reached a similar conclusion. Examining the contemporary documents from the time of the 1787 Constitutional Convention, author Robert Natelson asserted that the founders anticipated the Article V Convention device would serve chiefly as an agent of the states. The states would set a convention's agenda by specifying the questions it would address, with the convention bound to respect the limits of this mandate.[46] Congress, in this viewpoint, facilitates the will of the people acting through their state legislatures: if they call for a convention to consider one or more specific policy proposals, then Congress is obliged to call for an appropriately limited convention. Conversely, if the states were to apply for a general convention, then, by this reasoning, Congress would respect their intentions.

Congress's acceptance of the limited convention model was signaled by its incorporation of supportive language in most of the more than 20 bills introduced between 1968 and 1992 that sought to anticipate an Article V

---

[45] U.S. Congress, Senate, Committee on the Judiciary, *Constitutional Convention Implementation Act of 1984*, 98th Congress, 2nd session, S.Rept. 98-594, p. 25.

[46] Natelson, *Amending the Constitution by Convention: A Complete View of the Founders' Plan*, pp. 11-13.

Convention. For instance, S. 119, the Constitutional Convention Implementation Act of 1984, introduced by Senator Orrin G. Hatch in the 98th Congress, was generally similar to many of the convention planning bills introduced during this period. Section 6(a) prescribed a concurrent resolution that would summon an Article V Convention, which would "set forth the nature of the amendment or amendments for the consideration of which the convention is called." Further, Section 10(b) required subject-matter adherence to the state applications, and reserved the right to decide any related questions to Congress:

> No convention called under this Act may propose any amendment or amendments of a nature different from that stated in the concurrent resolution calling the convention. Questions arising under this subsection shall be determined solely by the Congress of the United States and its decisions shall be binding on all the others, including State and Federal courts.[47]

The limited convention model is not without its critics. Yale Professor Charles Black, for instance, asserted that the many hundreds of state applications for a convention to consider amendments on a particular subject matter should be considered null and void. He maintained that state applications requesting a single-issue convention were almost unknown in the 19th century, implying that they were not contemplated by the founders. He described the phenomenon as "... a child of the twentieth century [emphasis in the original].... The twentieth century petitions, embodying this theory, are on the point of law implicitly resolved by them, nothing but self-serving declarations, assertions of their own power by the state legislatures."[48] Professor Black went on to assert that limited conventions would be constitutionally impermissible for the reason that Article V contains no language that would authorize them:

---

[47] S.119, 98th Congress, "The Constitutional Convention Implementation Act of 1984," Section 10(b).

[48] Ibid., p. 203.

> It [Article V] does *not* [emphasis in the original] imply that a convention summoned for the purpose of dealing with electoral malapportionment[49] may kick over the traces and emit proposals dealing with other subjects. It implies something much more fundamental than that; it implies that Congress cannot be obligated, no matter how many States ask for it, to summon a convention for the limited purpose of dealing with electoral apportionment alone, and that such a convention would have no constitutional standing at all.[50]

Within his asserted context of convention autonomy, as noted earlier in this chapter, Walter Dellinger also argued against attempts to restrict a convention to a single issue or package of issues. His view of the convention's authority is among the most expansive advanced by observers of the Article V Convention process:

> ...any new constitutional convention must have the authority to study, debate, and submit to the states for ratification *whatever amendments it considers appropriate* [emphasis added].[51]

In his judgment, an Article V Convention must be free to pursue whatever issue it pleases, notwithstanding any limitations included in either state applications or the congressional summons by which it was called:

> If the legislatures of thirty-four states request Congress to call a general convention, Congress has a constitutional duty to summon such a convention. If those thirty-four states recommend in their applications that the convention consider only a particular subject, Congress must still call a convention and leave to the convention the ultimate determination

---

[49] Professor Black was writing in the context of the Article V Convention campaign to overturn the Supreme Court's decisions in *Reynolds v. Simms* (377 U.S. 553 (1964)) and *Wesberry v. Sanders*, (376 U.S. 1 (1964)), which extended the "one person, one vote" requirement to state legislative districts and congressional districts, respectively, ruling that the population of both must be substantively equal.

[50] Black, "Amending the Constitution: A Letter to a Congressman," p. 199.

[51] Dellinger, "The Recurring Question of the 'Limited' Constitutional Convention," p. 1624.

of the agenda and the nature of the amendments it may choose to propose.[52]

A Limited Convention Variant: A Convention to Consider a Specifically-Worded Amendment

Although many observers consider an Article V Convention to consider a specifically worded amendment constitutionally impermissible,[53] this limited convention variant continues to draw support. During the 1980s campaign for a balanced budget amendment convention, a number of state legislatures proposed specific amendment language. Some proposed a convention to consider amendments incorporating "substantially similar" language, while others advocated specifically-worded amendments. The House Judiciary Committee's study suggested the former could meet constitutional requirements, but that

> ... an application requesting an up-or-down vote on a specifically worded amendment cannot be considered valid. Such an approach robs the Convention of its deliberative function which is inherent in article V language stating that the Convention's purpose is to "propose amendments." If the State legislatures were permitted to propose the exact wording of an amendment and stipulate that the language not be altered, the Convention would be deprived of this function and would become instead part of the ratification process.[54]

Walter Dellinger further argued that specific language proposals "short-circuit" the checks and balances built into Article V by the framers. According to his interpretation, they intended to provide "sub-federal communities," i.e., the states, the authority to propose a convention to consider amendments, but deliberately avoided giving state legislatures the power to determine the exact text of the amendments to be proposed.[55]

---

[52] Ibid., p. 1640.
[53] js There a Constitutional Convention in America's Future? p. 6.
[54] Ibid.
[55] Dellinger, "The Recurring Question of the 'Limited' Constitutional Convention," p. 1632.

This issue has been recognized in recent Congresses. H.J.Res. 34, introduced in the 114th Congress on February 13, 2015, by Representative John Culberson, proposes an amendment that would expand the Constitution's Article V Convention language. The new language would permit states to apply for a specifically-worded amendment, and would require Congress to authorize a convention to consider such an amendment. Sometimes referred to as the "Madison Amendment,"[56] this proposal would address questions as to the validity of specifically-worded amendments noted earlier in this chapter. It is also intended to avoid the potential for a "runaway convention"[57] by limiting it to consideration only of the amendment applied for by the states.[58]

It may be noted, however, that other observers endorse the specifically-worded amendment convention on the grounds that the intentions of the states should be given great weight by Congress when it considers a convention call. Writing in 1978, William van Alstyne suggested that

> [i]f two-thirds of the state legislatures might perchance agree on the exact wording of an amendment they would wish to be reviewed in a called convention for discussion and vote, this would seem to me to state the paradigm case in which Congress should proceed with the call—and limit the agenda exactly in accordance with the unequivocal expressions of those solely responsible for the event.[59]

The "Runaway Convention"

Concern that an Article V Convention might "run away" has been a recurring theme in consideration of the convention alternative for many

---

[56] Not to be confused with the 27th Amendment, also sometimes identified as the Madison Amendment.

[57] The "runaway convention" is examined in the next section of this chapter.

[58] H.J.Res. 34 has been referred to the House Judiciary Committee's Subcommittee on the Constitution and Civil Justice. Rep. Henry Cuellar is a cosponsor.

[59] William W. Van Alstyne, "Does Article V Restrict the States to Calling Unlimited Conventions Only?—A Letter to a Colleague," *Duke Law Journal*, volume 1978 (sic), issue 6, pp. 1305-1306, at http://scholarship.law.duke.edu/cgi/viewcontent.cgi?article=2683&context=dlj.

years; as one scholar noted—"it is an age old fear."[60] The "runaway convention" has been generally defined as an Article V Convention summoned to consider a particular issue or issues (e.g., a balanced federal budget requirement) that ventures beyond its original mandate to consider policy questions and potential amendments contemplated neither in relevant applications by the state legislatures nor in its congressional summons. For instance, in 1967 Theodore Sorenson commented as follows on proposals for a convention to consider an amendment on apportionment in state legislatures:

> No matter how many and how sincere are the assurances from the backers of a new convention that their sole concern is reapportionment, no one can safely assume that delegates to such a Convention, once safely seated and in action, would wish to go home without trying their hand at improving many parts of this delicately balanced document.[61]

More recently, Virginia state legislator James LeMunyon recalled these anxieties, particularly the frequently-cited concern that the Bill of Rights might be targeted by a "rogue" convention:

> The principle [sic] problem for critics is that it may not be possible to limit the agenda of a constitutional convention. In addition to an amendment relating to a balanced federal budget, for example, a "runaway" convention driven by political fringe groups might propose revising or deleting existing portions of the Constitution, including the Bill of Rights.[62]

Other commentators have suggested that concerns over a runaway convention are overstated and alarmist. Critics note that the viewpoint elaborated above assumes an Article V Convention would be monolithic and dominated by a disciplined coalition dedicated to the imposition of an

---

[60] Almond, "Amendment by Convention: Our Next Constitutional Crisis?" p. 504.

[61] Quoted in Caplan, *Constitutional Brinksmanship*, pp. 145-146.

[62] James M. LeMunyon, "A Constitutional Convention Can Rein in Washington," *Wall Street Journal*, March 31, 2010, at http://www.wsj.com/articles/SB10001424052702304370304575152231710551888.

ideologically-focused agenda. The breadth of opinion and viewpoints in a nation as populous and diverse as the United States arguably acts as a deterrent. As one commentator noted:

> Delegates to an Amendments Convention would be selected by the people of their state, and so will almost certainly, in the aggregate, represent the political mainstream. The State Legislatures and the Supreme Court would also provide the necessary checks and balances against a Convention that exceeded its mandated scope. Finally, in the event some aberrant proposal does pass congressional and/or judicial scrutiny, it would have to be approved by the people of at least 38 states.[63]

To this should be added the element of time that would inevitably pass during and between the various stages of an Article V Convention. Supreme Court Justice Joseph Story took note of this element as early as 1833:

> Time is thus allowed, and ample time, for deliberation, both in proposing and ratifying amendments. They cannot be carried by surprise, or intrigue, or artifice. Indeed, years may elapse before a deliberate judgment may be passed upon them, unless some pressing emergency calls for instant action.[64]

The Senate Judiciary Committee, in its 1984 report on S.119 in the 98th Congress, argued that an Article V Convention would be more like Congress: broad, inclusive, and essentially moderate. The chapter echoed Madison's assurance that the size and variety of the nation would serve as a check to faction.[65] It also noted that the framers did not provide an unchecked grant of power to a convention: every amendment proposed

---

63 Marianne Moran, "FAQ: Article V Amendments Convention," National Conference of State Legislatures website, at http://www.ncsl.org/Portals/1/Documents/leaders/FAQ%20for%20BBA%20NOW%20in%20PDF%20July%2016%202010.pdf.

64 Story, *Commentaries on the Constitution of the United States* (Boston: Hilliard, Gray & Co., 1833), § 1824, volume 3, p. 688. Quoted in *The Founders Constitution.*

65 James Madison, in *The Federalist*, Number 10, "The Size and Variety of the Union as a Check on Faction," pp. 129- 136.

would be subject to the same conditions faced by those proposed by Congress—"... the notion of a 'runaway' convention, succeeding in amending the Constitution in a manner opposed by the American people, is not merely remote, it is impossible."[66]

The Role of Congress in Referring Article V Convention Amendments to the States

Although the Constitution states that Congress "*shall* [emphasis added] call a Convention for proposing Amendments," it is silent on the next steps in the process. Assuming an Article V Convention has met, drafted, and approved a constitutional amendment or amendments, the logical progression of the ratification process is referral of the amendment(s) to the states by Congress for their consideration and approval. The principal question here is whether Congress is *required* to refer amendments adopted by the convention. While a full legal analysis of this question falls beyond the scope of this chapter, scholars of constitutional law have generally concluded that Congress must at some point refer amendments to the states. It might be assumed that this is implicit, since the framers intended the convention to be an alternative to Congress's own amendatory power—refusal to refer an amendment to the states would seemingly frustrate their intent. Not all observers agree with this assumption, at least with respect to a blanket requirement to refer any and all amendments to the states: opinion on the issue is broad and diverse.

Congress, in particular, has historically claimed the right to determine the conditions under which a convention-proposed amendment might be referred to the states. From the late 1960s through the 1990s, Congress actively considered legislation to govern Article V Convention procedures. In most of these proposals, Congress reserved the right to decide whether an amendment or amendments would be submitted to the states for approval and ratification. This assertion of authority rested on the

[66] Constitutional Convention Implementation Act of 1984, 98th Congress, 2nd session, S.Rept. 98-594, p. 29.

assumption that Article V envisions a limited convention. The Senate report to accompany S. 119 in the 98th Congress stated this explicitly:

> ... the convention is without authority to propose any amendment or amendments of a subject matter different than that set forth in the concurrent resolutions calling the convention.... In other words, the convention, although a sovereign body, is subject to the limitations of its constitutional charter—the concurrent resolution by Congress—which itself merely reflects the intent of two-thirds of the States in applying for a convention in the first place.[67]

This proposed legislation was typical in providing that Congress could declare that it would not submit the amendment or amendments in question to the states because the subject matter differed from the issue or subject matter which the convention had been called to address.

Nevertheless, Senator Sam Ervin championed the right of Congress to withhold an amendment on the grounds of "procedural irregularities in the convention or failure of the amendment to conform to the limitations on subject matter imposed by the Congress in the concurrent resolution calling the convention."[68] He also cautioned that this authority was not unconditional, asserting that,

> ...unlimited power in the Congress to refuse to submit proposed amendments for ratification would destroy the independence of the second alternative amending process. Therefore, the Congress is explicitly forbidden to refuse to submit a proposed amendment for ratification because of doubts about the merits of its substantive provisions. The power is reserved for use only with respect to amendments outside the scope of the convention's authority or in the case of serious procedural irregularities.[69]

---

[67] Ibid., pp. 40-41.

[68] Ervin, "Proposed Legislation to Implement the Convention Method of Amending the Constitution," pp. 893-894.

[69] Ibid., p. 894.

The Goldwater Institute's 2010 study, which focused on the role of the states in the process, similarly found that Congress would be required to refer amendments approved by an Article V Convention to the states, but that the amendments must fall within the convention's mandate:

> Because the convention for proposing amendments is the state legislatures' fiduciary, it must follow the instructions of its principals—that is, limit itself to the agenda, if any, that states specify in their applications.... If the convention does propose amendments, Congress must send on to the states those within the convention's call.[70]

The Goldwater Institute study also offered a potential solution to this question: the chapter recommended that an Article V Convention could offer proposals outside its mandate by proposing policy recommendations. While these would not enjoy the same status as proposed amendments, they would arguably be accorded considerable attention in Congress, the states, and the policy arena at large, and might serve as the foundation for national debate on the issues they address.[71]

As noted earlier, however, other constitutional commentators hold that Congress is obliged to propose any and all amendments approved by an Article V Convention to the states, whether or not they fall within the scope of the convention's call. Writing in 1967, Morris Forkosch asserted the following:

> Congress has its own independent machinery to propose amendments in the first alternative, and to give Congress the power to review the proposals necessarily deprives the second alternative of its independence. As a result, Congress would become supreme, and Article V would automatically read that "The Congress shall call an advisory convention for proposing Amendments...." This would be an adoption of the very system rejected by the 1787 Convention.[72]

---

[70] Natelson, Amending the Constitution by Convention: A Complete View of the Founders' Plan, p. 24.

[71] Ibid., p. 25.

[72] Morris D. Forkosch, "The Alternative Amending Clause in Article V: Reflections and Suggestions," Minnesota Law Review, volume 51, issue 6, 1966-1967, p. 1079.

Professor Gerald Gunther similarly asserted that the congressional claim of any veto power over amendments proposed by an Article V Convention would directly contravene the framers' intentions:

> In my view, the text, history and structure of Article V make a congressional claim to play a substantial role in setting the agenda of the convention highly questionable. If the state-initiated method for amending the [C]onstitution was designed for anything, it was designed to minimize the role of Congress. Congress was given two ... extremely narrow responsibilities. First, Congress must call the convention when thirty-four valid applications are at hand (and it is of course a necessary part of that task to consider the validity of the applications and set up the machinery for convening the convention). Second, Congress has the responsibility for choosing a method of ratification once the convention submits its proposals. I am convinced that is all Congress can properly do.[73]

He also suggested that any effort by Congress to "veto" an amendment proposed by an Article V Convention might prove to be unsustainable. Convention delegates, jointly or individually, would likely make their case in the court of public opinion, arguing that congressional refusal to propose an amendment or amendments to the states would thwart "the opportunity of the people to be heard through the ratification process."[74] If the impasse continued, he predicted that Congress could be faced with an embarrassing political dilemma:

> ... might not Congress find it impolitic to refuse to submit the convention's proposals to ratification? I suggest that it is not at all inconceivable that Congress, despite its initial belief that it could impose limits, and despite its efforts to impose such limits, would ultimately find it to be the course of least resistance to submit all of the proposals

[73] Gerald Gunther, "The Convention Method of Amending the United States Constitution," *Georgia Law Review*, volume 14, number 1, fall 1979, p. 23.

[74] Ibid., p. 9.

> emanating from a convention ... to the ratification process, where the people would have another say.[75]

In the final analysis, the question of whether Congress can refuse to refer an amendment or amendments may also depend on (1) what manner of convention is authorized in Article V, and (2) a convention's ability to consider amendments beyond its mandate. If only a limited convention is permissible, Congress could arguably decline to propose an amendment that addressed an issue not included in its authorizing resolution. If, however, the states were to apply for a general convention, or if a legal or political decision concluded that even a limited convention could propose amendments beyond its mandate, then Congress would arguably be less justified in refusing to send an amendment to the states.

Convention Planning: Format and Procedures Proposals, 1968-1992

Congress has historically interpreted the constitutional authorization to "call a Convention for Proposing Amendments" as providing considerable discretion in setting standards and procedures for an Article V assembly. From the late 1960s through the late 1980s, when a convention appeared possible and perhaps likely, Congress considered a number of bills that would have established procedures governing such an event.

During the 90th through 103rd Congresses, between 1968 and 1992, 24 convention planning bills were introduced in the House of Representatives and 26 in the Senate. In general, they would have established a procedural framework for an Article V Convention, should one be called. Proponents argued that constitutional convention procedures legislation would be a valuable "stand-by" tool that would eliminate the uncertainties inherent in first-time consideration of such an event and would also facilitate contingency planning, thus enabling Congress to respond in a timely and orderly fashion should the constitutional threshold for an Article V Convention be attained. The Senate passed two constitutional convention

---

[75] Ibid., pp. 9-10.

procedures bills early in this period—S. 215, The Federal Constitutional Convention Procedures Act, in the 92nd Congress (1971), and S. 1272, a bill of the same title in the 93rd Congress (1973)—but the House took no action on either measure. The Subcommittee on Civil and Constitutional Rights of the House Judiciary Committee held hearings on the general issue, but no measure ever reached the House floor during this period.

As the prospect of an Article V Convention receded in the late 1980s and 1990s, the number of convention procedures bills introduced declined. No relevant legislation has been introduced since the 103rd Congress (1993-1994).

Characteristics of Convention Planning Legislation

Legislative proposals to set standards for an Article V Convention evolved during the quarter-century during which they were introduced. By the mid-1980s, they generally shared a range of quite specific requirements, including standards for state applications, size of the convention and delegate apportionment, delegate qualifications, convention procedures and funding, a set term for the convention, ratification procedures for any proposed amendments, and provisions for judicial review. The House Judiciary Committee's 1993 study noted broad agreement in the scholarly community that, "in the absence of guidelines in Article V itself, Congress must be able to act with respect to these matters pursuant to its power to call a Convention."[76] Some of the guidelines found in most convention planning bills of the period are identified below.

State Application Procedures and Contemporaneity Standards

Most constitutional convention procedures bills prescribed a standard format and content for state applications and set schedules for submissions to Congress and for congressional declarations of receipt. Most proposals

---

[76] Ibid., p. 16.

also included a contemporaneity provision, setting a time limit, usually seven years, after which state convention applications would expire.

Application, Receipt, and Processing by Congress; Call of the Convention

These measures generally authorized the Secretary of the Senate and the Clerk of the House of Representatives to receive and retain applications, declare when applications were received, and report to their respective chambers when and if the constitutional requirement had been met.[77] Most bills required a declaration by Congress in the form of a concurrent resolution that valid applications had been submitted by the legislatures of two-thirds of the states, and that the constitutional prerequisite for an Article V Convention had been met. Convention procedures bills generally set a time limit ranging from 45 days to two years for Congress to call a convention once the constitutional requirement was attained. An additional concurrent resolution would then call for a convention, designating the place and time of the meeting, usually not more than one year after the adoption of the resolution, and the nature of the amendment or amendments to be considered.

Convention Delegates: Selection, Number and Apportionment

Most bills used the formula for apportionment of electoral votes for President and Vice President to determine the size of the convention and apportionment of delegates among the states. Early proposals assigned each state the same number of delegates as it had Members in the House of Representatives, on the grounds that this apportionment would most closely approximate the goal of "one person, one vote."[78] Later proposals tended to assign each state a number of delegates equal to the combined

---

[77] In 2015, the House of Representatives directed the Clerk of House to begin the systematic retention and public availability of all state applications concerning an Article V Convention. For additional information, please consult CRS Report R000000, *The Article V Convention to Propose Constitutional Amendments: Current Developments*, by Thomas H. Neale.

[78] American Bar Association, *Amendment of the Constitution by the Convention Method under Article V*, pp. 36-37.

total of its Representatives and Senators, for a total of 535 delegates. In this case, the additional members reflect the "senatorial" electors, and were intended "to afford smaller states a weighted influence in proposing amendments, as they have in Congress."[79] Some bills also provided a three-member delegation for the District of Columbia, although the nation's capital does not participate as a political jurisdiction at any other stage of the amendment process. Most bills also provided that voting in the convention would be individual members per capita, rather than by state. This was a departure from the precedent set by the Philadelphia Constitutional Convention of 1787, in which each state cast a single vote, and from Article V's application and ratification processes, under which each state's application or instrument of ratification is equally weighted.[80] Most bills provided for popular election of delegates governed by existing state procedures. Although widespread agreement that delegates should be popularly elected might be assumed,[81] some contemporary convention advocates assert the states have complete discretion in choosing how delegates will be chosen.[82]

Convention Funding and Support

Most convention procedures bills provided that delegates and convention staff would be compensated from, and miscellaneous convention expenses covered by, appropriated funds. Delegates would be provided with immunity from arrest in most instances during the convention. Various federal agencies were authorized to provide a reasonable level of material and staff support for the convention as requested.

Convention Procedures

Convention planning proposals generally included the following provisions governing procedures.

---

[79] Caplan, Constitutional Brinksmanship, p. 119.

[80] This question is addressed at greater length later in this chapter.

[81] Is There a Constitutional Convention in America's Future? pp. 18-19.

[82] Natelson, Amending the Constitution by Convention: A Complete View of the Founders' Plan, pp. 22-23.

- The Vice President was designated in most proposed convention procedures bills to preside over the inaugural convention session, primarily for the purpose of election and installation the convention officers, as chosen by the delegates. After this initial session, the permanent officers would oversee the adoption of convention rules and procedures and preside over subsequent sessions.
- While earlier legislation would have provided for approval of proposed amendments by a simple majority of convention delegates, later versions generally substituted a two-thirds majority of delegates, voting per capita, for approval.
- Amendments were required to address the issue for which the convention was summoned. In most versions, as noted earlier in this chapter, Congress reserved the right to reject a proposed amendment that failed to meet this standard.
- Unless the House and Senate passed a concurrent resolution of disapproval, the President pro tempore of the Senate and the Speaker of the House of Representatives were required to refer approved proposed amendments to the Administrator of General Services[83] for circulation to the states for ratification.
- Valid grounds for congressional disapproval of a proposed amendment included not only a departure from the policy issue for which the convention had been called, but also failure to follow procedures prescribed in the authorizing legislation.
- Amendments proposed by a convention would be subject to ratification by state legislatures or ad hoc conventions at the discretion of Congress.

A Limited Term for the Convention

Most planning bills provided a term of six months or one year for an Article V Convention.

[83] This referral is explained by the fact that between 1949 and 1985, the National Archives was a unit of the General Services Administration. Since the latter year, it has been an independent agency, the National Archives and Records Administration.

State Authority to Rescind Ratification of Proposed Amendments

In general, state legislatures would have been authorized to rescind ratification of a proposed amendment any time during the process, but not after the constitutionally-mandated threshold of three-fourths of the states was reached.

Judicial Review

Most versions of convention planning legislation introduced later in the period would have established procedures for challenges to, and judicial review of, congressional rejection of a convention-approved amendment.

Additional Issues for Consideration

Beyond the fundamental questions examined above, the Article V Convention process presents a range of ancillary issues for the consideration of Congress.

The President's Role: Policy Questions

One question concerning the Article V Convention process concerns the President: what role does he have, if any? The Constitution arguably designates Congress as the exclusive agent in federal aspects of the process—in contrast, the President, the executive branch, and the federal judiciary are not mentioned in Article V. In this absence, certain precedents have emerged over time. For instance, *Hollingsworth v. Virginia*,[84] a 1798 Supreme Court decision, held that the President's signature is not required on amendments proposed by Congress, and many sources accept this as settled fact. As an example, the National Archives website states that "[s]ince the President does not have a constitutional role in the amendment process, the joint resolution [proposing an amendment] does not go to the White House for signature or approval."[85]

---

[84] *Hollingsworth v. Virginia*, 3 U.S. (3 Dall.) 378 (1798).

[85] "The Constitutional Amendment Process," National Archives website, at https://www. archives.gov/federal-register/ constitution/.

On the other hand, some argue that the Constitution's presentment clause, contained in Article I Section 7, clause 3,[86] requires that all constitutional amendments must be presented to the President. Whether this holding would apply to amendments proposed by an Article V Convention remains the subject of legal analysis beyond the scope of this chapter. Nevertheless, the President's role under an Article V Convention has been the subject of a range of policy questions and proposals over the years.

Advocates of a presidential role in the Article V Convention process have argued their point with considerable energy in the past. Constitutional scholar Charles Black emphatically asserted that the call for a convention was too important *not* to come under the President's purview:

> ... a convention call would have the force of law—significant, vital law, comparable to a law establishing any other body with power to act.... Can it be thought that Article I, Section 7, can be evaded by mere *nomenclature* [emphasis in the original]—by merely calling something a "Concurrent" rather than a "Joint" Resolution?[87]

Supporters of a presidential role in the Article V Convention process also note that the legislative models offered in proposed convention procedures bills in the past were more than simple "calls" for a convention. They prescribed forms and procedures for a convention, authorized use of federal resources and facilities, and covered their expenses through public funding. As commentator Arthur Bonfield noted,

> Congress must necessarily make more than a mere call for a convention. Such a call would be meaningless without the inclusion of the specific terms upon which such a body is to be constituted, organized, and conducted. These terms to be spelled out by Congress would appear to be similar to the general kinds of legislation with which Congress

---

[86] "Every Order, Resolution, or Vote to which the Concurrence of the Senate and House of Representatives may be necessary ... shall be presented to the President..."

[87] Black, "A Letter to a Congressman," p. 208. The author refers to the Constitution's presentment clause. contained in Article I, Section 7, clause 3.

normally deals. Consequently, no reason of logic dictates its different treatment in respect to the need for Presidential approval.[88]

From the standpoint of the broader national interest, the same author noted that as the President is the only federal official elected (albeit indirectly) by and responsible to all voters, "[h]is participation in this process that would intimately affect all Americans and our nation as a whole seems, therefore, especially proper and natural."[89]

Opponents of a presidential role reject this assertion. They maintain that the language of Article V is specific, providing no part for the chief executive. The Senate Judiciary Committee's 1971 report on the proposed Federal Constitutional Convention Procedures Act (S. 215, 92nd Congress) noted that, "[i]nasmuch as the function of Congress is simply to operate the machinery to effectuate the actions of the States and the convention, there is no proper place for a Presidential role."[90] Moreover, the committee went on to assert that the appropriate device for proposing an Article V Convention amendment to the states was a concurrent resolution, a legislative vehicle that, by tradition, is not sent to the President.[91]

In its 1974 study, the American Bar Association also cast doubt on the President's role in an Article V Convention. The study argued that the need for presidential approval of any action connected with a convention would impose an additional requirement on the process not contemplated by the framers. The chapter concluded that, under these circumstances, "the parallelism between the two initiating methods would be altered, in a manner that could only thwart the intended purpose of the convention process as an 'equal' method of initiating amendments."[92]

---

[88] Bonfield, "Proposing Constitutional Amendments by Convention: Some Problems," p. 675.

[89] Arthur Earl Bonfield, "The Dirksen Amendment and the Article V Convention Process," *Michigan Law Review*, volume 66, number 5, 1967-1968, p. 986.

[90] U.S. Congress, Senate, Committee on the Judiciary, *Federal Constitutional Convention Procedures Act*, report to accompany S. 215, Report No. 92-336, 92nd Congress, 1st session (Washington, GPO: 1971), p. 12.

[91] Ibid.

[92] American Bar Association, *Amendment of the Constitution by the Convention Method under Article V*, p. 27.

As the House Judiciary Committee's 1993 study noted, proponents of a role for the President might cite the presentment clause as justifying the chief executive's involvement, and that amendments proposed by Congress have traditionally been contained in joint resolutions, which are presented to the President, although not subject to his veto.[93] The chapter concludes, however, that, "[t]he purpose of the Convention alternative was to free the states [from] control of the Federal government in amending the Constitution. Presumably this includes the Nation's Chief Executive, as well as the National Legislature."[94]

The Senate Judiciary Committee's 1984 report on proposed convention planning legislation[95] made a strong claim for congressional primacy in the proposal process, apparently rejecting a role for the President:

> Although there is no explicit statement to this effect in Article V, there can be little doubt that the Congress is possessed with the authority to issue legislation on the subject matter of the "Constitutional Convention Implementation Act." Article V states in relevant part that, "the Congress ... on Application of the Legislatures of two thirds of the several States shall call a Convention for proposing Amendments." Congress' explicit authority under this provision is to "call" the convention. The power[s] invested in Congress ... are entirely a function of this responsibility, authorized under the "necessary and proper" clause of Article I, section 8, clause 18.[96]

Other sources, however, suggest that the convention planning bills of the 1960s through 1990s fell into the category of regular legislation, and if passed by Congress, would require presentment to the President for approval. The House Judiciary Committee's 1993 report argued that these are constitutionally distinct from the convention call, since they would appropriate federal funds and allocate staff, facilities, and other federal

---

93 "The Constitutional Amendment Process," National Archives website, at , at https://www.archives.gov/federalregister/constitution/.

94 Is There a Constitutional Convention in America's Future? p. 14.

95 S. 119, 98th Congress, Constitutional Convention Implementation Act of 1984.

96 Constitutional Convention Implementation Act of 1984, 98th Congress, 2nd session, S.Rept. 98-594, p. 21.

resources to support a convention. As such, it concluded these bills would require submission to the President for his approval.[97] This judgment implies a two-step process, in which Congress might pass a concurrent resolution summoning a convention, which would not be presented to the President, while the additional arrangements to implement the call could be contained in a law-making measure subject to presidential presentment and approval.[98]

A final issue of presidential involvement concerns the ratification process. The explicit constitutional language granting Congress authority over the mode of ratification "by the Legislatures of three fourths of the several States, or by conventions in three fourths thereof, as the one or the other Mode of Ratification *may be proposed by the Congress* [emphasis added]" arguably precludes any involvement by the President.

"Checks and Balances" in the Article V Convention Process

With their usual attention to constitutional equity, the framers incorporated various checks and balances in the amendment process, to which Congress has added an additional requirement since the early 20th century.

Ratification by Legislatures or Conventions

Article V provides Congress with two alternative ratification referral procedures for proposed amendments, stating explicitly that they "shall be valid to all Intents and Purposes, as Part of this Constitution, when ratified by the Legislatures of three fourths of the several States, or by Conventions in three fourths thereof, as the one or the other Mode of Ratification may be proposed by the Congress."[99]

The language authorizing Congress to choose ratification by legislatures or conventions was introduced at the Philadelphia Convention

---

[97] Is There a Constitutional Convention in America's Future? p. 15.

[98] Ibid., p. 14.

[99] "Congress has *complete freedom of choice* [emphasis added] between the two methods of ratification recognized by Article V—by the legislatures of the States, or by conventions in the States." U.S. Congress, *The Constitution of the United States of America, Analysis and Interpretation* (Washington: GPO, 2004), p. 952, at http://www.gpo.gov/fdsys/pkg/GPO-CONAN-2002/pdf/GPO-CONAN-2002-8-6.pdf.

by James Madison, during consideration of the amendment process in general. Although there had been considerable discussion of the need to provide for an alternative to congressional proposal of amendments, the records of the convention and available contemporary documents reveal little debate over the two modes of ratification, arguably suggesting that the duality met with general approval.[100] Earlier in the convention, however, the delegates strongly favored, and ultimately approved, ratification of the Constitution by ad hoc state conventions, which they presumed would be more democratic and reflective of public opinion. State legislatures, it was assumed, would be less open to change and more wedded to the status quo.[101]

Although the choice remains with Congress, observers have made competing policy arguments respectively, for ratification of proposed amendments both by conventions and state legislatures over the years. One commentator observed that "the convention is the only mechanism of ratification which assures the expression of the people.... It seems apparent, however, that the convention mode will be used only when there is powerful public opinion in its favor."[102] A contrary view was expressed by another scholar, who suggested that since amendments proposed under the Article V alternative will have been proposed by a convention, Congress should choose ratification by the state legislatures, on the grounds that

---

[100] U.S. Constitutional Convention, 1787, *Records of the Federal Convention*, 2:629, 15 September, in *The Founders' Constitution*, Web edition, at http://press-pubs.uchicago.edu/founders/documents/a5s2.html. It is worth noting that Madison's original draft did not require that a *convention* be called on application of two-thirds of the states, but rather, that *Congress should propose amendments* on application of two-thirds of the states. Madison, however, accepted an amendment offered by Governeur Morris and Elbridge Gerry that provided for a convention.

[101] Philip L. Martin, "Convention Ratification of Federal Constitutional Amendments," *Political Science Quarterly*, volume LXXXII, number 1, March, 1967, pp. 61-71.

[102] Ibid., p. 71. It is worth noting that Congress designated ratification by conventions only for the 21st Amendment, which repealed the 18th (Prohibition) Amendment. According to one source, pro-repeal Members of Congress "favored this mode of ratification because they believed that they clearly had popular sentiment on their side, and furthermore, they distrusted the response to the issue of the rural-dominated state legislatures." Alan P. Grimes, *Democracy and the Amendments to the Constitution*, (Lexington, MA: Lexington Books, D.C. Heath and Co., 1978), p. 110.

> ... there should be two different bodies, one to check on the other; the different sets of delegates to the Convention and to the states' legislatures may and should produce different reasons for so amending the Constitution.[103]

Thus the Constitution, in this seemingly uncontroversial delegation of authority, arguably endows Congress with a potential check to the work of an Article V Convention.

Approval by Three-Fourths of the States Required for Ratification

A second constitutional check to the Article V Convention alternative is that any amendments proposed by a convention must be ratified by a supermajority of three-fourths of the states. The framers' intentions in setting this threshold for both amendments proposed by Congress or a convention were clear. As James Madison wrote in *The Federalist*:

> That useful alterations will be suggested by experience could not but be foreseen. It was requisite, therefore, that a mode for introducing them be provided. The mode preferred by the convention seems to be stamped with every mark of propriety. It guards equally against that extreme facility, which would render the Constitution too mutable; and that extreme difficulty which might perpetuate its discovered faults.[104]

The framers intended that successful amendments to the Constitution, whether proposed by Congress or an Article V Convention, would reflect the measured and deliberate opinion of the nation, expressed through their elected representatives.

Ratification Within Seven Years of Proposal

Article V does not contain language requiring that proposed amendments be ratified within a specific length of time. Moreover, no

---

[103] Forkosch, "The Alternative Amending Clause in Article V: Reflections and Suggestions," pp. 1079-1080.

[104] James Madison, in *The Federalist*, Number 43, "Powers Delegated to the General Government: III," p. 315.

deadline for ratification was set by Congress for any amendment referred to the states between 1789 and 1918. Since proposal of the 18th Amendment, however, and continuing with the 20th and all subsequent proposed amendments,[105] Congress has set a deadline of seven years for ratification of these proposals. This standard is not found in the Constitution, but "[i]t has been accepted that Congress may, in proposing an amendment, set a reasonable time limit for its ratification."[106]

Would Congress have the authority to attach a ratification deadline to any amendment or amendments proposed by a convention, as opposed to one proposed by Congress? Proponents might argue that historic precedent suggests Congress does have this power, based on the generally accepted reasoning that amendments should be ratified within a reasonable length of time. To this they might add that this practice has continued for nearly a century, and has arguably been sanctioned by the Supreme Court.[107] Nothing in Article V, they might conclude, prohibits attachment of a deadline, asserting that since Article V makes no distinction between amendments proposed by Congress and those proposed by a convention, there is no constitutional barrier to the inclusion of a deadline for ratification.

Critics could point to the founders' original intent in establishing an alternative amendment process placed beyond the reach and influence of Congress. They could note that a congressionally imposed time limit for an Article V Convention's amendments would add an additional hurdle to the process of ratification, and that this would violate the spirit of the original text by making the ratification process more stringent, a requirement never contemplated by the founders.

A more problematic issue concerns *where* in the concurrent resolution proposing an Article V Convention amendment a ratification deadline could be placed. Two alternatives are available: for the 18th and 20th

---

[105] This includes the 20th through 26th Amendments and the proposed Equal Rights Amendment and District of Columbia Congressional Representation Amendments, neither of which was ratified within the specified time limit.

[106] *U.S Constitution Annotated*, "Article V, Mode of Amendment, Ratification," at https://www.congress.gov/content/conan/pdf/GPO-CONAN-REV-2014-9-6.pdf.

[107] *Dillon v. Gloss*: 256 U.S. 368 (1921).

through 22nd Amendments, Congress placed the deadline within the body of the amendment as proposed by the resolution. For the 23rd through the 26th Amendments, and for the proposed Equal Rights Amendment, the time limit was incorporated in the proposing clause, rather than in the body of the amendment itself. While it is arguable that Congress could attach a deadline to the proposing clause of an amendment generated by an Article V Convention, placing it *within* the body of the amendment could be subject to criticism as congressional interference in the process established by Article V.

Should Senators and Representatives Serve as Delegates to an Article V Convention?

This question has been the subject of legal discussion that is beyond the scope of this chapter, but various policy-related issues have been part of the Article V Convention debate since at least the 1960s. At first reading, the Constitution would appear to bar Members of either house of Congress from serving as committee delegates. Article I, Section 6, clause 2 states that, "[n]o Senator or Representative shall, during the time for which he was elected, be appointed to any civil Office under the Authority of the United States...." This point was acknowledged by the House Judiciary Committee's 1993 report, which noted the presumed constitutional prohibition, and that Members' service might present "great potential for conflict of interest because Members would be viewed as acting both as regulators and as persons regulated."[108]

Other commentators, however, have suggested that there is no apparent constitutional prohibition of Senators and Representatives serving in an Article V Convention. The American Bar Association's 1974 study determined that the constitutional prohibition bans Members of Congress from serving in one of the branches of the U.S. government, but concluded that service as a "state-elected delegate to a national constitutional convention does not meet this standard."[109] One scholar suggests that

---

[108] *Is There a Constitutional Convention in America's Future?* p. 20.

[109] American Bar Association, Amendment of the Constitution by the Convention Method under Article V, p. 20.

Members could make a substantial contribution to a convention: "in light of the delegates' function and possible impact on the constitutional scheme, it seems desirable that interested members of Congress be allowed to participate."[110] It could also be noted in defense of congressional participation that 41 of the 55 delegates to the Philadelphia Constitutional Convention of 1787 had served in Congress, and that during the convention, 10 delegates were simultaneously serving as incumbent Members of Congress.[111]

State Representation and Voting at a Convention: Equal or Proportional to Population?

As noted earlier in this chapter, convention planning bills introduced in Congress from the 1960s through the 1990s generally proposed that delegates be apportioned to states according to population, following a congressional model. Included in the various bills were the following figures: 435 delegates, assigned to each state according to its House of Representatives delegation; 535, which added two "senatorial" delegates to provide less populous states with a "weighted influence;" and 538 delegates, which included three delegates for the District of Columbia. It may be noted, however, that some commentators assert that Congress has no authority to set the number of delegates, and that the states can send however many they choose.[112]

While the size of a potential Article V Convention has aroused only modest controversy, debate has centered more closely on how the states would vote during proceedings, and on the crucial decision to propose an amendment or amendments: would delegates vote per capita, or would each state cast a single vote? Some advocates for an Article V Convention claim that a convention can only vote by state, not by delegates. The "Convention of States," for instance, asserts that

---

[110] Forkosch, "The Alternative Amending Clause in Article V: Reflections and Suggestions," p. 1073.

[111] More accurately, they were incumbent delegates to "the United States in Congress Assembled," which was the official style of Congress under the Articles of Confederation. Caplan, *Constitutional Brinksmanship*, p. 121.

[112] Natelson, *Amending the Constitution by Convention: A Complete View of the Founders' Plan*, pp. 22-23.

> The universal precedent for voting at an interstate convention is on a one-state, one-vote basis. It is not a convention of delegates but a convention of states. This is the reason Article V did not need to specify the number of delegates to be sent by each state. The states can send as many delegates as they like, but each state only gets one vote.[113]

According to this argument, an Article V Convention would be following the precedent established in 1787 by the Philadelphia Convention if each state cast a single vote; moreover, supporters could also note that Article V provides further justification by assigning equal weight to the several states in both the application and ratification processes, notwithstanding differences in population. A subsidiary question concerns voting within delegations at a convention under this rubric: assuming each state casts a single vote, what form would internal balloting take in multi-member delegations? How many votes would be needed to cast a state's single vote—a majority? a plurality? What would happen should the vote be split equally?

Others make the argument that contemporary democratic practice demands that convention voting power should reflect at some level the great differences in population among the several states. The American Bar Association declared in its 1974 study that "a system of voting by states at a convention, while patterned after the original Constitutional Convention, would be unconstitutional as well as undemocratic and archaic. While it was appropriate before the adoption of the Constitution, at a time when the states were essentially independent, there can be no justification for such a system today."[114]

The Role of the District of Columbia and U.S. Territories

Article V is silent on membership of an Article V Convention, so it is arguable that Congress might choose to include the District of Columbia or

---

113 Convention of States website, at http://www.conventionofstates.com/real_answers_to_article_v_questions.

114 American Bar Association, Amendment of the Constitution by the Convention Method under Article V, p.35."

U.S. territories if it summoned a convention, either as full members, or, alternatively, as observers.

As noted earlier, some versions of convention planning legislation did provide for District of Columbia delegates, but not U.S. territories. Although the federal district would not have a role in the ratification process, which the Constitution specifically limits to states, there is no apparent impediment to participation by its representatives in a convention's deliberations. The argument for participation by the District of Columbia can be made on the grounds that it has been part of the territory of the United States since independence, and that its residents have always been U.S. citizens. Within this larger question, Congress might consider whether representatives of the nation's capital could be accorded full membership in an Article V Convention, admitted as observers or non-voting delegates, as is the case with its representation in Congress, or not be included. Advocates might assert that what the Constitution does not deny, it permits, and that fairness and contemporary democratic values argue in favor of convention participation by the District of Columbia. Alternatively, it could be noted that Article V vests authority over the amending process exclusively in Congress and the states, and that inclusion of a non-state jurisdiction like the federal district was never contemplated by the founders. Some advocates might argue further that only states are authorized to participate in an Article V Convention, and that Congress lacks the authority to provide membership for any other jurisdiction.

The question of territorial representation at an Article V Convention seems more problematic. None of the convention planning bills introduced in the late 20th century provided for participation by the U.S. territories. A case could be made that these jurisdictions are controlled by the United States, their inhabitants are American citizens or nationals, they enjoy the privileges and protections of the Constitution, and that they deserve at least a place at the table, as observers or delegates, if not voting members. Here again, the counter-argument is that Article V vests authority over the amending process exclusively in Congress and the states.

Proposing an Amendment

The Constitution is silent on the vote required in an Article V Convention to propose amendments. As noted earlier in this chapter, convention planning legislation of the 1960s-1990s set varying standards: some bills required a simple majority vote of convention delegates, while others set a higher bar with a two-thirds vote requirement. Supporters of a simple majority could note that Article V sets two very specific super-majority requirements for constitutional amendments—the two-thirds vote for amendments proposed by Congress, and the three-fourths requirement for ratification by the states. They might argue that if the framers wanted a higher threshold for amendments proposed by a convention, they would have established it in the amendment. Other commentators argue a two-thirds convention vote is consistent with the requirement for amendments proposed by Congress, and that a super-majority would ensure that only amendments enjoying widespread support would be proposed to the states:

> Congress should also provide that an affirmative vote of two-thirds of the delegates would be required to propose any given amendments to the states. In this way, it would assure a symmetry of concurrence in the bodies empowered to propose constitutional amendments—whether the body was Congress or a convention.... A two-thirds requirement in such a convention would also guarantee that no amendment, regardless of its means of proposal, is ever submitted to the states before an overwhelming consensus as to its desirability is evidenced in a nationally oriented body.[115]

Here again, however, the question of congressional authority arises. Writing in *Constitutional Brinksmanship*, Russell Caplan rejects Congress's authority to set standards for an amendment produced by an Article V Convention and embraces the simple majority requirement:

> ... where the Constitution does not specify a vote ... a simple majority is sufficient to decide the issue, and Congress may not raise the figure.

[115] Bonfield, "Proposing Constitutional Amendments by Convention: Some Problems," p. 676.

> Since the convention decides its own approving vote, it could, by a simple majority, determine that proposing an amendment requires a supermajority, for example, two thirds or three fifths. But this hurdle can be imposed only by the convention itself, not from without by Congress.[116]

CONCLUDING OBSERVATIONS

The Article V Convention alternative for proposing constitutional amendments was the subject of considerable debate and forethought at the Philadelphia Convention of 1787. Clearly intended by the framers as a balance to proposal of amendments by Congress, it was included to provide the people, through applications by their state legislatures, with the means to call a convention having the authority to consider and propose changes to the Constitution, particularly if Congress proved incapable of, or unwilling to, initiate amendments on its own. It also has the distinction of being one of the few provisions of the Constitution that has never been implemented. As such, the convention alternative would present a wide range of policy and procedural questions should Congress ever be called on to consider or convene an Article V assembly. If this were to occur, Congress would not be without resources. This chapter has sought to identify and provide analysis of key issues for its consideration. In addition, other guideposts, if not simple answers, exist in the broad range of sources identified and cited in this chapter. These include the original intent of the founders, as preserved in the record; historical examples and precedents, particularly from the last decades of the 20th century; and the large volume of scholarly writing on the subject. Not least, Congress could also avail itself of the considerable body of study and debate developed by its own Members and staff during the more than two decades it gave serious consideration to the question of the Article V Convention alternative.

---

[116] Caplan, *Constitutional Brinksmanship*, p. 121.

INDEX

D

E

L

M

N

O

P

V

W